Hos, Hookers, Call Girls, and Rent Boys

Hos, Hookers, Call Girls, and Rent Boys

Professionals Writing on Life, Love, Money, and Sex

Edited by

David Henry Sterry

and R.J. Martin, Jr.

Soft Skull Press

Editors' note: People come and go so quickly in this world. There are many anonymous entries in this book. Identities have been disguised. Names changed. If there is a piece of writing which you feel may be improperly credited, please contact the authors at sterryhead@gmail.com.

Library of Congress Cataloging-in-Publication Data is available.

ISBN: 978-1-59376-241-4

Cover design by Torquere Creative
Interior design by Pauline Neuwirth, Neuwirth & Associates
Printed in the United States of America

Soft Skull Press
New York, NY

www.softskull.com

10 9 8 7 6

CONTENTS

2 · Love

3 · Money

4 · SEX

5 · THE SAGE STORIES

6 · NATIONAL SUMMIT OF COMMERCIALLY SEXUALLY EXPLOITED YOUTH

INTRODUCTION

David Henry Sterry

I JUST ORDERED a sixty-five-dollar steak. I have shoes that don't cost sixty-five dollars. Sitting across from me is the head of a television network. To my right is a well-known television producer. To my left is a well-known television writer. We are in one of those trendy, swanky, chic-y restaurants smack dab in the middle of Sunset Strip. It's full of women in short skirts with heaving cleavage and men with facial stubble wearing very overpriced cologne. There is hobbing and nobbing going on all around us and, periodically, successful-looking producer dudes come to genuflect before the head of the network, practically kissing his ring like he was the Pope.

This Hollywood Pope and these well-heeled and well-appointed television men want to make a TV series out of a book I wrote. It's about when I was seventeen years old, turning tricks not more than a stone's throw from where I sit now, in the heart of tony money. They're discussing handsome young actors who could play me and beautiful starlets who could portray the women who gave me money to have sex with them. My head is reeling, surrealing; my mind can't quite wrap around this full-circle moment.

I flash back to 1974, standing in front of what was then Grauman's Chinese Theater, alone with nothing but twenty-seven dollars in the pocket of my nut-hugging elephant bells. A very nice man wearing a T-shirt that said SEXY started talking to me as if he was my best friend. At a certain point, he asked me if I'd like to come back to his place. To have a steak. That steak would cost me a lot more than sixty-five dollars. In fact, it was the most expensive steak of my life. After he used me in ways I hate to remember but can't force myself to forget, I escaped with my life. As the sun was coming up, I was in a dumpster about to eat some fried chicken garbage when another very nice man approached me. Turns out, he was a talent scout for the sex business. A week later, I was having sex for money.

I was only in the business for nine months. One human gestation period. At the same time, I was attending a college run by nuns. Naturally, my favorite subject was Existentialism. When I retired from the business, I left Hollywood and I never again wanted to think about the fact that I'd been a prostitute. Over the next twenty years, I tried to bury it so deep inside of me that I'd never have to face that part of myself. But I kept putting myself in situations where death would be a likely outcome. Luckily, my skull is as thick and strong as my will to live. Nevertheless, it became clear to me at a certain point that I was going to have to go face-to-face, toe-to-toe, tête-à-tête with the demons that were eating me alive from the inside. Or I was going to die.

After a search that took years, I finally found someone to help me. A hypnotherapist. At a certain point, my doctor said that since I was making my living writing screenplays, perhaps I should try to write my own story. Due to my sick persistence, and using many skills I acquired in the world of industrial sex, my writing found its way into the hands of a literary agent in New York City. She was very curious about the fiction I'd written, which was not my true story at all. I still couldn't face the truth at that point. I couldn't write down the worst things that had ever happened to me.

We started dating. Me and the agent. In fact, on our first date we ended up back at her place. Suddenly it was four o'clock in the morning, and she asked me those questions you have to ask these days when you are interested in someone.

"So," she said, "have you slept with a lot of people?"

"That depends what you mean by 'a lot,'" I smiled.

"Well," she said, "have you ever had sex with a prostitute?"

Normally this is where I would lie about myself. Hide behind the veil of charm I have worn since I was seventeen years old. But after all that hypnotherapy, I had finally hit rock bottom. About three months earlier, I had been dumped by a fiancée I didn't even like. That's when I made the decision that I would no longer hide my true colors.

So in my normal, calm, big-boy voice, I said:

"Actually, I was a prostitute."

Instead of running horrified, screaming into the night, my New York literary agent got a quizzical, but definitely sympathetic look on her face and asked:

"Wow, that's interesting; tell me about that."

So I did. SEXY, the steak, the sex business talent scout. The rich Beverly Hills ladies. The Hollywood Hills lesbians who hired me to wear nothing but a black see-through French maid's apron and clean their house while they humiliated me and made furious love to each other. The Pacific Palisades woman who paid me to dress in the clothes of her dead teenage son and have sex with her.

When I was done, my literary agent said:

"That's the book you should write."

So I did.

• • •

WRITING DOWN THE worst (and the best) things that ever happened to me completely changed my life. The demons that had been feasting on me for so long were exorcised; they flew out of me as the words poured onto the page. At times, when I was writing *Chicken*, I'd suddenly realize there were tears streaming down my face. I was weeping and I didn't even know it. The release was so complete it liberated me in a way I could never have imagined. And when the book was published, many members of my family didn't speak to me for quite some time. The shame in our culture associated with being a prostitute is so profound it affects people in ways they don't even realize.

After *Chicken* came out, I was invited to a gathering with some writers and literati types, many of whom were college professors. My host was introducing everybody. He said, This is Harvey Shlmeel, he wrote a fabulous book about the 1919 Black Sox scandal. And this is Barry Shlmozzle, he wrote a marvelous book about the mating habits of the Tasmanian mole. And this is David Henry Sterry, he was a prostitute.

Deafening silence filled the room, time standing still, discomfort hanging heavy while feet shuffled, eyes averted, and throats were cleared. The whole rest of the night I was an object of curiosity, a sex freak geek in a traveling side show. Some wanted to talk economics, how much was I paid, how much work did I do? Some wanted to talk sex, tell me about the judge in diapers. Some just gawked. But they all had a certain over-entitled, condescending, smarter-than-thou-ness that simultaneously made my balls shrivel and my fists clench. It is that automatic assumption that an industrial sex technician is a) a drug addict; b) illiterate; c) uneducated; d) a slut. It slaps you in the face when you announce in public that you are a ho, hooker, call girl, or rent boy. Well, I finally told someone there that night, Look, I'm not a drug addict, I know lots of big words, and I got a very expensive education. Okay, I may be a slut, but I'm not alone there.

Nevertheless, for every painful incident, there were amazing, life-changing people, places, and things placed in my path. I still get emails from people all over the world in response to *Chicken*, telling me about ridiculous, abusive, crazy sex things that were done to them without their consent. After I do a performance of *Chicken*, there are always a couple of girls or women who linger after everyone is gone. They have a hard time looking me in the eye. They clearly have something very, very important to say, but they can't quite say it. Finally, they unload their stories. An uncle, a grandfather, a soccer coach, whatever. Somebody who knew better did something terrible to them, and they've never been able to tell anybody. It's counterintuitive in a way. I used to think that if I revealed the worst things about myself, people would be repulsed and would try to make me feel repulsive. And yes, some people do that. But the real result—and I have a large data pool to choose from at this point—is that people are drawn to someone who's willing to reveal the monstrous truth. Let's face it, the longer you live, the greater your chance of having suffering inflicted upon you, of having something dark, poisonous, and ugly living inside of you, making your life miserable. Since *Chicken* came out, I have become the poster boy for freaks. People feel they can reveal their freakiest shit to me. Because they can. Because they know I'm not going to say, I don't believe you. I'm not going to say rude things behind their back. I'm not going to reduce them or make them feel repulsive because they have revealed that they are a freak. It's my contention that we're all freaks. I just choose to fly my freak flag high.

• • •

Coming out as an industrial sex technician in such a public way led me deep into the billion-dollar sex industry, which I had not been a part of for twenty years at that point—except as a customer. It is a fascinating world divided into two camps. On the one side are people who claim that prostitution cannot be work: It is exploitation. Prostitutes are all victims. It should be illegal. On the other side are people who claim that prostitution can be work, if it's done with consent and respect, safely, in the spirit of cooperation. It is a way for independent business people to earn a lot of money very quickly. On this side of the sex worker fence, people have been trying for decades to decriminalize prostitution. They argue that prohibition doesn't work. We saw what happened when they tried to prohibit alcohol: It just put the means of production into the hands of gangsters. And this is certainly happening in the world of sex for money.

The people who toil in that trade have no recourse if something goes wrong—if they are beaten, raped, ripped off. Oftentimes, they can't go to the police because the police, sadly, are so often part of the problem. In fact, when one of the recent serial prostitute-killers was finally caught, he said he killed whores because he knew no one would miss them.

One of the saddest things I discovered as I penetrated deeper and deeper into this sex business war was that neither side seems to be able to easily acknowledge the truth of the other. On the prostitutes-as-victims side, there seems to be no room for people who want to have sex for money in safe, sane, sanitary conditions. On the prostitutes-as-empowered-sex-workers side, there seems to be very little acknowledgement that many people are actually trafficked, abused, and exploited. In my experience, there are many people who, given the state of the world, choose to have sex for money. And there are abused victims and humans who are trafficked against their will.

Of course, much of the divide is driven by money, class, and race. Many of the people in the prostitution-as-empowerment world come from middle- or upper-class families. People who have money have choices. They have better access to education. They're much more likely to end up as high-class call girls than ten-dollar crack hos. It's like the difference between working in a restaurant that serves sixty-five-dollar steaks and being held against your will, toiling feverishly eighteen hours a day in a sweatshop. Yet both those things are called prostitution.

As I tried to decide what was right and what was wrong about this strange new world into which I had thrust myself, I did what I have done my whole life: I leapt first and then looked. I reached out to both these sex worker camps. Since I was living in San Francisco at the time, I began by establishing a writing program in the basement of Standing Against Global Exploitation (SAGE), an award-winning organization that offers medical, emotional, and vocational help to people who've worked in the sex business. This in turn led me to work with girls who had been exploited and victimized. At the same time I accepted an invitation to be the token breeder white man on the Sex Workers' Art Show (SWAS), a traveling menagerie of musicians, artists, spoken worders, exotic dancers, and madcap activists, all of whom have worked in the sex industry, that bumped, ground, and belted its way all across the USA.

So after having been in the basement of SAGE doing these workshops, and having been through the blood, sweat, tears, and rapture of the survivors conference in Washington, DC, I decided to make an anthology of writings by people who've exchanged sex for money. I put out the word through the myriad of social connectors that exist in the world of sex for money. These are networks that very few civilians have access to, whether they be Internet or word of mouth. And it is a word-of-mouth business. Lots of words. Lots of mouths. It was quite magical how pieces of writing began to appear. From everywhere. From street hustlers to Ph.D.s. From some people who wanted to be anonymous. From some people who wanted their names to be public for all to see. I have been impressed over and over with this sense of community amongst whores, this spirit of generosity, of networking, that's woven into the very fabric of people who have sex for money.

This book is, I hope, a way of showing how people who make money in the sex business come in all shapes and sizes. They are mothers, fathers, uncles, aunts, brothers, sisters, and children. I wanted to put a face to people who are glamorized and vilified, worshipped and hated, sexualized and arrested; to celebrate, illuminate, and humanize humans who have lived in this ancient, yet completely modern, billion-dollar industry.

Oh, and by the way, that sixty-five-dollar Sunset Strip steak was very, very good.

1

Life

ANNIE SPRINKLE, PH.D.

I first met Annie Sprinkle in the '80s at a performance-art dive in Brooklyn. She was the headliner. I was the low man on the totem pole. I was doing a monologue that I hoped was cutting edge, avant-garde, and brilliant, but which I'm afraid was pretentious, incomprehensible, and wanky. Annie, on the other hand, was showing the audience inside her vagina. To this day, the inside of Annie Sprinkle's vagina is still one of the most interesting things I have ever seen. Her act truly was cutting edge, avant-garde, and brilliant. I was, and still am, in awe of Annie Sprinkle.

When I first did my one-man show in San Francisco, I invited Annie. Sure enough, she came. Afterward, she was so generous, warm hearted, and lovely. I was totally touched. Since the play is about sex work, to me it was almost like getting a benediction from the pope. Only in this case, the pope was not a gnarled, scary, old white man in robes. She was an earth mother goddess. Long live Annie Sprinkle.

40 REASONS WHY WHORES ARE MY HEROES

1. Whores have the ability to share their most private and sensitive body parts with total strangers.
2. Whores have good senses of humor.
3. Whores challenge sexual mores.
4. Whores are playful.
5. Whores are tough.
6. Whores have careers based on giving pleasure.
7. Whores are creative.
8. Whores are adventurous and dare to live dangerously.
9. Whores teach people how to be better lovers.
10. Whores are multi-cultured and multi-gendered.
11. Whores give excellent advice and help people with their personal problems.
12. Whores have fun.
13. Whores wear exciting clothes.
14. Whores have patience and tolerance for people that other people could never manage to put up with.
15. Whores make lonely people less lonely.
16. Whores are independent.
17. Whores teach people how to have safer sex.
18. Whores are a tradition.
19. Whores are hot and hip.
20. Whores are free spirits.
21. Whores relieve millions of people of unwanted stress and tension.
22. Whores heal.
23. Whores endure in the face of fierce prejudice.
24. Whores make good money.
25. Whores always have a job.
26. Whores are sexy and erotic.
27. Whores have special talents other people just don't have. Not everyone has what it takes to be a whore.

28. Whores are interesting people with lots of exciting life stories.
29. Whores get laid a lot.
30. Whores help people explore their sexual desires.
31. Whores explore their own sexual desires.
32. Whores are not afraid of sex.
33. Whores hustle.
34. Whores sparkle.
35. Whores are entertaining.
36. Whores have the guts to wear very big wigs.
37. Whores are not ashamed to be naked.
38. Whores help the handicapped.
39. Whores make their own hours.
40. Whores are rebelling against the absurd, patriarchal, sex-negative laws against their profession and are fighting for the legal right to receive financial compensation for their valuable work.

DO YOU HAVE WHAT IT TAKES TO BE A WHORE?

REMEMBERING OUR DEAD AND WOUNDED: WHY WE STARTED THE INTERNATIONAL DAY TO END VIOLENCE AGAINST PROSTITUTES

FOR TWENTY YEARS I worked as a prostitute at the best brothels in New York City (like Caesar's Retreat and Spartacus Spa) and even a few of the worst brothels in New York City, just for fun (like Pink Pussycat and the Hell Hole Hospital). From 1973 to 1993, I was the epitome of the happy hooker who loved my work—up until I eventually simply got bored with it. Over the years, like so many other sex workers, I was continually trying to explain to people that I freely chose my work, and I was not a "victim" in any way. This story is about acknowledging that I could easily have become a victim, that some prostitutes have or will become real victims of rape, robbery, bad laws, and horrendous hate and other crimes.

In 2003, "Green River Killer" Gary Ridgeway confessed to having strangled ninety women to death and having "sex" with their dead bodies. He stated, "I picked prostitutes as victims because they were easy to pick up without being noticed. I knew they would not be reported missing right away and might never be reported missing. I picked prostitutes because I thought I could kill as many of them as I wanted without getting caught."

Sadly, some Seattle area prostitutes, as well as their boyfriends or pimps, knew for years that the Green River Killer was Gary Ridgeway. But they were either afraid to come forward for fear of being arrested themselves, or when they did come forward, the police didn't believe them over the "upstanding family man" Gary Ridgeway. It seemed as though the police weren't working very hard to find the Green River Killer. If the victims had been teachers, nurses, secretaries, or other women, I suspect—as Ridgeway did—that the killer would have been caught much sooner. Ridgeway remained at large for twenty years.

From many years of being in the sex industry, I know that violent crimes against sex workers often go unreported, unaddressed, and unpunished. There are people who really don't care when prostitutes are victims of hate crimes—when they are beaten, raped, and murdered. They will say:

"They got what they deserved."

"They were trash."
"They asked for it."
"What do they expect?"
"The world is better off without those whores."

No matter how people feel about sex workers and the politics surrounding them, sex workers are a part of our neighborhoods, communities, and families, and always will be. Sex workers are women, trans people, and men, of all shapes, sizes, colors, ages, classes, and backgrounds, who are working in the sex industry for a wide range of reasons.

When Ridgeway got a plea bargain in 2003, he received a life sentence in exchange for revealing where his victims' bodies were thrown or buried. As the names of the (mostly seventeen- to nineteen-year-old) victims were disclosed, I felt a need to remember and honor them. I cared, and I knew other people cared, too.

So I contacted Robyn Few, the founder of the Sex Worker Outreach Project based in San Francisco, and we made December 17 the International Day to End Violence Against Sex Workers. We invited people everywhere to conduct memorials and vigils in their countries and cities. Robyn co-produced an open-mic vigil on the lawn of San Francisco's City Hall, which I facilitated. Since then (2003), each year hundreds of people in dozens of cities around the world have participated in this day to end violence—from Montreal (they marched with red umbrellas), to Hong Kong (they protested police brutality), to Vancouver (they did a candlelight vigil), to Sydney (they held a memorial ritual), to East Godavery, India (they organized a dance to overcome pain and trauma), to London (they distributed sex worker rights information while Christmas caroling). It looks like the Day to End Violence Against Sex Workers will continue for years to come.

The concept is simple. Anyone can choose a place and time to gather, invite others to gather, and share their stories, writings, thoughts, poems, memories of victims, related news, and performances, or read names of those who have been murdered. Or people can do something personal alone at home, such as lighting a candle or taking a ritual memorial bath. We encourage discussions among friends, by email, on blogs. People can also participate by making a donation to a group that helps sex workers by teaching them about dangers and how to best survive.

On December 17, 2008, about one hundred sex workers marched on Washington, D.C. for the first time. They said they intended "to take a stand for justice, and the freedom to do sex work safely. We are calling for an end to unjust laws, policing, the shaming and stigma that oppress our communities and make us targets for violence."

Every year when I create or attend a gathering on December 17, it is a deeply moving experience. I take some moments to feel grateful that I worked as a prostitute for so many years and came out alive. I remember those who didn't survive and I fear for those who won't unless real changes are made—namely safer working conditions and the same police protection other citizens get without recrimination.

ANNIE SPRINKLE, PH.D., is a prostitute/porn star turned artist/sexologist based in San Francisco and Boulder Creek, California. She has produced and starred in her own unique brand of sex films, photographic work, teaching workshops, and college lectures. Her internationally acclaimed theater pieces and visual art explore her life in sex and love. A longtime champion of sex worker rights and health care, she was a pivotal player in the '80s "sex-positive feminist movement." With her research into human sexuality, Annie became, in 2002, the first porn star to earn a Ph.D. Her books include an autobiography, *Post-Porn Modernist*; the Firecracker Award-winning *Hardcore from the Heart*; and a self-help book, *Dr. Sprinkle's Spectacular Sex: Make Over Your Love Life*.

SAM FORMO

I first met Samuel Brian Formo in the basement at SAGE. He worked there, helping hos, hustlers, and junkies kick the mean streets, the needles, the glass dicks, and the pimps. Sam was like a camp counselor, at the weirdest camp ever. Over dinner, my wife and ex-agent confessed that she has a mad crush on him (mind you, this is a woman who, as a girl, had posters of Boy George the Karma chameleon plastered all over her walls). But this is the kind of guy Sam is: a man whom smart, cool, popular boys and girls get a crush on.

Sam was an anchor in that group in the basement, where the very earliest seed of this book was planted. He was always a ray of gay sunshine, jaded but silly, sharp tongued but soft hearted, full of tough love, with an easy laugh. Even when he was bitching about something, he brought a panache and a pop to the party. Over the years, I've watched Sam evolve. I don't know anyone else who's worked both at SAGE, in the crack-ho end of the sex-for-money economic spectrum, as well as the St. James Infirmary, where you're more likely to run into a sex worker who's finishing up her Ph.D. at Berkeley. They are at the opposite ends of the sex worker bell curve, at the very center of the two camps that divide the sex worker world. But that's Sam in a nutshell. So I sat down and had a conversation with Sam, who's seen this world of prostitution, trafficking, survivors, and sex workers—both from the inside looking out and the outside looking in.

DHS: "What was the best thing about working in the sex business?"

SF: "What else could there be besides the money? I mean, seriously. The whole glamorized thing about money, the power you feel, and all the things you can buy. After you've been in it a while, that's not the issue. The issue is, what else can I do?"

Sam came up in Vallejo, California, in low-income white-trashy projects. "It was a cultural sinkhole. Kinda ghetto." He always felt like an outsider, and still does, pretty much everywhere.

His life has been steeped in irony since before he was even born. His mom wanted to name him Brian, but his dad knew a Brian who was an effeminate, queeny sort of fellow, so he vetoed the name. Naturally, Sam grew up to love men. He was a sexually precocious kid. When he was four or five, he hung out with the kids who lived behind him. "There was this one boy, he was older than me, I would give him oral sex. I'm sure he initiated it, I don't really remember how it started. It was scary and exciting at the same time. Later we moved and I used to hang out with this girl in the projects, we used to have intercourse. I was like eight or nine at the time. We used to do these little scenarios, like dramatic movie scenes, we'd have these wild movie kisses, thrust ourselves on the bed, tear our clothes off. It was fun. Then I would do it with boys. It was just as fun with boys and girls. Too bad it's not still that way. I wish it was."

Sam's mom was sarcastic, funny, and not entirely available. "I saw my dad as this aggressive thing to be wary of. We turned to my mom, but she was so stressed, she worked a full time job when we weren't on welfare. One time she was so depressed she couldn't even move from the couch." Sam's dad wasn't around much. Eventually he was arrested for selling drugs. "Dad had no idea how to be a father or a husband. Dad loved to party, although he did mellow out in his last couple of years."

Small wonder that by the age of sixteen, Sam had dropped out of high school and become a tattooed, pierced punk. Fashion was the first attraction of punk. Safety pins, torn stockings, ripped T-shirts, pointy shoes, pegged pants, mohawks, krazy kolored hair, ornate and beautiful, angry randy dandy peacock. Naturally even in the chock-full-of-outsiders punk scene, Sam felt like an outsider. High school was "absolutely positively a nightmare. It was the mid-'80s and I was a punk rock faggot freak. I was threatened every day, in this scary white redneck world. They threatened my life with guns. People would line up waiting for my bus in the morning. They'd throw dirt clods at me. Call me David Bowie and Devo. We got bashed by some guys one time. These guys in a car yelled at us and we waved, like, 'Hellooooo.' They took us in an alley and broke my nose. I wish I'd dropped out of high school earlier. Dropping out of high school was the best thing I ever did."

By his mid-twenties, Sam was a heroin addict, living in squats, couch-surfing, spare-changing for a living. Sam was an excellent spare-changer. He learned to play on people's sympathy. "It was great training for being a hustler. And a waiter."

By the time he was in his late twenties, Sam was performing sex acts for money. "The first time I worked I was so scared. I kept delaying. After it was over, he really wanted me out before the guilt set in. I didn't even wash my hands. I was so triumphant, I was like, 'Oh yes!' I had such low self-esteem, it did feel good to be the object of desire. I got three hundred dollars, but I had to split that with the agency. I was never really turned on by a client, I just went in like I had a job to do. It was my job to turn on the client. Most of the time that was really easy. I never got close to clients; I had a real sense of boundaries. I learned that from the girls at the brothel: stay away from all the Captain Save-A-Hos. Later I tried working on the streets. I was living with my friend Desi—can we use real names? She's dead, anyway. She was dying of AIDS, and we decided since we didn't have the money we needed for the drugs we wanted, and since she had experience on the streets, we'd give it a shot. Being on the streets was dismal. No one would talk to me, maybe they thought I was a cop. One time this car stopped. I got in. I was terrified. Negotiating was horrifying. I just couldn't do it . . . I never thought it was morally wrong to take money for sex. Still don't. My mom asked me if I had prostituted; I said 'Yeah.' She was not surprised. She didn't make me feel ashamed at all. My mom is awesome. It didn't even faze my dad. He was already an addict in denial anyway. His take was, 'Whatever.' He was totally indifferent."

At the time of this writing, Sam has been with his partner for five years. "That's a lifetime in gay years." He has worked as a food server, panhandler, apartment cleaner, cappuccino guy, freelance temp, scholastic map maker, houseboy at a whorehouse, rent boy, actor, performance artist, and writer. Of all his jobs, the worst was floral designer. "It was awful. There's no serenity in flowers."

NEW JOB

Janine

THE HIGH-BACK swivel chair barely contained the bulk of Janine. Her ass took on the shape of the scooped-out seat like a bucket full of sea castle sand. Her legs reached to the floor, two overstuffed sausage links tied at the end. Tiny feet peeked out from under the bulge of flesh where ankles should be. She was larger than life. In all ways she was larger than life. An enigmatic monolith planted firmly in the world by her girth.

When I entered the room, an office set up with desk, surveillance monitors, and six phones, she swiveled around at me, put down one of the phones, and told me to take a seat. I sat across from her in an armchair that also swiveled. She continued her phone conversation: "We have a tall, leggy blonde in her mid-twenties, a collegiate redhead in her early twenties, and a mature forty-four double-D brunette."

I was taken aback by Janine's voice. It was that of a twelve-year-old child. How could such a delicate voice come from such girth and authority? It was probably the biggest reason why she could pull in so much business. Men liked the idea that they might be having sex with a child. Her voice was as dainty as her hands, which were proportionate with her feet but incongruous with the rest of her and, I was to find out, became as cruel as billy clubs when her explosive temper got the best of her. When it did, the house shook, the walls reverberated with her energy, the girls scattered to corners and empty rooms. The poor sap who received her wrath would leave the office with a welt from the phone Janine had just thrown or a few clumps of hair missing. She was to be feared, but she also provided safety. She was a surrogate mother, a guardian angel, a partner in crime, and a brute.

As she put the phone back in its cradle without so much as a goodbye, thanks for calling, she swiveled back at me. "Hi. I'm Janine." And, barely missing a beat, "Are you gay?" This was to be my first question in the interview. My guess was that it was a requirement to be gay for this job. Supposedly it prevented complications as far as the girls were concerned. Hetero men spelled trouble.

"Matthew tells me you're doing drugs. Are you doing drugs?" Her frankness jarred me a bit but I figured since she put it that way all I could do was tell the truth. So I lied and told her yes, I did coke now and then, no big deal. It was the '80s after all. But at this time I was already dabbling in heroin, which was way too taboo. Matthew was the person who'd gotten me the interview. He'd found the agency in an ad in *The Village Voice*.

I wasn't sure how I felt about Janine just then. We kind of did this dance around each other, giving the once over, twice. Her mere presence was somewhat alarming but I played cool, not letting on that she scared me a little. Matthew had warned me about her extreme lack of boundaries. I didn't even know what boundaries meant at that time, but, looking back, I'm sure I had none.

The whole interview took all of ten minutes. It was punctuated by ringing telephones and doorbells; girls in and out of the office exchanging money, condoms, and lipstick; and Janine's shouts at them to get into or out of session. In between all this she swiveled at me and said, "You're hired. Come back tomorrow and Matthew will show you what to do." And then she turned and answered five phones. I beamed and let go of all the breath I didn't know I was holding in one big, quiet sigh. I had a job in a brothel. How underground chic. A sex industry technician. Or, in other words, the houseboy.

I wasn't supposed to tell anyone what I did but I craved the attention so I planned on telling everyone. I thought it was okay as long as I didn't disclose the location or the names of my co-workers.

Before I was dismissed, one girl walked her legginess into the office. I swear if she was accompanied by music it would have been something really '80s, like the Tubes' "One in a Million Girls." In slow motion, she took out a wad of cash, peeled off a few bills, and handed them to Janine, smiling. She had a permanent smile. Permanent on her face, permanent on my brain. She shined. I was introduced.

"Lana, this is Sam. He's our new houseboy," Janine said politely. I held out my hand.

"Hi. Nice to meet you."

Lana, with her glued-on grin, looked at me, pushing air through her teeth with her tongue, and gently took my hand, gave it a squeeze, not a shake.

"Hi. You too."

She was wearing a clingy knit dress that fit her like an elastic band. Her hair was streaked with candy-apple red and she had on stilettos with heels like nails. We exchanged a look that seemed to say, *I know you and I know what you do. We'll get along just fine.*

Just then the doorbell rang. Janine looked at the monitor, "Lana, it's Jack. He's your two o'clock." Lana rarely ever had time to breathe between sessions. She tucked the rest of her cash wad under the insoles of her shoes and teetered off into the living room. Janine pushed the button on the intercom.

"Hi Jack! Just a minute!"

The First Time

The lobby of the Plaza Hotel was just as grandiose as it should be. It was expansive and seemed much too bright for the time of night I entered the revolving doors. I strolled through like I owned the damn place. I'm sure as I breezed by the occasional straggler I left a nice waft of Fahrenheit behind. That was my hooker scent, to get 'em goin,' don't ya know. And my make-up was by Dermablend! A miraculous little cosmetic for those of us who are prone to perforation and puncture wounds! I had it dabbed up and down my arms like spackle trying to hide the track marks. So discreet.

"Hi. I'm going up to two thirty-three. I'm his nephew." This is what I was told to say. As they called up I looked around hoping to see some other hookers but the lobby became eerily quiet and empty as the desk agent spoke into the phone, "Okay, I'll send him right up. Thank you sir and have a good evening."

The trick, a dark-haired middle-aged man, looked very perplexed when he answered the door. Like he wasn't sure how to react or what to ask for. When I entered I had the feeling he didn't want me to speak so I lowered my voice to a whisper. "You can put the money on the nightstand, thank you," I said cordially, exaggerating my mouth around the words just in case he didn't understand. He silently obliged. Feeling slightly guilty I picked up the cash and stuffed it into my pocket. I'm not sure where the guilt came from. Maybe I was feeling a little sorry that this man had to pay me for sex. I thought about what his life must be like. He probably has a mousy little wife whose aging process is leaving her kind of hard around the face. Maybe he has a kid in college, one finishing high school. I bet he goes into bathrooms and cries because he's so miserable being a closeted homo. I bet, too, that he frequents gay cruising spots in some bumfuck town on the outskirts of where he lives. I almost wanted to tell him, "Ah, thanks, but that's all right, maybe you can pay me another time." But my hooker instinct told me not to.

"So what do you have in mind?" I asked, almost expecting him to respond with, "I dunno, what do *you* have in mind?" But he seemed to have put *some* thought into it. "Can you have a seat in this chair?" he asked, patting a chair he had moved next to the bed. He looked so serious. I wanted to reach out and smooth his brow but then I realized that he actually repulsed me. Good, that made it easier to get paid.

As I sat he proceeded to the bed and propped himself up with pillows. His robe fell open to reveal his strangely shaped, mushroom-head penis. "I want to watch you jerk off," he ordered, looking down at my crotch. I felt a wave of panic because I wasn't sure I could perform. I got stage fright and was feeling less-than. But then I thought about the three hundred dollars in my pocket. I pulled my pants down to my knees and unbuttoned my shirt, attempting to work my drug-dead dick. He didn't seem to mind that it wasn't fully erect. He appeared to be concentrating very hard while he diddled his toadstool and occasionally squeezed my thigh.

"Do you want me to cum?" I asked, my voice vibrating from the pumping action of my hand. He said, "OK. Yeah. OK." So I vigorously worked until it happened, using my little sample packet of lube. He squeezed my thigh like he was helping me out. A pitiable little ejaculation dribbled out onto my fingers and into my pubic hair. I let out my long-held breath and felt the blood rush back out of my red, throbbing face.

After I cleaned myself off I climbed onto the bed with him and straddled his legs. "Would you like me to finish you off?" I asked him, trying to sound sultry but really sounding winded and a little deflated. "Uh, OK. Yes. OK," he answered, like he was unsure of what he should say. "Do you mind if I use a little of this?" I asked, holding up my lube.

"What is it?" He asked, looking convincingly sincere.

"It's slippery stuff to make it more pleasant. It won't hurt, I promise."

"Oh. OK."

So I greased up his little knob and brought him to completion. That's hooker talk for "made him cum."

I offered to clean him with a hot washcloth and he declined, saying, "You can go now." So I quickly dressed and left the room, forgetting to wash my hands.

I left feeling really satisfied. I thought to myself, *Oh, I can do this. This is easy*, as I washed his dried-up jiz off of my hands in the lobby bathroom, hyperaware of the wad of cash in my pocket. I decided that sex work was merely an exchange of power. I decided that I was really ok with that type of exchange.

Jamie

As I got to know the girls at the house, I quickly learned who I could talk to, who I could get high with, who I shouldn't talk to, and who I shouldn't get high with. Some of them were really helpful to me and eager to show me the tricks of the trade. One in particular, Jamie, hooked me up with the outcall. Jamie was a constant, an old standard. Old reliable. She was sassy, brash, and approaching middle age. On the phone she was a "svelte, leggy blonde in her early thirties." This wasn't too far off but she was actually in her forties and leathery from too much sun. The leathery skin was a result of going to Florida a lot.

Jamie was a pro and spoke no nonsense. She did not indulge in other people's drama unless it directly affected her. When it was slow she'd say things like, "There's too much pussy in here. Where's all the dick?" And, "Aagh! Somebody come in here and fuck me!" When annoyed with someone or something, she'd say, "I can't with this one!"

She got good business and had several regulars. She did her job well. I don't think she knew how to do anything else. At least not anything as lucrative as selling sex.

Jamie introduced me to a friend of hers who worked as the phone girl. I trusted she wouldn't send me on a bum trip. She was all about the business.

A Hooker on a Drug Run

The door of 17D jerked open before my knuckles met the door's surface and I was met with a dimly lit dimwit who was shiny with sweat and wearing grey boxers that may or may not have once been white. He was pale and sort of chubby, maybe in his late thirties or early forties with greasy dark hair pushed into greasy dark wedges all over his head. He was pulling on his flaccid dick that seemed to have shriveled from the abuse it had probably endured. There was a wet spot on his boxers that could've been a piss dribble or pre-cum. Maybe blood, he was pulling so hard. He had a hungry look in his eyes but not for sex. I'd recognize that look anywhere. *Great*, I thought, *he's riding a hard coke jones and I have nothing to satisfy him. I'm probably gonna die.*

On the elevator ride up I'd noticed the gaudy '80s motif with the smoky mirrored panels trimmed with gold-colored metal slats. Very *Dynasty* or Trump Tower. The Jeffersons also came to mind and I thought *Oh yeah, I'm movin' on up* as I ascended to the seventeenth floor, staring into the eyes of my own reflection, blank.

I was totally on guard as I entered. He closed the door behind me without the slightest sound except a faint squeak and click. I tried to keep him in front of me at all times as he made an agitated move toward the shadowy living room. On a little end table to my right he pointed to three hundred dollars worth of unsigned travelers checks and asked, "Can you get me some coke?"

"With travelers checks?" I asked, somewhat in disbelief.

"They're just as good as cash," he anxiously argued.

"Aaalright, but I can't make any promises. And I'll need cab fare."

As fast as I had entered I exited, snapping the door shut behind me with an urgency that could only be that of a hooker on a drug run. On the way out I reminded him that this little errand would count as part of the hour. He sucked in his seemingly uncontrollable drool as he hissed, "Yes, OK. That's OK." My last glimpse as I left was of him standing there in his dingy underwear, shiny and desperate.

The "drug store" I had in mind was one of those corner grocery/deli places that had a little drug enterprise on the down-low. Fortunately they knew me from previous business dealings and I knew the rigmarole. First rule was to buy something legit. Second was to wait until the store was clear. Then you could throw down your cash and ask for it in a dollar amount. Like, "Gimme a twenty, please." It pays to be polite 'cause you want them to take good care of you and welcome you back. They would then quickly retrieve the drugs from some secret hiding place and slip the little tinfoil bindle into the bag with the rest of your shopping items and off you went to grandmother's house. Or in this case, the wolf's.

Lana

When I went into a room alone to clean after a session, I would notice how empty and soulless it was. As if any trace of life or personality had been sucked out of it, which was amplified by the vapid '80s decor. Lots of grays and mauves. I'd vacuum or dust and just feel sad and lonely. Maybe it was because of the fake plants and artificial light. The rooms were set up to resemble a sort of high-end bedroom or hotel. You know, *Penthouse Forum* material. They weren't supposed to look like anyone lived there or did anything that gave it an air of permanency. They were temporary spaces for temporary activities, like sex. I preferred to stay in the more populated areas, like the living room or office, and chat with the girls and Janine. That turned out to be what I did the best and most of.

I would sometimes catch Lana between sessions and we'd scheme to get high or do what we had in a vacant room. Queen Janine was very adamant about drugs on her premises so this took strategic planning. I'd lie on the bed and watch Lana rifle through her bag, pulling out make-up, candy, and pill bottles. I'd pop a Valium she tossed at me and swig a beer that I pilfered from the house liquor supply. I would be mesmerized by her obsessive-compulsive behavior as she primped. Each time she reached for something she had to retract in exactly the same way. Something to do with the need to be linear. She would also do this thing where she would press her tongue against her front teeth and push air through them, making a little hissing noise. She would do it while talking to you or while engaged in primping. She would hiss and primp. It only enhanced her beauty as far as I was concerned. She was a fabulous mess. We *did* get along just fine. When I think of her now I think about tragic beauties like Edie Sedgwick and Gia. I think about why it is that gay men worship this type of beauty, what they get out of such real pain. I was guilty. I found beauty in that pain too.

Coke-Dick

Now to my surprise the travelers checks were unacceptable. Go figure. I couldn't convince them that they were 100 percent legit, that they were transferable to exactly the amount they say they are. I begged and pleaded, my voice raising an octave or two, but no go. I was to return empty handed to a convulsing, slimy, slithering mass of jonesing flesh that just might envelope me like the Blob and I'd never get paid.

When I once again entered 17D I found coke-dick sweating and pulling some more and the way he looked when I told him no luck, I thought, *This is it! I'm going to be chopped up and burned, my ashes snorted, and I'll be discarded like so many baggies!*

Instead of killing me we retreated to his room where he threw himself on his bed, exasperated and defeated. I noticed several burn holes on the mattress that were the size of dinner plates. He lay back and grunted, "Play with my nipples." So I sat on the edge of the bed, reached out, and began yanking on his cone-shaped chubby-boy titties, working them between my fingers like sad little balls of dough. I stared at the wall behind his head and tried hard not to laugh. I thought about what it might be like to milk a dog. Finally the phone rings. Saved by the bell.

"Hello . . . yeah," he answers, " . . . I'm getting fucked."

Yeah, right.

"You comin' over? Come over . . . all right . . . how soon? . . . OK, yeah. Bye." Click.

I guessed that was a connection and I was free to go. Just like that. I guess I got lucky. Usually coke tricks are difficult and keep you there for the whole hour or more having you do everything possible, short of beating them with a bat, to make them come.

In the elevator ride down I avoided my reflection and looked at the stained carpet, outlining the geometric patterns with my eyes, humming along to an elevator version of "Do You Really Want to Hurt Me?" by the Culture Club. I didn't think of much; just about the cab ride home, copping my *own* drugs, and where I could spend those damn travelers checks. They were just as good as cash.

R. J. MARTIN, JR.

I first met Richard J. Martin at SAGE, where we ran the writing workshops that were the genesis of this book. He was introduced to me as a grant writer. He seemed like a courteous, well-spoken, and well-groomed fellow, but I felt a darkness lurking furtively in the corners of his eyes. Most of the people who work at SAGE are former junkies of one kind or another, so I just assumed that R. J. was a one-of-me, someone who'd been in the Life and had the scars and ghosts to prove it.

The next time I saw R. J. was at San Francisco State University, when I was brought in to talk to Alice LaPlante's undergraduate creative writing class. To see this fellow outsider amongst all the sweet, clean-cut civilian students made me irrationally happy. I gave him a big hug. He told me later how meaningful it was to be embraced in front of all those students, he who also felt like an outsider surrounded by all these normal citizens.

At that point I had an inspiration, that R. J. would make a great collaborator on this anthology. I imagined that as a grant writer he would possess many of the qualities I lack: organization, a meticulous stickling for detail, and the ability to make sure all boneheaded mistakes are eliminated. Turns out I was right. I would send him raw, messy material, and it would come back looking neat and pretty and pristine. But I had no idea what a hard-working motherfucker this man would turn out to be. And what great instincts he would have with regard to what to include and what to throw away. R. J., like so many people who've been to the bottom and come back, has a wonderful way of cutting right to the quick, dissecting the bullshit, and telling it like it is. And as an added bonus, he is, as I suspected, well versed in the ways of the dark seed-filled underbelly of America, where pimping and hoing and nefarious criminality thrive.

They say that writing a book is like giving birth. I would like to thank R. J. Martin for being a great same-sex partner during the impregnation, gestation, and creation of our love child.

PIMP SCHOOL

THEY SAY THAT prostitution is the world's oldest profession. Pimping, then, is the second oldest. You are a pimp. I know that because you said you were a pimp and being a pimp is just like being an actor: Once you say you are one, you are. You've made your choice and now you want the knowledge that will make you an elevated pimp, the kind that makes money.

In order to pimp hard and pimp right you have to understand that you are part of something larger than yourself—something that has gone on long before you and will continue long after. You also have to learn a little about the theory and concepts behind pimping. Most of the would-be players out there are long on *practice* but short on *theory*. You must understand that, like the prostitute, the pimp provides a service. Today, I'm going to tell you how you can provide that service, but you have to keep this to yourself until it's time to pass it on to the right person. That's part of showing respect for the game.

One of the country's most famous pimps, Fillmore Slim, once said, "You pimp with your mind and not with your hands."

He said this because people often confuse pimping with extortion and strong-arm robbery. Beating women and robbing them of their money is not pimping. If you want to make it by being an intimidator then go ahead on. It's easy. You just find somebody weaker than you and take their shit. Just remember to victimize people who are outside the protection of the law. Don't just focus on prostitutes. Beat on weak drug dealers, dishonest store owners, dope fiends, or anyone else that the police won't protect.

But being a pimp is harder—it requires a different mind-set and a different skill set. If you pimp right, you won't ever have to raise your hand to a woman and you'll always let her know that she is free to leave at any time. You will start to provide a service instead of standing around saying that you're a pimp and waiting to get paid. Things will go better for you. That's why we're here today.

I know you have a working knowledge of pimping practice; you've got game and Mack-ability, that's how you got in here. You've got your pimp clothes, your pimp rap, and you're working on a pimp car but you don't really need that until after you get started. You're familiar with terms like "turn-out," "catch," and "knock," which describe the ways you might get started. You've looked at yourself in the mirror for a long time and you know that you can do this. You've practiced standing the right way, talking the right way, and feigning indifference. That's good. You'll need all that stuff, and you'll need all those tools and skills and that kind of confidence to make it once you get your first working girl. Those things are essential to the *practice* of pimping.

Now, let's talk about theory.

What most young wannabe players don't know is that the quickest way to make money as a pimp is to fall in love with a working girl.

You think I'm crazy, but remember, the pimp provides a service. His service is to meet the needs of the prostitute. In return, the prostitute provides the pimp with all her money. This is the pimp equation.

No, to really be successful pimping you have to understand Maslow's Hierarchy of Human Needs—players call it the Pyramid.

See, the Pyramid is a triangle. To categorize human need you divide the triangle into five different parts, each of which represents a basic need that all human beings have.

The largest area of the pyramid, the part at the bottom, shows the most pressing of human needs: food, air, and water, called "physiological needs." Everyone needs these things to survive and everybody who is alive is getting them. You probably won't be able to find a prostitute who is not getting her needs met in this respect, at least not in America. However, at every other level of the Pyramid, there exists an opportunity for you to be a pimp. Because the pimp assesses prostitute need and then finds a way to fulfill that need.

At the second level of the Pyramid is the need for safety and security. You might be able to find a way in here. The prostitute may not feel safe. A ho plays a dangerous game. She is unsafe from crazy tricks, from unscrupulous police, and from intimidators masquerading as "pimps" (not like you), who might beat her or smear her makeup. To get in at this level you will say something along the lines of, "I want to protect you," but that is usually not enough. You need to combine this need with a need from one of the other levels of the Pyramid.

At the third level of the Pyramid are the human needs for love and belonging, such as the love of family and friends. Usually the prostitute is not getting these needs met. That's why the easiest way to get started pimping is to fall in love with a woman who is turning tricks. She has a need for love that is not getting met. The average guy on the street does not see her as a logical prospect for a love relationship and her family doesn't love her—they probably sexually abused her when she was a little girl and then lied about it. Her only friends are other prostitutes, who often are dishonest, confused, and needy themselves.

This is where a good pimp can make a living for himself, if he's got the right stuff to be a pimp. All of these women need love. A lot of them are good-looking, resourceful, and funny. If you can find a way to "have feelings" for them, you will be rewarded financially. The problem is, once you fall in love, you have to watch the woman you love go out and have sex with different men each night, and that is not easy. This is what separates elevated pimps from wannabes. It takes a man's man, a true player, a Mack, a pimp, to *really love* a woman who is having sex with other men every night. If you think you can do this, you are ready to become an elevated pimp. If you could never love one of these "bitches," then you're better off calling yourself a pimp and looking for a puddle of water inside Walgreen's so you can fall down, injure yourself, and then mount a lawsuit.

Of course, if you have good theatrical skills and knowledge of the Pyramid, you might be able to provide an *illusion of love*—that is, to make her think that you love her. But these women, through their work, become astute judges of human nature and they can spot a lie from down the street. They've heard pimp lines before, and although they may appreciate the attention, in the end they are going to support the man-pimp who they believe is "in their corner."

As you get near the top of the Pyramid, the area of need is less, but it still exists and may provide a way for you to be a pimp. At the fourth level, right underneath the top, is the need for "ego/self-esteem." Everybody wants to feel good about themselves and that is a hard thing for prostitutes to do. They need to feel respected—it's not as pressing a need as the need for food and water, warmth or love, but it is the kind of thing that can ruin a person's life if they don't get it. That is why so many sex workers are addicted to drugs. They feel bad about themselves so they shoot heroin every day to forget about it. A lot of them were abused as children—most of them, in fact—and they have been feeling bad for a long time. You, as a pimp, will understand the pathway that brought her into this life and you'll show some understanding and sympathy. You'll respect her and show her that she should respect herself.

At the top of the Pyramid is the need for self-actualization—the need to "be all that you can be." It's hard to find a way in at this level but it is possible if you provide a dream for the future—a way out. You explain that what she is doing now represents something temporary; that you know she is better than this so she is just doing it until you "get your insurance settlement," inherit some money, or make it as a rapper or a rock star.

If you meet the prostitute's needs at different levels of the Pyramid, simultaneously you will make money. You've got to meet needs at the third and second levels while you are trying to find a way in at the fifth level. Then you will have a devoted woman pulling for you. You will call her your "baby girl" or "hope-to-die-woman." Once you have that, you will enjoy the benefits of being an elevated pimp and know that it is time to expand your empire. Your hope-to-die-woman will help you to recruit new women. She will think she is your business partner.

The only other way to become a pimp fast is to provide a business opportunity for a prostitute—to show her she can make more money in an easier way than she does right now. See, it's all about relationships. If you have a relationship with someone who sets up dates for girls—a massage parlor, acupuncture studio, or the tricks themselves—you can go up to a girl who already has a pimp and offer her something better. A bigger cut of the money, a safer work environment, or maybe even a fun group of people to hang out with between dates. If you can connect with a pimp who is running a business, a house of prostitution, or an outcall service, and then see what their needs are, you might be able to be a liaison between working prostitutes who might take advantage of good business opportunities and the people offering those opportunities. It's important to behave like a businessman. Go to a massage parlor and ask if they need help. Make it clear that you have a "girlfriend" who is looking for work and that she does the kind of work that this business offers. Be friendly and ask them if there is some kind of bonus that you might receive if you bring them good earners. In these arrangements, the house gets half and the girl gets half plus tips. It doesn't leave much for you.

You make these choices and then you have to live with them.

The time will come when you want security and the Life will not have as much appeal for you as it does now. After you've learned that pimping is a job, you'll want a vacation. You won't want to be "high-siding." Showing your car and your hos around the track won't have any appeal because you will realize that the people out there are really crumb-bums and the only thing that separates you from them is your respect for the game. By that time you will want to move in different circles and get respect from a different kind of person. You will have become accustomed to a certain quality of life and may be unwilling to compromise that lifestyle. Your business may flounder and you will start to run "Murphy" schemes or blackmail or you may look at opportunities outside of pimping, like selling dope or doing robberies. Then you will make mistakes, you'll take chances you wouldn't otherwise take and you may wind up in the penitentiary. When you get out it's harder to come up. Maybe your hope-to-die-lady will send you some money for the prison commissary at first, but in time she'll find someone new. You may end up walking around the Tenderloin asking people for beer money and eating at St. Anthony's like so many retired pimps do. But you will have your memories. These are the choices we make.

You've got all the Mack-ability now. Remember your responsibility to all the players who came before you. Work on having a name that people will remember. "T-Dog" ain't makin' it. "Pair-a-dice" is already taken. So is "Iceberg Slim." Don't put yourself on Front Street and always show respect for the game that puts food in your mouth, gas in your tank, and respect into the eyes of the young players looking to come up. You the real thing baby. Skip the light fandango for me, Fast Ricky. 'Cuz every scam has a lifespan, and my time is about up.

RESPECT FOR THE GAME

The Police called Fillmore Slim
To identify the body of one Muriel Washington
A known prostitute
found dead in the bay

He was the only person
Who saved the newspaper clipping
December 12, 1974
with her mug shot

He would take it out many years later
And tell her story
On Tenderloin street corners,
or penitentiary cells

That is why
When she was alive
She worked the streets
And gave him her money

At the age of six
Frédéric Chopin was a gentle, sensitive boy
his parents stopped bringing him to the symphony
because he often burst into tears at the sound of music

SILENT

On the Big Yard
Art is everywhere
Etched into the skins
Of former foster care kids
Turned convict

One man walks the yard alone
He wears a shirt that he cannot take off
The ink of a thousand ballpoint pens
Pushed under his skin by the tips of old guitar strings and sewing needles
In group home midnights
Or D Block lockdowns

Across his shoulders; the letters "S O C A L"
And below this
A pictorial history of Los Angeles
The Pachuco Riots, the movie industry, and surf culture
Underneath the left arm
A lifelike rendering of Adolf Hitler
Underneath the right arm
A shamrock with the numbers 666 in the center
Four teardrops from his left eye
A Sistine Chapel of convict art
And down the back of two gigantic biceps are the words:

P
G R
A I
Y D
E

He is called "Silent"
Because he speaks to no one
And no one speaks to him
No one even speaks *of* him

Except for an old man who once said in chow line
"There go Ol' Silent . . . He don't talk to nobody . . ."

I wanted to speak to him
And when he ran past the Woodpile
Where the peckerwoods sat
I said "Good Morning . . ."

Silent kept running
But the Woods, playing Pinochle with their White Pride tattoos,
Had heard what I said
And one of them said to me: "Don't fuck with Silent . . ."

I decided this was good advice
But when we lined up to be searched after our day on the Yard
Silent stood next to me
He knew that I was the one who had spoken to him

You could see it on his arms!
How lonely he was . . .
I spoke to him, again
"You've got some really amazing tattoos, man . . ."

The room had been a maelstrom of convict clatter and clanging doors
Now it was quiet, as Silent regarded me with a blank stare
too late now
I looked back at him

Silent reached up and lowered the elastic band of his orange convict pants
No one could look away
We saw his tattoos
Black flames reaching down the shaft of an erect penis
A small "happy face" at the very tip

The guard turned
He addressed Silent by his real name
"Miller! What the *fuck* is you doin'?
Man, git yo' hands up against that wall!"

Silent covered himself slowly
He put his hands on the wall
They shook him down for weapons and other contraband
Then we moved back into the cellblocks
When they called for "Yard" at 11 A.M. the next day
I stayed in my cell

I left Old Silent
On the Big Yard
But I thought you should know
He was there

Gay Pride, motherfucker . . .

GEORGINA SPELVIN

I first met Georgina Spelvin in a movie theater in Portland, Oregon, where I was attending a showing of the greatest porn film ever made, *The Devil in Miss Jones.* She stood twenty feet high. I followed her through an astonishing odyssey, from her beginning as a wide-eyed innocent spinster virgin suicide to the fulfilling of every dark forbidden sexual pleasure—including, of course, the famous rendezvous with the greatest snake in the history of adult entertainment—to her existential ending in a cell, an unfulfilled love addict doomed to an eternity of emptiness. I was riveted by Georgina's eyes burning a hole in my soul like I was plugged into her and she into me. I'd seen many pornographic films at this point, and I'd seen many great movies. But I'd never seen a pornographic film that was also a great movie. With a great actress, giving the performance of a lifetime.

I had already been retired from the sex business for a year at that point. I was eighteen and going to Reed College. I was just beginning to become a sex addict: The seeds had been beautifully planted, fertilizer applied, just enough sun, and—in Portland—rain rain rain. *The Devil in Miss Jones* played at that little movie theater for years. I saw it over and over again. I must have jerked off dozens of times with Georgina Spelvin. I used to sit in the dark with all those other perverts and couples on dates (yes, a pornographic movie at that moment in history was something you took your date to) and meditate while I watched. Thought about my life and what I wanted to do with it. I couldn't picture the person I wanted to be, but I knew I didn't want to be the person I was: a torn up, ripped up, fucked up, utterly unlovable ex–rent boy. I even took one of my upscale upper-crusty uptown Reed College girl fuck buddies to see Georgina; we made out furiously and jacked each other off underneath my big coat. You just can't buy memories like those. So I really felt like I knew Georgina Spelvin in some primal, soul-mate way.

Imagine my surprise and delight when she suddenly showed up in my life. We met by appointment at a high-end delicatessen in Beverly Hills, not even a stone's throw from where I turned tricks when I was seventeen. There they were, those eyes, sparkling and shining with the same fire I remembered. She was charming, gracious, welcoming, down to earth, smart, salty, with this truly goofy humor right out of vaudeville.

She said she wanted to write her life story. I felt so grateful when I sold my memoir that I decided I would help people tell their stories. I had no idea this decision would bring me face to face with this lady who had helped me through some very lean years of my life. We worked really hard together on her book. I gave her voluminous notes, the way that my mentor had given me voluminous notes. Georgina Spelvin worked her ass off. And then I got the sweetest message a book doctor can get: My patient, the writer with the manuscript in hand and dream in heart, was going to be a published author. Hallelujah and hallelujah once again!

Writing a good book about your life is a very, very hard thing to do. It requires not only the skills of a wordsmith and a storyteller, but it also demands self-knowledge and introspection, a desire to dig into the best and the worst parts of yourself, and a willingness to reveal them to the world. You learn a lot about someone when you work on their memoir with them. And I learned that the soul that rocked me as a teenager watching her twenty feet high came from a fire burning deep inside that shines still fierce and strong in Georgina Spelvin.

Some people, when you push them, just stop. Not her. She has a real old-school work ethic. Nose to the grindstone. Elbow grease. Of all the book doctor clients I've ever had, and I've had many of them, Georgina was the most fun to work with. An easy laugh, a dry, ironic, naughty sense humor, and a lifetime of observing the human condition the way only she can. I am proud to call Georgina Spelvin my friend.

THE ACCIDENTAL HOOKER

The Devil in Miss Jones, a surprisingly acclaimed porno film released in 1972, took me, its principal actor, across America in a spate of personal appearances. The film emporiums that featured such fare ranged from small "mom-and-pop" shops in far-flung outposts like Fortuna, California—a wide spot in the magnificent Sequoia forest—to splashy palaces in the urban heart of many a major city.

The smaller venues, such as the charming one in Fortuna, were clean, cozy, and attended by almost as many couples as single men. The city shops, which generally featured strippers as an adjunct to the films, were less so, but still had an air of socially acceptable naughty fun. A few places were adjacent to bars where the girls were "invited" to socialize with the patrons, downing the watery drinks purchased for them and making any arrangements for further activity they cared to. I was never asked nor expected to extend my stage appearances beyond the stage in this manner. It was clearly understood, I was not a whore. Not me. I was an actress: a porno star. I did my fucking in front of lights, cameras, and a select few crew members. And I was paid, not by the men with whom I was participating in assorted sex acts, but by ephemeral beings known as "producers." Hell, even the courts had ruled that performing in sex films did not constitute prostitution.

My tour took me to one of the lately arrived stroke houses on 42nd Street in New York City. The fabled Great White Way, whose hallowed boards I had traversed as a dancer in the '50s, had been overtaken by the newly allowed hardcore films of the '70s. The name Georgina Spelvin graced almost every billboard along that street of dreams. It was not quite the dream I had envisioned when I arrived from Texas, toe shoes in hand, in 1954.

The current venue was up a flight of poorly lit stairs over one of the many "book" stores jammed cheek to jowl amongst the old theaters. This was in the dark ages before VCRs and, subsequently, DVDs took porn out of the theaters and into the bedrooms where it belongs. In these early days, the "book" stores had only slick magazines, a few primitive sex toys, and the ubiquitous back room where loops (short films that played over and over at the drop of a quarter) could be viewed in relative privacy. The smell of working men's sweat-caked jackets, tobacco, and congealed jizzum permeated the premises.

The proprietors, as courteous and concerned as any I had encountered, directed me to the tiny dressing room behind the raised and lit platform that served as a stage. The other two girls who would share the room had not yet arrived.

Against one of the three longer sides of the oddly shaped room, a clean white towel covered the counter space before the mirror. Bottles, jars, and tins of makeup were neatly arrayed along the back of the space. Colorful spangled, feathered, and flowing gowns were carefully hung on hangers beside the dressing table. A framed photograph showing a good-looking black couple with two children, one a babe in arms, leaned against a minuscule TV sitting beside the area covered by the towel. Several pairs of stiletto-heeled shoes sat primly under the table in a tidy row.

The dressing table area on the other side of the room was completely obscured by a teetering pile of makeup, wadded up G-strings, assorted food and drink containers with crusted remains clinging to their edges, shoes, magazines, combs, brushes, emery boards, nail polish bottles (both open and closed), and totally unidentifiable masses of assorted detritus spilled over onto the floor and much of the adjacent countertop that seemed to be my station.

I was standing in open-mouthed amazement at the mess before me when a tall, graceful, ebony-skinned creature with carefully coifed tresses piled atop classic features walked into the room and set her purse and tote bag down on the chair before the neat table.

"Just shove that pig's stuff off onto her side of the floor. She spreads like a disease. Hi, my name's Keisha. You must be Georgina." A strong hand reached out in welcome. I grasped it in grateful camaraderie. "Don't worry about Miss Piggy. She won't get here until precisely forty-five seconds before she goes on and will be out of your hair long before my set's done and you go on. She works the streets in between shows." The last bits of information were delivered as my roommate slipped quickly from her modest street wear and donned a dressing gown pulled from the copious tote bag.

"Those your kids?" I asked, referring to the photo.

"Oh yes," said with a sigh that indicated huge amounts of love coupled with huge amounts of trouble and concern. "They're a lot bigger now. That's an old photo, but it's one of my favorites. We were visiting my husband's folks in Alabama when that was taken. He still had a good job then, and we could actually take vacations."

"What does he do?" I asked the now seated stripper.

"He's doin' three to fifteen at the moment," she replied with a sardonic twist of a smile as pancake makeup was daintily applied over prominent cheekbones. "Got busted for a lousy nickel bag. That's why I'm shakin' my booty for the boobs out there. It pays better than flipping burgers and I can run home between shows."

"You live that close by?"

"Yeah, on 45th between Eighth and Ninth." Makeup now going on the long, shapely legs.

"We used to call that 'The Dance Belt,'" I exclaimed with joy. It had been the preferred residence of the Broadway Gypsies, as we referred to ourselves, in the golden age of musicals.

"Right. There's still a lot of dancers living in our building. Most are pretty old, now."

My fleeting glance at my own image in the mirror behind her was unstoppable.

"It *was* a long time ago," I concede.

During the course of our conversation, I had cleared a space for myself and set out my sparse makeup needs on the table now claimed as my own. I hung my sleek, shiny, black jumpsuit on the only empty hook in the room, then pulled forth my tap shoes from my own copious tote and placed them on the floor beneath the table.

"What the fuck are those?" asked my new companion. "Tap shoes? You gotta be kidding. You gonna *tap dance* for these bozos?"

"Why not? I take my clothes off first," I assured her.

"Tap shoes." She shook her carefully coiffed head in bemusement.

At this point, the third of our contingency could be heard in the hall just outside the door of our sanctuary.

"I don't care what your stupid fucking policy is. I can walk in or out of this scum hole with any damn person I want. Who the hell do you think you are? My fucking mother, for Christ's sake?"

The door was popped open by the impact of a scarlet booted foot. A pile of take-out containers was held so that the face was obscured, but I had no doubt as to the identity of the party behind them.

The boxes were placed on the chair, cleared for the occasion by the same booted foot. A black wig was ripped off and tossed on top of the pile on the dressing table. The new arrival shimmied out of the tightest pair of hot-pink hot pants I had ever seen. As the dropped drawers were kicked aside to lie in a crotch-crusted curl under the table, the face leaned toward the mirror and a fresh layer of glossy red lipstick was applied throughout the course of the following exchange.

"You the fuck films star, Georgiana?"

"Georgina," I correct with a smile.

"Wanna go shoppin' between shows? I know the best place to get great stuff for our kind of people."

I guess my blank stare prompted an explanation.

"You know. Whores and pimps. I get a discount at the place. They got everything. Great boots. Look at the platforms on these fuckers. Three fuckin' inches."

The boots under discussion were unzipped, liberating calves as pudgy as the thighs and now bare buttocks above them. When the frothy blonde show wig was slapped into place and the apparition turned toward me, I could barely suppress a giggle. An exact replica of the famous Muppet, Miss Piggy, stood before me. The front-opening corselet hastily buckled into place and copious folds of sheer, marabou-trimmed *penoir* tossed over it enhanced the effect.

Keisha was right. Exactly forty-five seconds after the boisterous arrival, the familiar strains of "Love to Love You Baby" oozed through the speakers. The round little fist clutching a large bottle of Jergens lotion punched the door open, and the porcine performer clattered through it, teetering on platform mules and wafting a cloud of heavy perfume.

I looked into the mirror and caught the eyes of my new friend rolled skyward in that familiar expression that suggests there's just no accounting for some folk. My giggles finally spilled over and the two of us almost laughed ourselves into a coma.

The assumption that anyone who made fuck films was automatically in "the Life" bothered me a bit at the time, but I considered the source and thought no more about it—until a year or so later.

Older than the average porn actor to start with (I was thirty-six when the film was shot) I had definitely outlived my usefulness as a fornicatrix in films. The jobs had simply dried up. I was broke, as usual. An old pal and porn producer, Henri Pachard, called to see if I would do a quick shoot for him. Would I! When he learned I was tap city, he sent me two hundred bucks to help cover my rent. In the course of our conversation, I said things were so bad I was seriously considering turning tricks to survive. I was being sarcastic, but he gave me the number of an "old friend" of his: "a really great gal who keeps a nice clean stable." I not only wrote down the number, God help me, I called her.

She was, indeed, a wonderful woman with a fine sense of humor and the requisite heart of gold. My faith in the world's first profession was restored. She said she would make some calls and let me know as soon as she had a booking for me. It sounded so much like a nightclub gig, I sort of just accepted it as another performance opportunity and crossed my fingers.

I really didn't expect to hear from her for several days, but her return call came within a half hour. I was a hot item on her circuit, it seemed. She wanted to know how many tricks I wanted to turn per day, explained the sixty-forty split I could expect (which seemed fair to me; it was, after all, her linen), and asked how soon I could report for duty!

Boy. How many tricks per day? The most number of times I had fucked in a single day for films topped off at three—and one of those had been a girl-girl thing, which is much easier on the tissues. Nevertheless, it seemed silly to spend money on gas to get there and not make as much money in a day as I could.

"What's the usual number of sessions in a day?" I asked naively.

"Some girls are good for one an hour. Others only want to do one a day."

No help at all. "How much will I make for each trick?"

"Because of the films you've done, you're sort of a Boutique item," she explained. "I can get two hundred dollars a session for you."

"That's eighty for me?"

"Right. If they want to get kinky, you're free to set your own price and I don't take any off that."

I suppressed a slight shudder.

Hmmmm? What about all those books I'd read where girls were paid in the thousands? Oh well. Let's see . . . my rent was $325 a month. If I did two tricks a day I could survive until I could figure out what to do about my life.

"Can I try two sessions tomorrow and see how it goes?"

"Sure. Most clients like nooners. Do you need a rest between, or can I schedule a twelve thirty and a one thirty?"

"Go for it. What time should I show?"

"Come on over around eleven to eleven thirty. I'll show you where everything is and we can have a bite of lunch."

"Who will I be . . . never mind. I don't wanna know. You just tell me their first names when they get there."

"That's why they're called 'Johns,' dear. You don't really need to know their names. If they want you to call them something, they'll tell you."

"Oh." Pause. "OK. Well, I'll see you tomorrow."

I lasted one day.

The next day I applied for work at a temp agency.

Not that the "Johns" weren't nice guys. They were both regular sorts. More interested in my work in films than in the current activity, I think. Took forever to get them off.

It wasn't the working conditions. The apartment was luxurious and scrupulously clean. Gabby, the "Madam," was a delightful gal. We became friends in spite of my bombing as a whore.

And bomb I did. Truth be told, cameras turn me on. Fucking without benefit of erotic excitement was just plain hard work and downright painful.

Fortunately, my mother had insisted that I learn to type if I planned to pursue a career as a dancer. My guardian angel was back on duty. The temp agency sent me to a job where I learned the trade that sustained me for the next twenty-some-odd years: desktop publishing.

I still hold the firm belief that prostitution should not only be legal, but deserves some respect for its ineradicable place in society. The "working girl" who makes a proper business of her business is as deserving of success as any entrepreneur.

Yet, I despair of the downtrodden, drugged slaves of the demented control freaks who take all the earnings of their "stable" and abuse their "stock" shamefully. There are good and bad managers in every business.

Fucking for demanding clients is damn hard work. You can't just lie there "and think about your canning," as it was so colorfully phrased by a tight-lipped matron when asked what she thought about connubial relations in the film *Night of the Hunter*. It's also way more dangerous than it needs to be. However, not until the double standards of sanctimonious citizens are shelved, and a realistic attitude toward the natural urges of the human condition is achieved, will anything nearing a proper place for The Necessary Trade be assured.

Meanwhile, do your part. Take a hooker to lunch.

HAWK KINCAID

I first saw Hawk Kincaid onstage. He was singing "I'm on Fire" by Bruce Springsteen. I love that song. *I got a bad desire . . . I'm on fire.* Yes, Hawk sang with a beautiful voice, but it was more than that. He inhabited that song. Haunting, plaintive, hungry. Fire. Hawk's hotness does not come from the fact that he is beautiful and/or cute. Although he is very cute—I'm not saying that. But Hawk beams. He sang, "At night I wake up with the sheets soaking wet and a freight train running through the middle of my head." I was transfixed. At one point he got very quiet, and this huge crowd got very quiet with him. There's something so mystical and powerful about eight hundred people suddenly so quiet you can hear your own heartbeat. And then Hawk let it loose and tore it up. And brought the house down. And then I found out that Hawk, besides being an amazing performer and singer and Springsteen interpreter, is also a Renaissance man. Poet, artist, activist, bon vivant, and man about town. He interviewed me for his website, HOOK, which was a revolutionary cyber information center for men in the sex business. So I thought I would return the favor. Included here is my interview with Hawk, and after that, a poem of his. And if you look at the front cover of this book, you will see another of the many talents of Hawk.

AN INTERVIEW: HAWK KINCAID & DAVID HENRY STERRY

HAWK WAS BORN and grew up in the middle of America's hinter-heartland: Central Illinois. His was a nomadic childhood, and his parents divorced when he was in the second grade.

> **HAWK:** I won't be so trite as to say my mom was the purest woman on the planet: she had great qualities and human flaws. She spent a lot of herself trying to get approval from my grandmother, from everyone. I remember her caught up in the frustrations of fulfilling expectations. I have brought much of that into my own life—as if what I do is never enough. I make myself acutely aware of whether I am following a path that I determined for myself instead of by others. I have memories of her as constricted, and that is what I find myself running away from. My brothers disagree with me, but I think she regretted not being able to explore more diverse interests. I don't want to regret that for myself.

Hawk's dad had difficulty finding a passion for anything in life. And apparently had a very hard time being alone.

> **HAWK:** For me, my father's a solid, caring family provider who embraced everything from theater to philosophy, but never really made them a life's passion. He took to "Dad" things, like golfing, fishing, mowing lawns, and watching TV with beers in hand. Eventually he shacked up with my stepmonster, a failed actress gone alcoholic. Wicked-tongued and passionate, she provided him with alternating pieces of trauma and joy. My father and I never talk about these things or in any detail about my website, HOOK, or my personal life. I still don't chatter well with my father. My family says I spend too much time thinking about the past, the reasons and impacts of our decisions, but I fear the inevitable reproduction of the life I grew up with, and that's why it's important to me.
>
> I have shown my brothers HOOK and we have talked about it in various ways and circumstances. My father should know by now, as I have never hidden my involvement with sex work. But I don't bring it up. I can't

tell you if that is because I don't want to talk about it and I avoid him or because his opinion would mean so little. I imagine it more the latter.

Hawk was a chubby, unattractive redhead, as a child. According to him, anyway. Often made fun of and quiet, he yielded to television whenever he could.

HAWK: I can't recall many friends growing up because we kept switching neighborhoods and because my family did not encourage that kind of social behavior. One of the biggest forces to change that was a babysitter named Pauline. She was passionate, loudmouthed, and, in a world where things seemed so sterile, she was an opposition. Not dirty, but touched: the glasses in her kitchen, her aged beads and curtains that separated rooms, her velvet paintings. Some of my fondest memories from childhood are at Pauline's, lip-synching to Chicago records, hanging bags of Avon samples on doors in rich neighborhoods, the smells and all. It felt more real than my own family, which was so concerned with appropriateness.

Hawk went to a private high school and remarks, "Public junior high made me understand why kids kill themselves." He's always had a hard-on for religion. Literally.

HAWK: I have terrible memories of getting hard-ons in church, and perhaps this is the source of my persistently negative association with the church, religion, and formality. When I get a little sleepy sometimes I accidentally get a hard-on. Jesus notwithstanding, the notion of sex and church has never been linked in my head, but my body was uncontrollable. In church I always devised plans. Used to pinch myself. I never understood it. But the body is like that. My mother's cancer. My constant battle with flab. The body infrequently does what I want it to.

Hawk is very self-conscious about his body.

HAWK: I gotta fight getting fatter. I think that feeling unattractive is the propulsive force for a lot of guys in the business. Certainly for myself, the flattery of men responding positively to you affects your mood, your sense of self. But that tends to be an addictive path. Looking outside to find that validation is a long self-destructive cycle. I've seen a lot of people fall into some bad behaviors to maintain that position. To give priority to strangers over their lovers, friends. Gaining pleasure from giving pleasure, or craving being appreciated is simply human—but needing that in ever increasing amounts will kill ya.

DHS: Do you feel like you are a beautiful person?

HAWK: I have good energy.

DHS: Do you feel like you're attractive?

HAWK: I ain't a model.

DHS: How do you deal with being naked with various clients?

HAWK: It isn't that hard. I had clients who were big gym bunnies, jocks, younger than me. They didn't hire me to be pretty, they hired me to play a part, to make them interesting for a period of time. I am unique in this business in that I don't represent normal images seen in magazines and idealized in the gay world. How many of us do? At times, I think that is where I found success. I never pretended to be pretty, I simply was genuine. I found clients interesting, and that was something they liked. Truth is that I am jealous of pretty men. Beautiful people paid to be beautiful have to spend their energy there, and my success in the business was not on being beautiful outside; it was about the conversations, the conviction, the energy, and the other attributes I leveraged. It will never be my job to be beautiful.

Hawk first had sex with a female when he was seventeen. He recalls, "I remember her as baby-powder-smelling underwear with roses or flowers on it. Pink. Definitely pink." He now identifies himself as queer. His first sex work experience was with a man. He was in college at the time, staying with some bigoted, ignorant, distant family members, who accused him of gangbanging, doing drugs, and screwing girls.

HAWK: Eventually they accused me of trying to kill some family members by doing my laundry (I know, it sounds insane—it was). So, I got a house-sitting gig and met a guy who introduced me to doing bodywork. As weird as it sounds, because of the long hours I had been working, it was ideal. The work was rough, a bit scary, but it just made sense. I mean, I had been working ten-hour days for nothing at an internship, and then trying to work for a record store for three to four hours and making twenty to thirty bucks after taxes. I could turn around one hundred dollars in a session doing massage, and with tips, upwards of two hundred dollars. Since I was uncertain about housing and scared about being so many miles from my home and my family, it was the right choice.

Hawk was nervous the first time he had sex for money, but he now feels he should have asked for more money. "Never shortchange yourself," he says. "I never felt guilt about the money. Just guilt about the sorrow." When he first started doing bodywork, he was paid more for doing "extras."

HAWK: The extras sometimes involved sex, sometimes because I liked the client, sometimes for affirmation—hell, I even dated one of my clients and he is still one of my dearest friends. I think that's the strange part of the sex industry, that even in my most panicky moments, it was often an attempt to connect to people. The money part has always been hard for me. Not just in sex work, but even now as a freelance designer, I dread the billing aspect, because I like what I do. Charging for it seems the right thing to do, but it doesn't always feel right. Sometimes, I think the generosity I have stems from feeling awkward about asking for compensation. Leftover deposits of Midwest Protestantism. That being said, having sex for money was never wrong. It wasn't a moral issue. It was the feeling that these are vulnerable people, and I am cautious about business operations or personal behaviors that leverage people's weakness. That is the source of guilt for me. Not the morality of prostitution, but the sense that making people feel better about themselves is a paid-for operation. Sex can be an industry—but self-esteem just feels diluted when you commercialize it. It's why I don't trust bartenders or psychologists. They make a living off of your sorrows.

Hawk's specialty was breaking and entering, also known as B&E. This involves surprising a client, tying him up, and fucking him. His ads as a sex worker featured a rough, tough persona.

HAWK: Bondage was definitely my thing. And spanking, paddling, and abuse. I preferred bondage, though, because I could tie them up and leave for a bit, come back and be mean, hit them, and then leave. Low maintenance. It also gave me control with clients and meant I had little contact if I wanted. Kink was where I made most of my money, and now, when my partner brings up some kinky ideas, I always resort to cuddling 'cause kink is what I did with customers, and I think it reminds me too much of that. Cuddling is something I do with people I care about.

This might be something to deal with in the future, I think . . . not to vilify radical sex in general, but I just think that it has taken me a long time to rethink sex and contact in positive, constructive terms that don't mean fear. I think people are often afraid of contact, but now, it is what drives me. Laughing during sex. Joy during sex. Porn doesn't cover that for me. And there is a cool aesthetic to that kind of aggressive image: That was an image I maintained with clients, but it is not what I want to come home to.

My partner says I'm a lot of false advertising since my ad looks so rough, but my real identity is more cuddly and fuzzy. I am softer than I let on, especially when working—but that was the edge. To be in control maintained my safety, my security, and solidity in that market. It gave me the elements I needed to walk in and out of the industry intact. It was a fun image but definitely a lot of work.

Hawk often found that his clients were turned on by being controlled.

HAWK: It's what all people want, for the most part. Freedom from responsibility, from having to make choices. Most men seem to equate sex with freedom from thought. Sex is a way to avoid loneliness most of the time. To forget about it for a short time. People want a psychiatrist who doesn't make them self-consciously aware they are seeking treatment. We play doctors, and the more you understand that what they need more than sex is care, you are good to go. With a client, it's all performance. I don't think it's about being turned on. That doesn't matter. It's like theater, and you treat it like theater. They don't know and they certainly don't care. They don't want you to be real. Real people have problems, dramas, credit card bills, etc. They want you to be simple, and they will want you to be a separate part of their lives. They want you, most importantly, to leave quietly.

Being in the sex business has never really inhibited Hawk in his relationships, but he had commitment problems anyway.

HAWK: A few guys shied away from me when they found out what I did, but in the gay world, I think that prostitution is hardly news to anyone. I've been honest my whole life about being in the sex business. Oftentimes I think guys have sex to make a connection. The quality of the sex is bad, and I know I used it for that, as well. When we get hooked up in a relationship, suddenly you don't need to have sex, so you don't. Or the thrill of sex was not knowing the other person well, and when you get someone you know, the thrill is gone. I often associated sex with those two elements: work or loneliness.

Hawk acknowledges that there are diehards who want to reminisce about the beautiful badass days of street hustling and the hyper-masculinity it conjures.

HAWK: But they have short memories and are probably lonely or bored with the reality of today (and were just as bored in the reality then, but choose to forget). It was a messy, self-destructive lifestyle that was either littered with rape and drug abuse or self-involved ego issues. I made it in and out of the industry with my body and health intact. I could lay down my own rules, and I was never in a position of being abused. I have been ripped off—my own damn fault—for a check. Yes, a *check*! Of course, he voided the check and I never got my money. But if that's the worst mistake I made in years of taking clients, then consider me lucky.

After having been in the Life for a while, Hawk decided to start a website for male sex workers. Thus HOOK was born.

HAWK: HOOK was a project that grew from my frustrations with the silence around the male sex industry. The only discussions I could find treated male prostitutes as victims or were the self-destructive biographies that the press loves to promote. There were other stories. Not just mine, but many stories.

I consider myself unique in this particular industry because as a sex worker, I have gone in and out again a few times, maintained being sober the entire existence, and have spoken publicly in all forums about the issue. The idea of HOOK was to pull together true stories and tips from guys in the business. When I was in the business, one thing I did share with others was the lack of connection. The separation between different sides of my life, and often the inability to really find an ear that understood. Where was I to vent? Especially since a lot of guys took up drugs or alcohol to release those feelings (which often made them worse). I wanted to provide a format that would open up that dialogue and help people avoid some of the common mistakes. The point was to say, "Hey, this happened to me, and here's something you can do to prevent it from happening to you." In the same vein, a lot of guys are in the business for immediate cash and lose sight of long-term goals or what to actually do with the cash or how to get more cash while making better decisions. Often the fast cash comes with the worst decisions, like more money for barebacking, i.e., having unprotected sex. And HOOK serves as a publication by, for, and about guys in the business. We don't push people into the business on a float of "Whore Pride," and we don't tell people to get out. What we do is simply tell it like it is as best we can. Through guides and tips and materials, we attempt to build something that is fun, comfortable, and, most of all, helpful.

You can find the history of HOOK at http://hookonline.org/program/ap.htm.

ANAL GEOMETRY

Two dozen years,
and I am still a stranger to my ass.
Truth is that we have never even met,
shaken hands or done much
other than bump into each other
on occasion or simply rub each other the wrong way
in private moments,
the lesser known stories of the rich and famous begin
with the parts of them they don't know.
I'd like to hold a conversation,
take it to lunch.
Ask it if it blushes at the attention,
or perhaps it is a feminist/radicalist ass
that rustles up deep-seated anger
toward your comments,
and suggests you
pay more attention to my breasts.
It could be fluent in many languages.
I don't know.
We've never met.
Or maybe we've met, but my ass was too shy
to say something—like boys who dance as close as they can
to get a good luck—just hoping one of you has the balls
to do something about it.
My ass would.
I can tell. A good conversation and my ass might
turn the whole world around.
Ask your ass.
I bet there is a high percentage of asses
that can fit physics and cultural criticism,
lawn ornamentation and world peace into the same sentence
much better than I did.
My ass would be a doctor. Of mathematics.

It would. It could calculate inches
and diameters and expose the world to
virtual communities where the size of the penis
actually reflects the real person.
We'd throw a party for it.
Dress up my ass in a nice suit.
It might make a speech
and bring the house down
to its knees
begging for more.
Because I never could.
I'm not an ass.

HAWK KINCAID has worked as a host in a restaurant, a shoe and record salesman, a tour guide, and an art teacher for kids. He graduated from Drake University in Des Moines, Iowa, summa cum laude, majoring in broadcast news, minoring in Russian studies and cultural studies, with honors in cultural studies. He is the founder of HOOK, the world's premier website for male sex workers, and is also currently an activist for sex workers, a graphic designer, a photographer, and a performance artist.

SOMETHING ABOUT THE BOY

I LEFT HOME when I was seventeen years old. That is, I left the place where I was born—Savannah, Georgia—and an explosively abusive, single-parent upbringing in the public housing project where I grew up; and after a freshman year at the University of Georgia, 1964 to 1965, decided that I had had enough. Georgia (the university thereof) at that time was an ag-frat-jock school. Translation: You were either an agriculture student, a frat boy, or a jock; if you shared none of these distinctions—and I definitely did not—your happiness there was in dire question. I was gay, knew it, and already acted on it. Ergo, my very existence at the school was not only unwelcome, it was even against the rules in the student handbook, which stated that students could be expelled for "perverse sexual activities." Although I was in the honors program, I was isolated in a freshman dorm, where I had threats against my life and was hazed regularly.

I had started going around with some bohemian kids, older ones from the art and drama departments, who were living off campus and already smoking dope and shacking up, and who hated the ra-ra Southern ag-frat-jock mentality. "You should go to San Francisco," said one of my hip friends who lived in the squalid series of outbuildings and garages known as the Zebra Shacks. "You can do anything there." I decided to take his advice.

So, in June, when I was still seventeen, I put together a canvas suitcase and thumbed from Savannah to San Francisco, with about seventy-eight dollars in my wallet and no idea what to do once I got there.

The city opened itself up to me with the most intense blast of wind I'd ever felt. As Mark Twain said, "The coldest winter I ever spent was a summer in San Francisco." I stayed at the downtown YMCA (which was scary; it was filled with strange men, a large number of them staring at me constantly) and spent my first several days in the city trying to find a job. It was impossible. Everyone in the world wanted to come to San Francisco to do what I was doing—namely, getting away from somewhere else. Finally, almost down and out, I heard about farm work in the San Joaquin Valley, not far from San Jose, the center of California's big ag business. There I was, back in the old world of the U. of Georgia: agriculture!

It was a cheap bus ride into the valley's endless rolling countryside, and for the next couple of weeks I slept out in the fields in a sleeping bag, hitching myself up with various people in a casual but amazingly intimate way. A pair of very butch lesbians who called each other "Sister" decided to "adopt" me for a week, so we ate out of the same pot, slept beside the same fire, and picked apricots and blackberries together. Then I took up with a straight couple, a big blonde named Judy and her redneck husband Bill, who were traveling with Florence, their three-year-old little girl. They could have sprung directly out of *The Grapes of Wrath*. Judy would disappear into the closest fruit town and hustle when the pickings got low. Bill was a mean sonovabitch when drunk, but it was fun swimming naked with him in the irrigation canals that crisscrossed the area.

I moved on after we met a tall, skinny, sun-wrinkled drifter named Tom, who waded up to me one evening in the canal, whispered, "If you ever need anything, boy, just let me know," and started feeling me up under the water, a bit downstream from Bill, who often talked loudly about bashing queers in the face and casually murdering them. I found another hick fruit town, filled with pickers, truck stations, ranches, and fields of produce. I was doing OK on my own, until one evening a group of the local teens drove by me and started shouting some very unappreciated things, honking the horn while attempting to run me down. Being from the South (where we traditionally take no shit), I shot them the bird as they passed. A second later, they screeched to a halt, piled out of their car, and gave chase. Luckily I flagged down two of the local sheriffs.

"He shot the bird at us, Josh!" the kid with the fists said to one of the sheriffs.

"No reason to kill him," the officer said matter-of-factly. He ordered the kids back into their vehicle and told me I had a ten-minute lead to get my butt out of Dodge. "There are fields all around here, boy. Get lost in one and don't come back!"

Good advice. The next morning I was on the road to Los Angeles. I arrived toward sunset in downtown L.A., an area I would describe as part skid row and part zoo. I spent my first night at a Christian mission for down-and-out geezers and then was released into the dawn with nary a clue what to do next. Until I realized that being seventeen and comely from the California sun could be helpful. Men seemed to buzz around me at every point, near bus stops and otherwise. That evening I found a particularly buzzy place close to the downtown YMCA (the Village People were right: the YMCA is "good for every boy").

"What are you out for?" a man about thirty asked me in his car.

Suddenly totally tongue-tied, I couldn't say a word.

"Why don't you just get in?"

I did.

He offered me a cigarette. I didn't smoke but decided this would make me seem more grown up.

He pressed the gas again, and asked: "Is this going to be business or simply pleasure?"

Again stone silent, I just shrugged.

He smiled. "You *are* new at this."

He drove me to a restaurant and bought me dinner. A hamburger, French fries, and a Coke. I gobbled everything. At seventeen, you are always hungry. Then he took me up to Mulholland Drive. The view was gorgeous. We just looked at it. It then occurred to me that this guy was as shy as I was, and I had no idea how to break either his ice or my own. He drove me back to the Y, then suddenly handed me a ten-dollar bill.

"There's something about you. You seem too nice a guy to take advantage of," he said, then drove on.

I had no idea how lucky I had been, but my whole adventure so far had been characterized by luck. I got a room for the night at the Y. In the communal shower, older men propositioned me. I had no idea how to deal with that, but had just enough money for my Y room for another night.

The next day I went back into downtown L.A., into the area around the Greyhound station and Pershing Square, infamous for its street preacher crazies and its quite open sex market. I got hungry and went further down a side street filled with cheap eateries. There I met a man named Blake. In his early thirties, he was short and muscular with blunt features, a thick neck, and brazenly bleached platinum blond hair, which he admitted was "totally whore-able, I know," but had been dyed for a show he'd been doing. He was a professional singer, grand opera quality, from a good family in Miami, down on his luck—but then so much of downtown L.A. seemed to be filled with guys down on their luck, escaping from someplace, drawn by magnetism to this sinkhole. He had no place to stay, had been up all night on coffee, and I had nothing to lose. I snuck him back into my Y room, no easy feat, past a burly guard who had turned his head. Blake was dying for a shower; we showered, then made love in my room. Like real *love*, as in, "Wow! This is what it feels like!" I had never done anything like that before: as in real, pure, physical sex . . . as in . . . this could be magical.

I asked him how he'd been making money, and he told me hustling. "L.A. is filled with queens who'll pay for it. If they'll pay a guy like me, imagine what they'll pay you?"

I did not want to imagine. But what else was I going to do? I had no money, no education, and no family—when you come out totally queer by sixteen, family becomes pretty much beside the point. It's never there anymore, except in isolated, disapproving ways.

We got up the next morning and hit the streets. I was broke, with just enough money for a cup of coffee. That seventeen-year-old hunger was hitting hard. We went back to Pershing Square, and I scored several times that afternoon. Older men (a laugh; sometimes older meant twenty-eight, maybe even thirty-two) would pick me up and take me back to one of the numerous "trick hotels" in the area, where you could get a place for $4.50 or less. They would blow me or I would jerk them off. Since I was a teen "trade" hustler and very fresh meat, it was not expected that I'd do more. As evening approached, I met up with Blake and we got a room together.

The sun-filled days seemed to last forever. There was hanging out in Pershing Square, and picking up johns—Blake, because he would do everything, characteristically got paid more than I did for doing almost nothing—and going to all-night movies, eating cheap greasy food, and even getting to the beach, to Will Rogers State Park, the famous gay beach in Santa Monica. All of this was good, until one day in Pershing Square when I met Rodney.

Rodney was my age, exactly seventeen, and the most beautiful boy I'd met in my life. He was of normal height, but perfectly formed, as if someone had taken a pair of drafting calipers and formed this incredible creature out of classic proportions, with wide shoulders, a perfect honey-skinned chest, and arms, legs, and facial features to match. He had greenish blue eyes and a gaze that was both disarmingly innocent yet capable of destroying anyone. He was from Nashville and had been hustling since he was fourteen. He came from a lower-middle-class family (not completely impoverished, as I had been), and had started working local parks where older married men would meet him, buy him anything he wanted, and then take him back to offbeat hotels. He took small jobs, like babysitting, so his parents wouldn't ask him how he ended up with so much money to buy clothes or spend on things. With his deep, soft Southern drawl, he told me: "I tell 'em from the start: Honey, I don't do nothin' but lay back and let you do all the work. And don't even think about fuckin' me!"

He had his shirt off in Pershing Square. I was taken with him immediately in the most *boing-boing* way. Blake shook his head.

"This is going to be a disaster."

But, like a hurricane, when you are seventeen and in love, how can you avoid it?

He joined us. Kid hustlers don't like to be on their own. The three of us would sleep in the same downtown hotel room, with Blake, who was the only one who'd "do everything," enjoying both of us. I could not imagine going down on Rodney. He had his strict code, and guys who sucked him were johns. I was not going to be a john. But we would make out passionately. He had the kind of beauty I could imagine Tennessee Williams falling for and writing a play about.

One evening, he and I ended up on busy Hollywood Boulevard: hustler central. Suddenly a big blonde teen-movie-surfer-type kid approached us.

"Would you guys like to go to a party? We have a car waiting."

The "party" ended up being in a beach house in Santa Monica; present were two older men, in their forties, and Jeff, the young surfer, paid to procure for them, and of course Rodney and me. What happened was exceedingly "professional" for them. In fact, it shows why teen hustlers are often killed. After the two older men and Jeff had pleasured themselves with Rodney and one of them had fucked me, against my will, they proceeded to dump us back on Hollywood Boulevard, at 3 A.M., like discarded toys. Since the two older men, one of whom told us he was a local deputy sheriff, were twice our size and Jeff was built like a WWF wrestler, there was absolutely no possibility of us putting up a fight. I can only guess what might have happened if we had.

I felt humiliated. Blake always warned, "Ask for the money up front, before the sex," but there was no time or place to do it—we were two kids, and these guys had perfected their snow-job-for-a-blow-job act to a T.

"What do we do now?" I asked Rodney.

He looked around. The area was almost empty.

"Just walk back to downtown."

We were on a dark side street when a cop car cruised by, slowing down. We had to do something; there was a vacant lot nearby with a house going up on it. We dashed into the lot, taking refuge in some unfinished basement construction. A second later, flashlights were aimed in our faces.

"Come out now, or we'll come in after you!"

I was hungry, exhausted, and now everything felt like a dream. One of those painful nightmares that seem too real not to be real. We were shoved in back of a squad car and handcuffed. Rodney was separated from me, and I was stripped and thrown naked into a freezing detention cell with a bare concrete floor and a toilet. A dirty Army blanket was thrown in after me. I couldn't sleep, except in fits. Some boys caged in other cells shouted at me and Rodney, who was jailed close by, "Queers! Faggots! Eat shit, you faggots!"

I was kept there for several days without being able to shower, brush my teeth, or wash. I was told that I'd be shipped back to Georgia—one-way train—or held indefinitely in the cell. One of the guards barked at me, "Your friend's goin' back to Nashville soon. Wanna say goodbye?"

I did. Rodney, back in his clothes, was allowed into my cell. We were in such a state of frozen shock that we had almost nothing to say to one another. I just remember him leaving and the cell door slamming.

Several days later, I was given my clothes and sent on a bus with other young offenders to Los Angeles's huge juvenile hall, home of thousands of other boys, some of whom were in for murder and armed robbery, and others for lighter offenses. I was told that I was busted for being underage on the streets, and (of course) for "suspicion of male prostitution." My mother, a barely functioning schizophrenic, was called, and was told that if she agreed, I could be "shipped" back to her but at her expense. She said it was not necessary. I was asked by a court officer if I knew anyone in Los Angeles who would vouch for me and agree to be my guardian until I turned eighteen, which would happen in September, a mere two months away.

I could only think of Blake, but how could he pass muster and get me out? I remembered that he had been thinking about getting a job at a downtown music store, so I gave the name of the store to the officer, along with Blake's name.

"Is he a homosexual?" the man inquired.

"No, sir."

"Then why is he interested in somebody like you?"

"He's just a nice guy," I answered.

The officer grinned. I was fooling no one, but at least this would be a way for the State of California not to have to feed me for a while.

I stayed in juvy for the next three weeks. It was actually fairly OK in comparison to a lot of my earlier life. Juvy, amazingly, was well racially integrated, and there was a clique of about eight queer boys in my unit of forty-eight kids. We hung out together, playing cards, telling jokes, supporting each other. A few were young cross-dressers who as long as they minded their own business were not bullied or bothered. It was completely different from the world I had left in Georgia, where as a barely passable sissy I had to hide every single moment. We were locked every night into single-person cells, about as big as a coffin, so that no "sex-play" could take place either between boys or adult supervisors. There was a strict rule that you were never allowed to be alone with another person, even with an adult. I was fed regularly; I actually got fat.

At the end of the three weeks, I was told that the court had been able to reach Blake, and he had agreed to be my guardian until I turned eighteen. I felt happy about being able to leave juvy, and yet strangely protected there. Since I had graduated from high school at sixteen and already had a year of college (where I made Dean's List all the time), I was a rare bird there. The social workers and adult supervisors treated me with a certain respect and kindness I had not had in a long time. However, being locked alone in a tiny cell at night was horrible; I felt trapped in it.

I showered and was given clean clothes to leave in. A court officer accompanied me to the courtroom where a judge who meant absolutely nothing to me asked me if I knew why I had been held. I told him I did. He asked me if I'd obey all the rules of my probation and stay in contact with the court through a probation officer until I turned eighteen. I promised I would.

I was then led into another room, and there was Blake, wearing a second-hand suit, his hair no longer platinum. He shook my hand, and we walked out together.

"A pioneer of gay literature" (*ForeWord Magazine*), poet/novelist **PERRY BRASS** has published fourteen books, including *How to Survive Your Own Gay Life*, *The Lover of My Soul*, *The Harvest*, *Angel Lust*, *Warlock*, and *The Substance of God*. His newest is *Carnal Sacraments, A Historical Novel of the Future*. A finalist six times for the prestigious Lambda Literary Awards, he has been given IPPY Awards from *Independent Publisher* for *Warlock, A Novel of Possession* (2002) and *Carnal Sacraments* (2008), which was also named a *ForeWord Magazine* Book of the Year Award finalist. Perry Brass has had fifty poems set to music by such composers as Chris DeBlasio, Ricky Ian Gordon, Christopher Berg, Mary Carol Warwick, and Paula Kimper, and has been included in twenty-five anthologies, including the groundbreaking *Male Muse* (1973), the first-ever openly gay poetry anthology, edited by Ian Young; *The Gay Liberation Book* (1974), edited by Len Richman and Gary Noguera, with contributions by Tom Hayden, John Lennon, and William S. Burroughs; and *The Columbia Anthology of Gay Literature* (1998), edited by Byrne R. S. Fone. He lives in the Bronx, New York, where he reads, writes, and watches the Hudson River.

ZOE HANSEN

L.E.S.

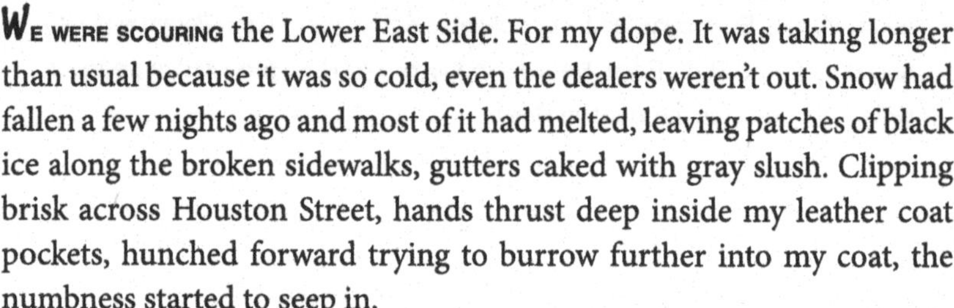

We were scouring the Lower East Side. For my dope. It was taking longer than usual because it was so cold, even the dealers weren't out. Snow had fallen a few nights ago and most of it had melted, leaving patches of black ice along the broken sidewalks, gutters caked with gray slush. Clipping brisk across Houston Street, hands thrust deep inside my leather coat pockets, hunched forward trying to burrow further into my coat, the numbness started to seep in.

We were looking for Leroy, a thin, cool black dude. Leroy was a peacock: tight dark striped pants, black frilly shirt, and a wide-brimmed black hat over mushroom-cloud 'fro were his plumage. We had a friendly dealer/customer relationship, and I appreciated that often he would serve me ahead of the crowd that waved cash in his face.

We would wait, ten or fifteen sick junkies scattered along the street, standing in deserted doorways, hidden in the shadows, waiting and waiting for our man. The moment Leroy came through the door from where he hid his stash, we would descend upon him like starving children, running, pushing each other aside to get served first. Ludlow was a deserted street; there were no businesses except El Sombrero—"The Hat"—a Mexican restaurant.

I was walking with Marilyn. She was petite, thirty-three, Puerto Rican. Marilyn had light skin and long brown hair. I don't think she had had a haircut in a decade, so it hung loose and ratty. Marilyn was just five feet tall, which added to her childlike appearance. When I looked into her eyes, I felt as though she was clinging to a thin lifeline, so much pain came from those eyes. Years of hard-core drug abuse had ravished her small frame, deep grapefruit-sized pits all over her body. She told me it was from speed balling. She had stuck herself so many times that she had no veins left. Large craters ran down her legs, along the insides of her thighs and hips. It was as if someone had taken a dull penknife and cut away at her flesh, leaving gouged-out, deformed limbs. I marveled at the skilled artistry with which Marilyn found a vein in her stomach area and actually hit it. We sat for hours upon hours in her bathroom shooting speedballs and talking. She was raped at thirteen, two children followed at fourteen and fifteen, heroin at sixteen. Marilyn worked as a prostitute outside on Allen and Chrystie streets. She got ten dollars a trick and turned them in their cars and doorways. She had been raped and beaten countless times; I would listen in silence and horror to her stories. But somehow Marilyn's soul hadn't been hardened by her miserable life. On the contrary, she was sunshine amongst the disease, degradation, and death. She showed me a lot of love. When I asked Marilyn what she wanted from life, she thought for a few moments and shook her sad head, choking up. She wanted a normal life, and a man to love. She was only in her thirties but had long given up on that dream. Some of us chose this life, but for Marilyn, the life chose her. Marilyn told me she just wanted to be loved.

I was starting to feel a bit sick, so time was of the essence. We were walking a fast-paced speed walk, dead serious faces. Being eager to find the dope man and to avoid arrest made *the walk* a highly tense activity. Marilyn instinctively knew where to go cop; working the street made her more familiar than I was to what spot was open, or what rated as *good* that particular day.

Marilyn said she heard that Golden Child, which was a heroin brand name, was strong today. We turned onto Stanton Street, a few buildings in. She stopped and eyed the broken stoop in front of us; I followed carefully. She kicked the front door, it creaked open, we slid into a dark hall littered with garbage. It took a minute for my eyes to adjust. One naked bulb was shining at the end of the heavily graffitied hall. At the foot of the stairs was "the man," the one holding the dope. My heart speeding, adrenaline rushing, bowels turning over, I felt terrified, excited, and alive.

The dope man smiled at Marilyn, and they exchanged words in Spanish. Suddenly two large dirty-looking white males were right behind us. I told the dealer I wanted seven bundles. I said it a bit too loudly. I was not being careful; for some reason I was feeling bold and fearless. Sometimes it's good to show no fear to these people. Then just as I said "seven bundles," one of the large white guys asked me quietly for a few dollars. Without thinking I turned and spat, "No, fuck off!" and waved him away. It wasn't usual for me to be so nasty and rude, but my personality was changing. I had been speedballing solidly now for three years, every single day. Sometimes I found myself saying things I wouldn't usually say, and taking risks that were unnecessary and dangerous. I was surprised by my answer to the man. When I thought about it later, I hadn't been intimidated because they were white and unfamiliar. They certainly didn't look like they were from the neighborhood, they were outsiders. I just felt like telling him to fuck off and I made no attempt to stop myself.

I handed over the seven hundred dollars to the dealer. He carefully counted out seventy bags into my palm, in seven bundles of ten bags each. I put the rubber-banded bundles down the front of my jeans, in my underwear. I often wore tights under my jeans when I went to cop, so I could slip bags down the legs of my tights and they wouldn't fall out. I looked down at the bundles. I could feel them through the jeans, but you couldn't see them. Marilyn smiled and we skipped out of the building. I had a lot of dope and felt safe and secure knowing I could blast away for a few days. As I turned with Marilyn to go back down Clinton Street, the large fat white man who had asked me for a few dollars came up behind me, pointed right at me, and said, "OK, you . . . you're under arrest."

Everything stopped. I looked at him in disbelief. But at the same time, I had been at this game for years now, and amazingly it had been uninterrupted by the police. I deserved it now. The karmic laws of nature meant it was just my time. We all have to pay our dues and getting arrested was part of the life. All these thoughts were running through my head as I surrendered, way too easily. Marilyn backed off. I looked at her; she had a confused look on her face. Why was Marilyn looking like that? Didn't she realize these were cops? Arguing wouldn't do any good. No tears. I'm not much of a crier anyway.

I was lead to the curb where a dirty twenty-year-old Ford was parked. I assumed this was a police undercover car. As the dirty white guy, obviously an undercover officer, led me toward the car, I assumed I was to get in it. I was still somewhat in shock and mindlessly following along. As I stood before this *undercover* police car an alarm went off in my head. *Police cars have four doors, not two . . . don't they?* But I was already half in the backseat. Then I was pushed in. Now, I started to sweat, scared beyond belief. My heart was racing, I was so nervous and confused. My biggest fear was being dope sick in a cell. The image I had created when being told of someone's arrest and subsequent detox while in "the tombs" scared me to death. We had all heard the horror stories, the vomiting, shitting, and pissing while huddled on a thin foam mat, still stinking of the last person's sweat and urine. I would have done anything, truly anything, to avoid heroin withdrawal behind bars.

O God help me I am going to be so, so sick in the jail cell . . . Please help me . . . I won't be able to stand in court to even talk to the judge. Please God, no . . . help me, help me . . . I swear, I'll never do another hit . . . well, maybe not never, but I'll cut down . . . I'll do anything, anything, please God help me . . .

Suddenly I realized that these two cops hadn't shown me a badge. Now a part of me began to wonder, "Are these two really cops?" I was just so totally confused. But what if they are cops? I had better get rid of these bundles. I took them out from my underpants and slipped them out of the tight elastic band spilling the loose bags under the seat in front of me.

I looked out to the street. We were behind a slow-moving line of cars. There was Marilyn; she was screaming at me, "They're not cops, they're not fuckin' police! Get out! Get the fuck out!"

I looked away, thinking she'd lost her mind. Why was she screaming like that? If they weren't cops, who the hell were they? But they had to be cops . . . didn't they?

The one driving was thinner and had longer black hair. The one who stopped me on the street looked like a redneck from the country. In fact, they both looked like country boys. Now I was really getting suspicious. I'd so easily gotten into a stranger's car. I bit my bottom lip hard, what a fucking idiot I was. He didn't show me a badge.

I started yelling, "Show me a badge, you're not cops . . . Show me a fucking badge NOW!"

I was really starting to freak out. And I began to hit the passenger over the back of his greasy head. I was pushing his head while yelling. The passenger started fidgeting around with his wallet, which was one of those cheap material billfolds that secures with Velcro. He sheepishly opened it as though somehow a police badge was magically going to appear. He showed it to me. He actually opened up a very empty dirty wallet. I couldn't believe this.

"Are you fucking kidding me? Where's the badge?" I looked at him incredulous.

And here's the weird thing. This hulking grubby guy seemed to get embarrassed. Maybe for a brief moment he really thought he was a cop. I was totally at a loss for words . . . what now?

I was sitting in the backseat leaning over between both these men. I looked closely at them and I could see now they definitely were junkies and sick. Knowing they were dope sick made the possibility of them hurting me, even killing me, become quite real. A nonviolent person can summon supernatural strength, although briefly, when dope sick. A normal sane person could easily become the next Jeffrey Dahmer while riddled with the hideousness of heroin sickness.

The traffic was heavy as we crawled along Clinton Street. Looking back, I could have screamed and shouted, maybe gotten some attention from the people outside. But I also was thinking, *If I do that, and the police do come, I'll get arrested for possession.* I thought it unlikely the police would screech, arrest the two junkie "kidnappers," heroically save me, escort me home in a police cruiser, hand my dope over to me, and bid me "Good day." Ha! Not bloody likely.

We were now driving toward the Brooklyn Bridge. If they took me over that bridge I was dead meat, as I'd never been off Manhattan soil. I had to get out of that car.

That was when the passenger said, "Give me the dope."

I told him that before I got into their car I dropped it in a garbage can on the street. I was trying to still hang onto my precious drugs. I saw them exchange glances. They were probably thinking that the whole fucking plan was a total wash if I had dumped the drugs. But then the man in the passenger seat started to get angry, really nasty. He turned around and told me he was going to fucking rape me, torture me, that no one would ever find me where they were taking me. My heart was beating so fast. At that moment of intense fear I had no control over what came out of my mouth. I pleaded with them to let me go.

The driver wasn't being nasty like the fat guy. I was starting to realize he wasn't really into this whole plan and was beginning to get nervous at his friend's crazy anger and threats of torture. He asked me if I was a junkie. I told them, "Of course I am. Why else would I be buying dope, you fucking morons?"

The fat guy didn't like that. He kept telling me to hand the dope over. As I looked at his profile in the backseat, I could see beads of sweat drip. I watched it rolling down the sides of his face, landing on his torn grubby blue T-shirt collar. It was cold outside but he looked like he was going to burst. His face was red and puffy, his hair was limp from grease and sweat, his face was shiny.

I reached down under the seat and picked three bundles off the floor and handed them to the fat guy. To them that was payday. I stuck two bundles back into my underwear. They slowed the car down. We were creeping to the beginning of the bridge, and the driver was telling his partner to let me go. Then he started yelling, "Let her go, man!" He asked for the rest, figured if I gave up three bundles I must have more. I pulled the rest out from the elastic band, so they couldn't count it so easily. I was desperate to escape with some for myself.

Again the driver told his partner to let me go. But the fat guy was grinning and telling his buddy that I was going to suck them both off, no way were they going to let me go now!

The open window next to the passenger seat was my only way out. And I had to get out that instant. We weren't going that fast. I saw a wide white sidewalk and a metal fence and parked cars on the other side, and not a soul in sight. I gathered my courage together.

I lifted my ass off the backseat. My head bumped the torn lining on the car roof; I threw myself forward, aiming my head for the open window. I felt the front seat thump my stomach as I dove for the opening, pushing the front seat forward with my body. I grabbed and pulled myself across the man's shoulder and head. I now had my head and torso out of the window. As he was pushed forward in the seat, I heard his head hit the dashboard. My arms grabbed at the open window and pulled myself through, using the car door. I was on top of the fat guy and he was pushing me off of him, but also trying to keep me in the car. I was half in, half out of the car. Then with a final move, something between a wriggle and kick, I hit the sidewalk on my side and rolled to a stop.

I did it! I got out! My heart was racing, I had never fought so hard to save myself. People in horror movies did things like this, not people in real life. I scampered to my feet, which took some wild-looking crawling and scampering moves, till I was up and running. Everything was in slow motion, and I heard my keys fall from my jeans and hit the ground. I saw them in slow motion, falling, falling, falling. I ran and ran for my life, and I didn't stop until I was back in familiar territory.

I couldn't believe what had just happened. I was panting, sweat pouring from my forehead. I finally stopped when I got to Second Avenue and Fourth Street. I flopped down on a milk crate, breathing heavily, wheezing. My head fell into my lap, and I closed my eyes. My head was so scrambled from drugs, things got distorted and I tried desperately to make sense of it. Would anyone really believe me that I'd been kidnapped. Had I been kidnapped? I didn't even know. I felt the front of my jeans to make sure the two bundles were still there. I felt the bump, relieved that I had at least two bundles, but that would only last tonight, shit. I had to get more money now, and go through the whole shit of scoring again tomorrow.

I was most pissed about losing five fucking bundles. I'd stopped, a while ago, thinking of dollars in real currency. To me a hundred dollars was a bundle, or ten bags. Twenty dollars was two bags, five dollars was not enough for a bag, just cigarette money. The fact that I could've been tortured, raped, lost my life, was not nearly as important as the heroin I lost.

ZOE HANSEN grew up in London. She studied fashion design at Kingsway Princeton, where she lasted a year, and then at sixteen got a job at Antenna, a hair salon known for hair extensions and their musician clientele. She befriended Boy George, who put her in his "It's a Miracle" video. In 1984, armed with two hundred dollars, she left London for New York City's Lower East Side. She started in sex work by answering the phones for an escort service and eventually going on out calls. She began writing everyday and moved into the Chelsea Hotel, where she wrestled with heroin addiction. In 1999, she achieved stability through methadone maintenance and felt it was time to open her own brothel, Sterling Ladies, which was on Park Avenue and Twenty-First Street. It was the first of five brothels she opened during the next three years. Zoe closed her businesses just before the birth of her son. She feels it's time to hand the torch on to a younger generation of females, who can endure the busts, the raids, and the outrageous women, but who are ready to learn about themselves while enjoying the sex industry and making a lot of money. She is now working on her first book and living in the East Village.

MELISSA PETRO

MARIPOSA

MEXICO SMELLS LIKE piss and burning garbage. Barefoot children sell gum to people in taxis at stoplights. They are tiny piñatas swaying in the breeze. In the city, eggs are frying, roosters crow. Men in broad-rimmed hats sell wares from off their backs. Pause. Take a picture. There is a deformed beggar. Give him a peso and he will thank you. Buy a blanket from the Indian woman and she will bless the money. Take a picture: women weaving. A man with a puppet, making it dance. A mariachi band. A woman in costume. Take a picture in a church. Another cripple. A wild dog, tits swollen, sick with mange. There is a drunk asleep on the sidewalk, pants split at the seam, exposed. Another animal. Another child, this time selling bracelets. Be seduced by her smile, her dirty face and wagging palm. Take a picture for a peso. Take a picture with her, she won't mind. Only a peso. Cheap. Plastic. Everything less than a dollar, a knockoff, a deal. Take a picture: two dogs, identical, asleep in the sun. Take a picture: graffiti on a crumbling wall, written in English, it reads: *tourist go home.*

Walk to where the sidewalks narrow to nothing, to the place where people throw trash in the gutters and garbage is everywhere, plastic soda bottles and tin cans and chicken bones. Where whores stand in doorways of hotels near the second-class bus station, I am too afraid to look. In the market, where everything is so alive it is on the verge of death—fruit so ripe it is nearly rotten—I am bruised and tired of walking.

I walked all day today, I wrote, *to where the sun meets dust and the land is not just brown but many browns: cinnamon, cocoa, chili, brown blood, cockroach wing, pony-colored earth. I walked all day today but all I found was nothing; nothing was there. A town, identical to the last. A church, dim and cool as wet clay, where I sat for who knows how long. I just sat there and did nothing, and for just a moment, everything felt OK.*

I walked all day, through one town to the next, until I reached what looked like a farm, where I found a little girl and a little boy playing in a dirty stream. I went to take a picture and the little girl froze, terrified, and something in me said don't.

It was a long day in the sun. I have a picture of a lunatic with a shotgun and another of military men in uniforms guarding a governmental palace.

Picture me in Mexico. I am nineteen years old. My brownish blonde hair is in two braids. I am in jean shorts and a striped T-shirt, a book bag at my feet. At the time of my enrollment, Antioch had what they called "co-op," a program where students alternated academic terms on campus with terms of work or volunteer experience anywhere in the world. I was in Mexico on co-op, volunteering at a preschool for indigenous street children. It was my first time out of the States.

Home was Ohio, just outside Cleveland. It was my mom, and my brother. And my boyfriend, Rick, who had been my boyfriend since high school and who I missed so badly that I called every day, sometimes two or three or four times a day, until I'd spent all my cash on calling cards and we'd both run out of things to say. Home was Burger King and Dairy Queen and Walmart and Target. It was cable TV and spaghetti sauce in a jar. As far as I knew this stuff didn't exist in Mexico. I was farther away from home than I'd ever been. I was alone and I was scared. The feeling was acute, like a physical pain, somewhere sharp and bright inside. At times it felt unbearable.

After less than a month, my job at the preschool fell through. I was bored. I was running out of money. One day at a grocery store, my credit card was denied. It had reached its limit. I don't remember what I thought at the time but I must have thought something like, Oh well, I guess something is going to have to happen. That's when I met Angel, who introduced me to sex work.

Angel had a sidekick who never spoke. When a customer came in, Angel took care of business while this brown-eyed boy no older than fifteen prepared the tools with a surgeon's grace. Needles and ink, Vaseline, rubber bands, latex gloves—everything was silently laid out at Angel's disposal.

Angel told me if I didn't like the way it turned out he'd give me my money back, but it wasn't the money I was concerned about. It was the permanence of what I was about to do to my body. It occurred to me that maybe I should be afraid of him, this older man with a needle and a shit-licking grin that never left his face. But I didn't feel afraid. I felt excited. The parlor was clean, Angel spoke English, and I trusted he was an artist. It was an ordinary day.

I committed to a design, a butterfly. The needle drilled in. The sensation of needle into flesh was nauseating. Angel sang softly in French as my comprehension dissolved. I felt swarmed with sensation, the beautiful unnamed fear—the fact that I was doing something irreversible—was adrenaline producing. I had only come to look, and now look at me, I thought. My shirt hiked up around my neck, Angel hunched over me, digging into my back, all under the observant gaze of the silent sidekick.

It was Angel who first introduced me to La Trampa. He asked me if I was interested in making some money and, to his mild amusement, I said yes. We met later that evening and, together, took a cab to the club. La Trampa was like a neon flare off the highway in the middle of the night. Something potentially dangerous and thrilling and just what I felt I needed. The tattoo was burning and greased-up with Vaseline, it felt like I'd been punched in the shoulder and I couldn't believe I'd gone through with it. Angel did all the talking. I stood back and watched. The guy at the door called for a round-bellied, older-looking Spanish man I presumed to be the owner. There was a lot of nodding over to me as the three men talked. The owner eventually turned to me and asked in Spanish, Is this what you want to do, are you sure? I said yes and asked Angel to ask them if I could start that night.

That first night I was handed over to Lila, the floor manager, who showed me around the club. The rules of La Trampa were simple: every dancer was called to stage three times nightly to perform three songs per set—the first fully dressed, the second topless and the third fully nude. Girls made money in three ways: customers bought them drinks, they sold table dances—where, in Mexico, you'd literally dance on top of the customer's table—and they sold private dances, called privados. La Trampa, translated, means "the tramp" or "the trap, or snare." I liked the idea of that. The place looked clean—no drugs, no strange liquids, tons of security—and as far as I was concerned the women were performers.

Everything Lila said she repeated once or sometimes twice, like she was used to dealing with foreigners or like she'd given the same speech a hundred times before. Lila took me through the club's main room, past the booths where the privados took place, and into the dressing room, where she introduced me to Paco, the housemother. A housemother's job is to attend to the dancers—fix costumes, apply makeup, break up catfights—and prevent the theft of personal belongings. "Don't spend too much time in the dressing room," Lila instructed. "Time is money. Spend your time on the floor."

Onstage, everything becomes louder and hotter. The room is lined with mirrors. I watch myself as I dance. I tell myself that I feel beautiful. I feel sexy. I feel powerful. I feel in control. I am desired, wanted, loved, perfect. The DJ says something in Spanish and the room goes insane. Below me are men, faces distorted by sound. When my first stage show is over, I can't wait to go again.

Paco called me mariposa. I went by Melissa. This is my real name and I didn't bother to change it, even though most customers mistook it for molesta, which, in Spanish, means "annoying." I got a kick out of seeing the confusion on a customer's face when I'd introduced myself. It didn't matter what my name was or if I didn't have a name at all. It was enough that I was white and American.

They'd start by asking where I was from. In the beginning I'd say "Ohio" and they'd ask if Ohio was near California or New York. I began introducing myself as "from Ohio, west of New York." Next they'd almost always ask about my family, and how many brothers and sisters I had. I'd say I had a mom and a brother. They'd ask for a dance.

In the booth, I made my customers sit on their hands. I'd tell the guy before the dance that if he wanted to touch he could take another girl. As I'd lead my customer to the next available booth I'd sometimes catch another girl's act. She'd straddle her client, one leg catapulted over any which shoulder, vagina inches from his face. Most of the girls who worked at La Trampa were professionals—part of an organized cartel that travelled club to club as monthly features. They'd roll in one week and the next week they'd be gone, another crew arriving at their high heels.

Sometimes as she was paying me out for the night Lila would ask how I was getting along—how the other girls were treating me—and once or twice she asked about my "no touch" policy. Why not? She'd asked. Because I don't have to, I'd think. Because I'm not a whore. Because the men love me and they pay me just to look. "You're new but you'll learn," I remember Lila telling me one night as she handed me my cash. "Your body is your business. The more you understand that, the more money you will make."

But I didn't think of it as business; I didn't think of it as work. I was doing something sexy and exciting, something wild and spontaneous. I was getting loads of attention and making heaps of money. I was living out a fantasy, in a fantastical scene, and nobody back home would ever have to know.

At La Trampa I sometimes feel suspended above myself. I am in disbelief that I am doing these things. I am dancing naked on a table in a strip club in Mexico. This new world is unnatural and its unreality resembles fiction. I enjoy it because I am good at it. It feels like driving a car too fast on the freeway, in control but on the verge of something else. The table is wobbly and the act requires security guards on both sides to hold it steady. I feel fifteen hundred feet in the air. At La Trampa I begin to feel at home.

I leave the club at dawn. I sleep until noon, one, or sometimes two in the afternoon. I wake up when the sun is high and hot, the city noisy and congested. I keep the money I make hidden under my mattress. I count it last thing at night before going to bed and again first thing when I wake up. As a stripper in Mexico I make more money in one night than a farmer might make all week. I make more money than I could possibly spend. I enjoy making it for the sake of making it. I work as often as they let me.

I told my mom I found a job babysitting. I talked on and on about how well it paid. I mean really, mom, it's unbelievable. I took funny things that happened to me in the club and I'd change around the setting. I made things up. I lied. My mom liked my stories. She was proud of me. I never even considered telling my mom the truth.

I remember one day washing my clothes by hand in a tub of water in the courtyard. All the time I am being watched by the hacienda owner's daughter, a little girl about five years old with long brown braids, thick black eyelashes and pink jelly shoes. The little girl likes to watch me and slaps her hand to her mouth and giggles like crazy whenever our eyes meet. I am hanging wet clothes on the line to dry in the sun, a sun in a sky as wide and empty as an ocean. I think about home and how far away that seems when, just then, a jet plane breaks across the perfect sky. I remember feeling, in that moment, a clutching panic. The feeling of something important having been abandoned or forgotten—a curling iron left plugged in, a stove left on on another continent—or maybe it is that I have been abandoned, all or part of me, cast off or left behind. I remember thinking of my father and feeling afraid. This memory lives in me like a snapshot: the image, the feeling. The smell of the detergent, the way it burned my nose and hands, and the way you can never get blue jeans clean washing them by hand, and they were always stiff and shrunk when you dry them in the sun.

I met a woman at La Trampa named Salma. Salma named herself after the movie star, Salma Hayek. I don't remember her real name. I remember she was beautiful and she idolized me. Que linda—how pretty—she'd say about me to others when she thought I couldn't understand. Salma considered herself a real dancer and would drive the men crazy by performing traditional dances onstage. Not until the very end of her set would her top come off to expose her perfect breasts for just one moment before she'd scoop them up and carry them offstage. She had a great body and a wicked wit.

Salma and I would do what we girls call "doubles." Together with one man in a booth, I'd sway stupidly as Salma grinded on our customer's lap, let him touch and kiss her breasts. One night she invited me closer and we danced together. She kissed me and touched me in ways that a woman had never touched me before. I did it for the money but it was also true that I enjoyed it. Salma arranged more and more doubles. Together we made more and more money. I allowed more and more contact. I began to let certain customers touch me in exchange for tips.

One weekend Salma and I traveled by bus to Mexico City on business. Salma's business—not mine. Three hours into the trip I started to feel sick. By then, having lived some months in Mexico, it was a familiar feeling—an elevated temperature, a cold sweat, the agony of illness, agony becoming familiar, normal. It occurred to me that this was the first time Salma and I had met outside of the club. Petite and professional in a pink skirt suit, you'd never know. When Salma asked me what I was doing in Mexico, I told her I was a student. She asked me what I was studying. At Antioch I concentrated in an interdisciplinary major combining the three social sciences—psychology, sociology, and anthropology—with a minor in women's studies. All this felt too hard to explain. I said psychology. She laughed and said something like Then it makes sense that you do this kind of work. When she asked me if I worked as a dancer in the States I flashed Salma the brave sort of smile I'd have given a customer and said no, never. Then why do you work at La Trampa? she asked. I told her I needed the money.

I asked Salma to tell me her story. Most of it I missed. My Spanish was still poor. She said something about growing up in Puebla and that she had no interest in school. To understand this you must know what I didn't at the time, that Puebla is the poorest state in all of Mexico. We crawled through Puebla as she spoke, the highway a ribbon through the dead earth. Salma called herself an entrepreneur and said she'd done "this kind of work" all over Europe—Paris and London and Milan—and I knew she was saying all this to impress me. She was thirty-two years old, near the age, in her industry, to begin thinking of retirement. For Salma, that meant finding a husband. Salma asked me if I had a boyfriend and I said that I did, but the fact was, by then, I hadn't talked to or even thought of Rick in weeks. Salma asked me if I would marry him and I said yes. Even in the moment I knew that it was ridiculous to feel so sure of this but I did, as if something very important depended on it being true. Salma told me that she was married once and that she had a daughter. I imagined Salma's daughter, a skinny little girl in braids with Salma's enormously seductive eyes. Her daughter lived in Puebla, she told me, with her grandmother. Somewhere off in that dead earth. At some point Salma asked me if I had many friends in Mexico and the truth was I did not. I said to Salma, I have you, you're my friend right? And she smiled and said something like, Of course, Beautiful, I'm whatever you want me to be.

The bus rattles to a stop on the side of the road. We park next to a leaning shack selling tortas, sabritas, potable water, sodas, and candy. I stay on the bus while Salma goes to get me something to drink. From the bus I study the roof of the shack. It's made from Folgers coffee cans cut in half and hammered flat and I wonder what it must sound like when it rains. The people from the bus line up in front of two women at a grill. At their feet, an emaciated dog steals a greasy scrap from a pile of rotting garbage. One of the women notices the beast and shoos him off with the chuck of a rock. I wonder where I am and if this place has a name, and if it matters. Salma returns with a Fresca. She brings her palm, cool from having gripped the bottle, to my forehead. She tells me I have a fever and instructs me to lie down. I let her seduce me into an uncomfortable sleep.

Comprehension dissolves into images of dilapidation: corrugated faces, plastic flowers, jars of rainwater, rainless sky, tires on fire, scrap metal on the side of the highway. At one point I am afraid. I could die here, on this bus, on this road, in this country, and nobody—not even Salma—nobody so much as knows my last name.

My time was running out. Soon I would be returning to the States, where everything would go back to normal. I would go back to college and I would lead a normal life and all of this would be unreal.

In Mexico City we stayed with Salma's manager—you could say pimp—an overweight Spanish woman who, for the duration of our visit, sat in the kitchen chain-smoking, watching Spanish soap operas while talking on her cell phone, managing beautiful girls like Salma all over the country. One evening Salma went off with a light-skinned man in a nice suit and came back with a thousand dollars. Not a thousand pesos but a thousand U.S. dollars. I was impressed. Envious, even. At times I think Salma was trying to get me a job with her manager, because I remember the two of them asking me all these questions, and then talking together, conspiratorially, in Spanish of course—quickly and quietly—the way people talk when they don't want me to understand what they're saying, the way adults will sometimes speak in front of children.

We slept in the same bed. Salma wanted to have sex with me, but I was sick, and afraid. I didn't want a lover—I wanted a friend, someone I could trust. She took care of me as best she knew how. She brought me gifts—chocolates, balloons, Vicks VapoRub—but she left me alone for long periods of time. I did not feel safe in her pimp's home.

Salma disappeared from the club a couple weeks later, which by then I'd learned was not uncommon. A stripper comes and goes and there's a new girl just as beautiful and willing, eager to take her place.

Two or three weeks before returning to Ohio, La Trampa took me off the schedule. They told me it was because I was working illegally, but I think it had more to do with my "no touch" policy and the fact that I was collecting cash on the side. I floated around to a couple other clubs. None was as nice as La Trampa, and one or two of them were downright dangerous. By then I was ready to go home. I used the money I had saved to buy my mom a plane ticket to visit me during my last week in Mexico. It was her first time out of the States.

MELISSA PETRO's academic writing and creative nonfiction has appeared in *Research for Sex Work*, *Sex Work Matters*, and *Post Road*.

APRIL DAISY WHITE

The first time I saw April Daisy White was at Book Soup, a fantastic book emporium smack dab in the middle of Sunset Strip, a stone's throw from where I used to turn tricks as a kid. Arielle and I were down there as part of my tour for *Chicken*. We knew that there were going to be a number of sex workers and a number of Hollywood producers, so after my performance, when we spotted two women in their late twenties talking to each other—one a spangly, sparkly, thigh-high-slitted, fake-titted, huge-haired, face-painted tart, the other a striking blonde with no makeup, in a simple flowered dress and flat shoes—there was a natural assumption that the one who looked like a classic prostitute would be the ho, the hooker, the high-end call girl. The other one could easily have been script reader, working hard for some hot-shot movie exec. Of course, as you have probably guessed by now, just the opposite was the case. The one who looked like she could have been walking up and down Sunset Boulevard picking up Hugh Grant and giving him a blow job in the Hollywood Hills at three o'clock in the morning was a Hollywood producer. Simple unadorned flower-dressed woman was ex–sex worker April Daisy White.

So gracious is she, April Daisy White, with a certain old-world European savoir faire, je-ne-sais-quoi gentility and grace about her. Which is not surprising since she spent so much time growing up in France. She also is a spectacular physical presence. She's a personal trainer, and, I swear, I always feel like such a big fat slob whenever I'm around her. Not because of anything she does, just because she looks like such an embodiment of robust good health. And I so do not.

Over the next year or so, April Daisy White let me stay at her house in Los Angeles when I came down from San Francisco on business. You can tell a lot about somebody when you stay at their house. April Daisy White has good food in her house. She makes sure you have really excellent sheets and bedding. Nice towels. Superior beauty products in the bathroom. She even made sure I had an Internet hookup in my room. Trust me, if April Daisy White ever asks you to stay at her place, definitely take her up on the offer.

The more I came to know her the more I realized we shared this strange bond I feel with people who entered the sex-for-money world at an early age. Growing up too fast. Pleasing adults. Getting attention and a sense of self-worth exclusively from our sexuality. We had these long intense conversations that would go deep into the dark night, conversations I can't have with almost anybody else, because if you try, they either nod their heads sympathetically like you are a miserable wretch, or they think you're making the whole thing up, or they're paralyzed by their own weird feelings about the whole thing so they have no idea how to respond, or they're disgusted and treat you like some depraved, degenerate, disgusting, sick sideshow traveling circus freak.

I am happy to report that it's a great, great feeling to know that you're not crazy. And that you're not alone.

THE FIRST TIME

THE SAME QUESTION keeps coming up. I'm wondering about that first time. I'm trying to figure it out. I can't pinpoint a real first time because maybe there is no real first time. There are many first times, new choices, each new decision. Maybe *I* don't care so much about the first time. Maybe I'm just wondering because everyone always asks about it.

"When was the first time? What made you do it? What sent you over the edge? What was the way in?"

I don't know. The way in wasn't just once, not one time. The first time was lots of different times. The first what, anyway? I mean what are we really talking about? Because the real first time I didn't know that it was the first time, not the thing they're calling the first time. So can that be the first time? But you could call that the official first time. But then after that there were many more times that could qualify as the first time, too. I didn't know those as the first time either. There was a time when I did know what I was doing and what it was called, and maybe that's what people want to know about. That could be the official first time. I'm enraged and I want to explode, trying to make sense out of this. I can't fucking organize it into any neat box.

"Miss White, when did you commit your first act of prostitution?" I am on the witness stand of the Van Nuys courtroom in a black wig, wearing dark thrift store clothes that I've never worn before. I'm trying to be someone else. The courtroom is filled with people I've never seen, reporters, court reporters. Jury men and women, what seems like the entire LAPD vice squad, and various other guests. The room is packed. I'm fidgeting with a black string on my incognito jacket. The judge is to my right on what feels like a high chair that reaches up to the sky. His black sleeves move like a bat with each objection. The room smells sweaty and angry. Sasha's lawyer, Mr. Scottie, is wearing a gray generic lawyer-type suit and he looks as jerky as he sounds. He is a gray box. Sasha, my madam, is sitting opposite me at an angle, and her blond hair strobes the entire courtroom. She looks like a younger version of Angelina Jolie wearing a fake white Chanel suit. I'm here to testify against her. I'm worried she hates me; maybe she'll have someone follow me later. I focus on the pencil in Scottie's right hand. I'm scared. I'm tired. I've been answering fast questions for over an hour. Hoping for help, I look at Mr. Wallmark, the D.A., who is sitting directly across from me, but he looks down.

"Miss White? The question." Scottie calls my attention.

I'm not sure what Scottie means by his question. I grip my hands around my cool wooden chair and anchor myself. I turn to my lawyer, standing at my left. By now I've figured out that I am the star witness for this D.A. I know Scottie, his opponent, is just trying to get me, and I don't want to cry again. I want to ask my lawyer, Gayley, how to answer this question, but I know Scottie will object. I turn toward the judge instead.

"I don't know," I answer.

Scottie looks at me stunned and brushes the lapel of his ugly suit as if he had smooge all over it from sloppy eating. He flicks it with thumb and index finger. The heavy maple doors of the courtroom slam as yet another looky-loo enters and stands at the back. Scottie hovers at his big desk and looks at his notes, stalling for time. Sasha whispers to him. The judge picks his fingers and rolls his eyes, waiting for Scottie. The first juror lady adjusts herself in her seat. I look over at her and she smiles me some silent encouragement. Mr. Wallmark's chair scrapes the floor as he stands to interject. Scottie cuts him off.

"OK, so you don't remember. Can you tell us about *when* you first became a prostitute?" Scottie bounces back and forth between his heels and his toes. He's throwing me that same question I can never answer. The one that always stumps me, the one about the first time. The room gets blurry. My eyes narrow like they did when I was little and I squinted my way down the Champs-Élysées so that all the light would go soft. The room hums. The judge looks down. Wallmark waits. Scottie revels. Gayley looks at me. Everything goes blank.

"Voila! Take this five hundred franc note." Sámi handed me the biggest, most colorful money France ever made and put it into my thirteen-year-old hand. I wore my *escarpin* to the agency; all models were tall and I wanted to make the best impression with my high heels. Sámi wore the most beautiful Armani suit, well pressed, and the tan color matched his skin. I looked at all the magazine covers on the wall. I recognized every face. I wanted to be one of them one day, one of the ones on his office wall, one of his favorites. Sámi's office was big, bigger than any office I'd been in. The walls were plum and the room was dark like a cave with furniture from Versailles. I crinkled the bill between my fingers. He must like me, he gave me money. The office smelled like eau de cologne, Sámi's cologne.

"Merci monsieur." I smelled the 500 francs and put them in my little purse. I felt valuable. I smiled and Sámi smiled back. I smoothed my pleated skirt down on his white couch. The phone rang and Sámi ignored it; I was important. The rain and thunder started to pound on the street below, the room got darker. Sámi took off his jacket and swung it on the back of his desk chair.

"Non, non, don't call me monsieur, call me Sámi. I want us to be good friends and I will make you a famous model like all these." He gestured and spun around, pointing to all the girls on the magazine covers filling his office walls. "If ever you need something you come to me. I'm just going to lock this door now. Privacy. Oui. Bon, bon. Now why don't you put your mouth on my cock?"

"Miss White. You have to answer the question. Miss White?"

The judge is talking to me from above. I turn to my lawyer, unable to speak into this room filled with people.

"Your honor, I'd like to ask for a sidebar." Scottie touches his few strands of hair.

"OK, OK, let's retire to my chambers. Miss White, just sit there and wait."

The judge and all his men file out. I watch them follow the man in the black robe with the bat sleeves. They move out one by one while I sit there staring out into the crowded courtroom.

I WAS A BIRTHDAY PRESENT FOR AN EIGHTY-TWO-YEAR-OLD GRANDMOTHER

"DAVID, I'VE GOT a fantastic job for you, Friday night, this is a two-hundred-dollar job!" Mr. Hartley's straight-shooter baritone reaches down my throat all the way to my seventeen-year-old balls and squeezes.

"Wow," I say in what I hope is a loverstudguy voice, but which I suspect smacks of eunuch, "that's great, excellent, thanks, I uh—"

"David," Mr. Hartley sounds like a benevolent dictator in a three-piece suit, cheerful as the day is long, but a master alpha, "this is a very special job. Very special. I'm really counting on you, David. This is a very important client. And if you do this job well, I can absolutely guarantee there are going to be a lot of exciting opportunities on the horizon for you. You understand me, David? Do we understand each other?"

I have no idea what he's talking about so I say:

"Sure, absolutely, I got it—"

"This is a unique opportunity for you, David. I want you to be completely prepared. It's a rather unusual job. But I think it really matches your skill set."

My mind races. Will there be barnyard animals involved? Ritual sacrifice? Unmentionable fluids? I see myself in a slideshow of perversion. What will you do for money? Where do you draw your line? How much of your life are you willing to sell for two hundred dollars? And remember, this is 1974 money, so that's like one thousand dollars now.

"David, this client, who I must emphasize is extremely important, has decided that she wants to treat her friend to a very special birthday gift. And that birthday gift is you. So get ready to put on your birthday suit." Mr. Hartley laughs at his own joke. He has a machine gun of a laugh, rat-a-tat-tat. "I kid, of course. Seriously, though, you are being given as a birthday present to a wonderful, charming, sophisticated, mature woman."

Mature. Oh, I see. Mature.

"David, it's our policy at the Hollywood Employment Agency to give our clients all the information they need to succeed. We believe that preparation is essential to success. And for this job, it's very important that you understand that the client will be celebrating her eighty-second birthday."

GULP!

"It's very important to us, David, that our people are comfortable performing the jobs we ask them to do. I want to make sure you're comfortable with this. Are you comfortable with this, David?"

No. No. No. I'm not comfortable with this job. I don't honestly think I can fuck an eighty-two-year-old. That's what I say in my seventeen-year-old man-child idiot head. Out loud I say, "Sure, absolutely, I'm on it."

"You're on it," Mr. Hartley's Uzi of a laugh rattles around in my skull. "That is droll, David, very droll. That's exactly why I thought of you when this job came in. I have every confidence that you won't let me . . . down." Bam bam bam, Mr. Hartley laughs fast and staccato. "I kid of course. David, I want you to call me as soon as this job is done. Do you understand? Do we understand each other?"

"Absolutely, for sure, y—"

Mr. Hartley gives me the 411 and then I disconnect.

Immediately my shattered brain sees this horrifying picture: An ancient naked wrinkled saggy droopy granny is spread-eagled in front of me, and my poor placid flaccid penis is a lifeless piece of useless meat; I have to give the money back; I am shamed, spiraling down humiliated, a brutal failure rejected by Mr. Hartley and Sunny, drummed out of the business, shunned by all my *Chicken* peers, the only family I know at this point that accepts me for what I am, my paycheck, my refuge, my people.

This is what I'm picturing when I knock on the door at the ultra fancy-ass swank swish hotel. It smells like old money in the hall. I realize suddenly that I'm having trouble breathing. Heart racehorsing pounding against my breastplate. A sticky clammy sweaty nervy jumpy freaky tweaky moisture oozes out of many of my pores. Under my arms are wet, I can feel it now.

The door opens. There she is. In a styley Chanel-type suit, pretty in pink. She definitely has a helmet hairdo, but it's not severe—it's well done if you like that kind of thing. She's got a huge honking diamond ring. She's got diamonds around her neck, but they're small, not gaudy; they look good. She has on pink shoes the same color pink as her outfit.

She's small, but she looks totally trim for an eighty-two-year-old. Has wrinkles on her face, but they're not grotesque. She has makeup on, but it's not grotesque. But the best thing about her is when she smiles. It's a really really nice smile. A smile that welcomes you in. She seems nice. Sweet. Smart. Fun. Not at all what I imagined. Deep relief, heavy sigh. I hope I'm doing this good when I'm eighty-two years old, that's what I think.

She welcomes me in like a hostess greeting an international dignitary. Would I like some champagne? Would I like some chocolate-covered strawberries? Would I like some pâté and cheese? It's all spread out on this fancy silvery tray. All that beautiful food and incredible flowers that smell so excellent. The curtains are closed. The lights are low. Candlelight makes everything soft. I've never really had much champagne at this point. In fact I don't know that I've ever had champagne. Well maybe at boarding school, but that was definitely cheap shit champagne so that doesn't really count. She gives me a long, thin, beautiful glass of champagne. Like I'm an adult. She does it with respect and kindness.

I know what to do. I've been trained well by my mom. So I say: "I want to wish you a very, very happy birthday, and if there's anything I can do to make your dreams come true, I'm here for your pleasure."

I've rehearsed that speech. I'm very happy with the delivery. I hold up that long thin beautiful glass full of the sparkly bubbly. She smiles, almost shyly—demure, I guess might be the word. She clinks glasses with me. We both drink.

I love the way the champagne shoots tiny little tickling giddy meteors up onto my lip and nose. I love the way it feels inside my mouth—like the most sophisticated Pop Rocks ever. Smooth, smooth, smooth, it goes down tingly and frothy all the way. And it tastes good.

She tells me her name is Dorothy. But her friends call her Dot. I think that's a cool name. Dot. She's talking about the champagne. She knows a lot about champagne. This is from France, from some famous champagne place. As soon as I am done with the first sip I can't wait for another one, so I just bend my wrist and let it guzzle down my muzzle all twinkly and sparkly. One more big gulp and the whole long thin champagne glass is empty, the contents now inside me. It comes on quick. All of a sudden my head is light on my neck, floating there, and my face feels happy, my bones all jangly, my blood rushing around in a good way. It just feels a lot more great to be alive than it did five minutes ago.

Dot insists I have a chocolate-covered strawberry. It doesn't take much persuasion, really. Oh my God. That chocolate on that strawberry, it is just about the best thing I've had in my mouth—apparently it is some top-drawer chocolate from Belgium—it has a hard crunch to it when you bite into it, but then it gets all melty in your mouth, and the way it plays in symphony with the juice of the strawberry, perfectly ripe, flooding, singing with the chocolate . . . When I finish I see her watching me with a big grin on her face.

Dot tells me she really likes to watch people enjoy themselves. I tell her how much I am enjoying myself. And the crazy thing is, I totally mean it. Usually I just say it whether it's true or not. But it's much easier when it's actually true. She asks me if I want another one. I say no. But I really do want another one. Then she asks me if I really want another one but I am just saying I don't. Like she can look inside my head. Which I guess isn't so hard, since I am practically drooling to have another one. But then she totally insists that I have another chocolate-covered strawberry. So I do. I have two more after that. I could eat every single one. But I am there to do a job. I figure another chocolate-covered strawberry might impair my ability to perform.

Dot is one of those people who hates to have air in a conversation. She is telling me all about her husband, how they met, how he proposed to her. He was such a romantic, he took her to Europe, he took her to South America, they went to Broadway shows, apparently he was a massively charming fellow. She shows me a picture of him that she has in her purse, and I must admit, he was a dapper motherfucker. It's a black-and-white picture, and he's in this sharp suit with these two-tone shoes with his hair all slick and this debonair devil-may-care smile on his face.

Once he died, she couldn't live in their old place anymore. He'd been dead for ten years or more. He was older than she was. It's sad but it's happy. But it makes me like her so much, that she has all this love for this guy. They were married for like fifty years or something. I just can't fathom being married to somebody for fifty years, at this time in my life. But she says he was a pistol and a firecracker and a bundle of fun. Apparently, they used to have these parties with all their brilliant, zany, fabulous friends. And they used to get all dressed up and talk about art and politics and life and death and war and taxes. It's fun listening to her talk about her life. Makes me hope that at some point I can have a life. Some fantastic wife, brilliant, crazy, zany friends, some big house with a pool and lots of rooms where people can party. Sounds nice. Kristy, my girlfriend. I see her being my wife. Getting set up by her parents in some fabulous swank Beverly Hills pad.

This is such a great job so far, that's what I'm thinking. But of course there's that nag in the back of my head—what is it going to be like when I have to perform? There are many things in life you can fake. An erection is not one of them. I'm trying to imagine a way that I can get it up and get it off. I believe I can do it. That's what I think. But then the very next second I think, well what if I can't? What if it just hangs there like wet spaghetti?

At a certain point I can tell she's got something on her mind that she can't quite talk about. Her monologue stops and she hems and haws and tuts a little. I don't know what the hell to do. I'm scared to death of what she wants. But I want to give her what she wants. I really want to please her. She's been so nice to me. And I want to succeed at this job. Be an American. Be a man. I'm scared to death of what she's going to ask me to do. Does she want to ride me? Will I be able to achieve liftoff with her lying naked on top of me? I believe I can. I know I can't. Does she want to do something weird to me? Something bizarre that old people do that I don't know about?

Finally she gets up her nerve and she says: "I've had this fantasy for a long time. I've never talked to anyone about this before, but I figure, what the heck, if not now, when? If not here, where?"

The suspense is killing me. I just know I'm not going to be able to perform.

"I've always wanted someone to kiss me . . ." she motions with her head down towards her nether regions, "down there."

Is that it? Thank you, Lord, for delivering me from the wilderness. That's all she wants? I can do that with my eyes closed. In fact many times I have. And then I think, can you imagine wanting to have someone go down on you for sixty years? Having a husband and not being able to ask him to do that? I went down on Kristy the first time we had sex. I've performed cunnilingus with every girlfriend I've ever had. It seems like one of the most basic sexual things you can do. My mind is officially boggled.

But I feel such relief. The world, which was weighing so heavily on my shoulders, has been lifted. I assure Dot that I would be more than happy to make her dream come true.

She gets under the covers. She doesn't take her clothes off. This is getting better and better.

Here are the best jobs in order.

1. All they want to do is talk.
2. All they want to do is talk while I'm naked.
3. All they want to do is talk while I'm naked and playing with myself. And when I say playing with myself of course I mean masturbating.
4. Cunnilingus.

So this is the fourth best job there is, as far as I'm concerned. Which is very high up on the list. Extremely low maintenance. Actually, anything that doesn't involve erection is good.

Dot wiggles and wriggles under the covers. I guess she's taking her old lady underpants off. She doesn't tell me to take my clothes off, so I don't. I crawl under the covers. I suspect there will be wrinkly grandmother flesh. But what do I care? Cunnilingus is cunnilingus. Luckily I was trained in this art by the first girlfriend I ever had. She was much older than I was and rigorously demanding, although in a very sweet way.

So it takes a while for me to burrow myself in, but eventually I find myself between her legs. It's very dark in there. Like a cave. I like it. And when I get myself up there it smells good. Fresh. Manicured. Everything is quite smooth leading up to the area. Which is a very pleasant surprise to me.

At first she seems very stiff. Tense. Ironing-board-like. I take my time. I go slow. I kiss all around the area softly and very gently. Some lips. A little tongue. But very light. And the more I do it the more she softens. And then she's moving herself toward my mouth. And there's little moans and sighs and groans and gasps coming from outside the covers. How cool is this? I'm thinking, she's totally into it. I feel so useful at this moment. I'm a success here. Doing something that requires skill and special talent. I'm a success at this, a thousand dollars for making someone happy. That's an excellent job.

So now her hands are on my head and she's pulling my head into her area. And to tell you the truth, her area is much like any other area I've been in, vis-à-vis women's nether regions. Especially since I'm in this black cave where I can't see anything. I think it actually helps.

Dot is gently manipulating my head so she's getting it exactly where she wants it and I'm just applying the appropriate pressure. It's like we're dancing and she's leading while I'm following. And she's getting all the symptoms of excitation. It's all happening. I could not be happier.

Dot now seems to be climbing the ladder of the stairway to heaven. I don't know how long I've been going at this now, but it doesn't seem that long. And she's already manifesting all the physical symptoms of pre-orgasm.

Sure enough, here it comes. Here she comes. She is diving off the board into the pool of sexual ecstasy. It's happening right here. I am making this happen. I have such a sense of joy and satisfaction. She's been so nice to me. Plus, I know that Mr. Hartley is going to get a great report. I'll get more business. Sunny will be so proud of me. One thousand dollars for fifteen minutes of oral manipulation. To make this sweet and lovely human feel good. To make our dreams come true. Or at least one of them, anyway.

It's clear we're done. So I burrow out from under the covers and head into the bathroom. To give her a chance to put herself back together. I wash. She tasted great. Can you imagine? An eighty-two-year-old great grandmother tasted great.

Sure enough, when I come back out, she's totally put together, like nothing happened. Except for the bloom in her cheeks and the sweet smile of satisfaction on her lips.

Dot thanks me profusely. She asks me if I would like to take a chocolate-covered strawberry with me. I confess that I would.

I grab a chocolate-covered strawberry and head for the door, full-to-overflowing with a sense of well-being. Even though my parents don't care to talk to me, even though I have no home and no family except for a bunch of prostitutes and a pimp, even though I have no future and I'm wracked by nightmares and lusting for revenge on the men who attacked me, at least I'm good at this.

As I leave with my chocolate-covered strawberry, Dot surreptitiously slips a crisp green bill into my hand while she plants a very nice kiss on my cheek. When I pull back, she playfully wipes the lipstick off my cheek. It's a tiny little gesture, but it feels so intimate and connected in a world where connection is virtually impossible for me.

I thank her sincerely—wish her a happy birthday.

She thanks me right back.

Then I'm gone.

It's a one hundred dollar bill. And that's 1974 money. So multiply by five. Five hundred dollars she just gave me. Plus the two hundred that was in the envelope on the fancy platter with the food. I love that. I wish all my clients would do that. An envelope. That way I don't even see the money until after the job is over. It's better that way.

I open the envelope. There's the two hundred dollars. So that's the equivalent of fifteen hundred dollars to drink champagne, eat chocolate-covered strawberries, and make one pretty great grandma woman's dream come true.

America, what a country!

2

Love

CANDYE KANE

I first met Candye Kane at a Sex Workers' Art Show at the grande dame of Olympia, Washington: the Capitol Theater. In the dressing room it was all garters and mohawks, sweet songs and dirty talk, porn starlets and shameless harlots, strippers and hip-hop hipsters, feather-headdressed breast-baring transsexuals and call girls in summer dresses, burlesque babes with toys and bad-ass rent boys dildo juggling, and lots of hugging. Oh look, there's a fully shorn uncircumcised penis hanging like a newborn featherless bird with a big silver stud pierced through its head. There were thirty of us in that dressing room built for ten, and the estrogen/testosterone levels were staggering; you could actually hear the hormones moaning. There was a lot of sex in that room, ladies and gentlemen. I stopped to think how many partners all these people had had in their lives and careers. I myself have maybe had sex with one thousand partners. Let's say I was average (you have no idea how comforting it was to be able to say that about myself for the first time in my adult life). Well, that's thirty thousand sex partners. That's the entire population of Juneau, the capital of Alaska, for God's sake, and for some reason that made me smile. That dressing room is the only place I've ever been where, when someone yelled, "Does anyone have a spare nipple clamp?" three people replied, "Sure," and one person asked, "What size?"

At the time I was using a hot pink Barbie book as my personal journal. I left it on the table in the dressing room when I went to do my stretching, and when I came back, there was this big red lipstick kiss inside, and the note: "I don't know whether you're gay or straight, but you're really cute. Candye Kane."

I had just come out as a sex worker, I was brand new to this strange world, and she made me feel included, on the inside, welcomed. And this was such a rare feeling for me at that time. Now mind you, Candye Kane is and was a huge star in that world. Everybody backstage knew and loved Candye Kane. And I was finding out why. Then I saw her perform. Oh my Goddess! It was just her on the massive stage with her guitar, belting out in a vast voice an amazing song she'd written about how you have to love people and forgive them. And on a screen behind her played one of her movies from her days as a porn queen. There was Candye Kane, twenty feet high, twenty years younger, jacking off and having a shaking, shuddering orgasm, while right in front of herself, she was playing and singing this jaw-dropping song. Well, the crowd poured forth a glorious roar that raised the roof and shook the floor. I've been alive a while now and it was one of the most staggering, breathtaking performances I've ever seen.

I've known Candye Kane for half a decade now, and I've never seen her be anything but gracious, bighearted, big-brained, fierce, and lovely. Do yourself a favor, go out, get one of her records, put it on, and be prepared to be blown away.

THE BABYSITTER'S SECRET

She was a thin and beautiful woman. She wasn't very tall but she had tanned and toned legs that she often rested atop her desk while she laughed on the telephone. Her laugh started low, trilling high and then coming to a soft low note at the end. She smelled of baby powder and strawberries. She seemed always to be happy and smiling. I liked going over to her house even though it was a tiny, upstairs apartment above a grocery store, not a big house with a yard like the one I lived in. I liked her because she never yelled at me, even when I knocked over a whole quart of milk and it spilled all over the table and made a big stain in the rug.

She had lots of costumes that she let me try on. There were feather boas in red and black, sequined dresses, rhinestone earrings, and tiaras. She had drawers full of makeup, lipsticks, and loose powders, eye shadows in every color like a crayon box. She had two big fans made of feathers and shoes with heels so high, I could grow five inches just by slipping them on. It was a dress-up party every time, and even her name seemed exotic and mysterious. Lorelei. I'd say it and it teased my tongue, rolling around between my teeth like a whisper, like a warm summer breeze. Lorelei.

My mom would drop me off on weekdays after school. It was a short drive between school and Lorelei's house and I stayed there until it got dark. Sometimes Lorelei would cook me dinner before my mom came to fetch me after work. Lorelei wasn't a great cook but she was my best friend and so I forgave the soggy sandwiches and tomato soup from a can.

As soon as mom left, I raided Lorelei's wardrobe, trying on chiffon shawls, fur coats, and diamond crowns. I wrapped myself up in a feather boa and slipped on her ultra-high-heeled shoes. Lorelei powdered my nose and applied bright red lipstick to my pre-teen mouth. She took out a Polaroid camera and snapped pictures of me modeling my fabulous movie star outfits. I felt like a real celebrity when Lorelei was behind the camera, giggling and giving me directions:

"Smile bigger! Now make a pouty face. You're mad because you can't have more ice cream. Tell the camera!"

After my dress-up and modeling session, Lorelei would close the curtains in her room and swear me to secrecy.

"I'm going to practice my show now, Candye. Promise me you won't tell anyone!"

I promised my very best, most solemn promise to keep her secret. She slipped a cassette tape into her stereo and placed a chair in the middle of the room.

As the room filled with what sounded like tropical drumbeats from a faraway land, Lorelei danced. She started out slowly at first. Using the back of the chair as a prop, she would bend and sway, right and left to the music. She seemed to have no bones as she bent her arms and pretty red-nailed hands in opposite directions, removing one long black glove and then another. She would spin around, flicking her long red hair behind her, turning and smiling at me over a boa-draped shoulder. My favorite part was the fan dance, when Lorelei would duck and hide behind the fans, playing peek-a-boo with me through the fans' lush feathers. Little by little, she removed her clothing: the gloves, the Chinese bathrobe, the wrap-around skirt with the Velcro fasteners. By the time the first song had ended, she was seated on the front of the chair, wearing only the boa and a special bikini, a little bit breathless, waiting for her next number.

The next song was faster, with loud guitars and pulsating rhythms. Lorelei would thrash her long hair from side to side and spin around on the chair until her legs were on the back of it and her head was hanging off the front. She'd mop the floor with her hair and then jump up suddenly, gyrating wildly and spinning around again and again. She had some bongo drums and she flailed on the bongos right in time to the music as she moved her muscular legs back and forth faster and faster. Just when I started getting dizzy watching her, she would dip down and do a cartwheel, landing on her feet as she spread her legs slowly and ended up doing the splits right on the floor. Rolling out of her split, she bounced back up to her feet, ending the dance by tearing off her bikini top, to reveal two little silver pasties covering up each nipple of her tiny, perky breasts. As the song ended, she raised her arms above her head, triumphantly holding one side of the bikini top in each hand. I would clap like crazy until my little hands were raw and Lorelei would take a bow and laugh and laugh. Then we would go to the kitchen and drink ice-cold lemonade while Lorelei tried to answer my questions and explain her dance moves.

I tried tirelessly to imitate Lorelei's moves, practicing the splits and trying to do somersaults. I was a clumsy kid and I could never get the moves quite right. Even the teacher of my ballet class took me aside one day.

"Maybe dancing isn't your talent. You seem to have a lovely singing voice."

I knew I could sing but what I secretly wanted to do was be a dancer like Lorelei. But I couldn't share my secret with anyone. I couldn't tell anyone that my best friend was a stripper who practiced her show in front of a ten-year-old. Sometimes I wanted to blurt it out to the world. When "Mame" came on TV and Auntie Mame came out in a feather boa, I wanted to say "That's just like Lorelei's boa!" but I didn't. Lorelei and I had our own secret vocabulary. It included words like "pasties," "g-string," "bump and grind," "stilettos," and "corsets." I kept my own private dancer and my own private words a secret from everyone I knew. It was my secret. It was Lorelei's secret. It was our secret.

Lorelei started doing a hula-hoop dance. She could spin that hula-hoop better than anyone at my school. I wanted so much to bring her to school with me so she could win the Friday hula-hoop contest and I would finally be popular. Lorelei tried to explain to me that grown women who are strippers are not allowed at schools. I didn't understand what was wrong with the world. Why wouldn't Lorelei's dancing be allowed? Sometimes I didn't understand why I had to keep it a secret. Her dancing was beautiful and fun. It made me feel free like riding in a convertible or spinning on the sand at the beach over and over again until I fell down, dizzy. There wasn't anything bad or scary about Lorelei's dancing. She was like an angel or a mermaid—a mythical creature that could only appear to you in a dream.

I started having dreams about her when I wasn't at her house. In my dreams, she would be wearing a costume like a fairy or a bride. She would spin and do her beautiful dance. Sometimes in my dreams, she would float above the ground, above my head, in a flowing white gown just above my reach. Sometimes, I would dance alongside her and my somersaults and cartwheels would come out just right.

One day, after school, my mom drove past Lorelei's house and dropped me off a few streets down at a new babysitter's place. I was upset and asked my mom what happened to Lorelei. My mom said Lorelei was sick and that I couldn't go over there for a while. I missed her so much. The new babysitter was fat and had a big wart on her nose. She made me do my homework and she always followed me around as if she didn't trust me. I played outside in her driveway and practiced my spinning and my splits all alone, hoping to be able to impress Lorelei when we saw each other again.

It's strange how time passes in the eyes of a child. Days turned into weeks and weeks turned into months, months into years and there was still no Lorelei. I started getting breasts one summer and my mom made me cover myself up with a T-shirt. I couldn't walk around in my cut-off shorts anymore without a shirt. I now had teeny little boobies with nipples that stuck out a bit. I thought about Lorelei and her silver pasties and I vowed that one day, I would knock on her door. She would be so surprised when she saw me, and I knew we would go back to being best friends again.

Then one day, I started junior high and had my first kiss. I didn't need a babysitter anymore. I wore bras, came home alone after school, and made myself soggy sandwiches. I didn't dream about Lorelei anymore, either. Now I dreamt of handsome boys in boxer shorts and well-defined biceps in football jerseys. I dreamt of smoking cigarettes in the back of the gym and groping male hands in the backseat of my consciousness. Lorelei seemed a far-off distant memory. She was just another face and phase of my lost childhood. Sometimes it seemed like she had never existed at all.

One day, I came home from school and there was a package addressed to me on the front porch. It wasn't my birthday. I didn't recognize the handwriting on the box, but I was so excited to get a present, I ripped and tore into the brown wrapping paper with a Christmas morning vengeance. As I pulled off the last remaining pieces of tape, I suddenly smelled that old familiar scent of baby powder and strawberries. I knew it was from my old friend. I opened the box and inside was a red feather boa, a white fan, and a rhinestone tiara. I felt a butterfly deep in my stomach as the memories flooded back to me. Lorelei looking over her shoulder, Lorelei dancing in the breeze. Underneath the boa and the fan was a Polaroid picture of me all dressed up in her costume with red lipstick smeared across my face. I had grown so much, I hardly recognized the girl in the picture. There was a letter in the box, and I tore open the white envelope.

Dear Candye,

By now I am sure you have heard that I have breast cancer. I have fought very hard to win but I know now that I don't have much longer to live. I don't want you to see me sick like this. I want you to remember me strong and happy like I was when we spent time together. I have instructed my landlady to send you this box when

I am gone to heaven. I want you to know how much I appreciated you and our afternoons together. I never had any children of my own and so you were the closest thing to a daughter or a little sister that I have ever had. I loved playing dress up with you and dancing with you. I will never forget how well you kept my little secret. Your mom always thought I was a secretary. She never knew how I made my extra money. I know it must have been hard for you to keep such a secret but you have never let me down. Thank you for being such a good friend. I know you are growing up to be an amazing young woman. I have always thought you would end up an actress or an entertainer of some type. Maybe you will even be a dancer someday. I hope you will take care of these costumes and maybe they will cheer you up and remind you of all the fun we had together. Be a good girl and always be true to yourself. See you again someday, somehow.

Love your friend,
Lorelei

I held onto the boa and squeezed shut my eyes, trying hard to keep the tears from coming. It didn't work. I cried until I couldn't cry anymore, remembering my sweet friend and our special secret. Now she really was a memory after all, floating above me like an angel. I felt like she was in the room with me, watching my tears flowing onto the wooden porch. I pictured her face, her long red hair and her funny smile as she tore off the Velcro bikini and threw caution to the wind. She was the first stripper I ever met and the only grown-up person who treated me like an adult when I was a kid. I took my box of Lorelei's secret things and hid it under my bed. I didn't tell a soul about the package or the news I had received.

Ten years later, I am standing backstage at Show World Center on 42nd Street in New York City. I am twenty-four years old, and this is my first strip show. I am nervous and shaking. My knees are knocking. In another minute, the announcer will call my name and I will come out and strip to my G-string in front of God and everybody. My name is announced, my cassette tape starts, and I saunter across the rickety stage. There is a simple chair in the middle of it and I stand behind it, using it as a prop. As the drumbeat starts, I bend back and forth, swaying to the music, channeling my babysitter, Lorelei. I am not in this seedy strip joint that reeks of cigarette smoke and spilt sperm. I am a thousand miles away, in a Hollywood Boulevard apartment, smelling strawberries and lemonade. I imagine I have no bones in my arms as I remove my long black gloves one by one and look over my shoulder at the yawning men in the audience. I spin around, squeezing my ample breasts in my hands, undulating and grinding on the edge of my chair. I remember her face. I remember her sweet smile. I remember how she danced for joy, for life, unashamed and beautiful. I am not a singer yet. I am a stripper and a porn model, occasionally turning tricks for cold, hard men and colder, harder cash. I am the girl next door who society shuns. But when I think of Lorelei, I become a fairy bride, a mermaid angel, or a mythical creature who understands and cherishes the mystical power of a simple secret.

CANDYE KANE may still be a secret well-kept from the mainstream, but in most underground circles, her diva status is legendary. She has been making music professionally for over two decades and has toured worldwide since 1992, performing for amazingly diverse audiences. She played at the French Embassy in Rome for the President of Italy; headlined the Rhythm Riot, a rockabilly and R&B festival in the U.K.; and belted it out alongside Ray Charles at the Cognac Blues Festival. She slayed 'em at the Cannes Film Festival, kept them enthralled at New York Gay Pride, and, most recently, helped organize a thirteen-city tour of the Netherlands for special-needs kids. Candye Kane's a diva who is here to help us celebrate our sexuality, shatter stereotypes, live our dreams, and have a damn good time on the dance floor.

AUDACIA RAY

HOT FLUSH OF CASH AND LUST

DATING YOUR COWORKERS is a really bad idea. Every article I've ever read on the subject advises this with various degrees of emphasis. These articles usually make cracks about mixing business and pleasure, and they tend to be in the sorts of magazines that also give fashion advice about what is appropriate business-casual attire. But since I'm in the business of pleasure and my workplace dress code leaves me pondering whether I should only wear perfectly matched bra and panty sets or if I could squeak by with a black bra and red panties—I figured that those other rules didn't really apply to me either.

And that's how I found myself dating a fellow sex worker in the messiest way possible.

In the late summer of my twenty-fourth year, I devoted myself in earnest to the task of making my living as a naked girl for hire. I had dabbled in the business for a while—accompanying a domme friend on a call where a second girl enthusiastic about ball-kicking would be handy, taking up random foot-fetish clients who responded to craigslist ads I'd posted that weren't written with them in mind, and answering a call for models who needed only to pretend to be asleep while being carried around were the toe-dipping beginnings. All of those things fit pretty well with my open-minded New York queer twenty-something lifestyle. I'd then progressed into more formalized escorting work, with an online advertising campaign, a consulting business set up through a trustworthy accountant, a rapidly growing wardrobe of pencil skirts and button-down shirts, and a diverse portfolio of lingerie.

After making some embarrassing mistakes as a non-pro (which is to sex work what a baby dyke is to queer culture), I established a mental list of dos and don'ts and learned how to say no to obnoxious or blatantly illegal requests from potential clients. I knew how to check references and screen clients carefully. I knew how to count my cash out into labeled envelopes and put non-suspicious amounts into my bank account. I was settling into being a businesslike middle-class sex worker, with a weekly quota, savings, and a plan.

While self-respecting middle-class escorts who fancy themselves as having careers in the business regard craigslist as the bottom of the barrel, I never quite cured my perverse adoration of the Erotic Services section. The ads were short, crude, and poorly spelled; offered blatantly illegal services; and re-posted a bajillion times a day. I found the messiness and immediacy compelling, and there were a few diamonds in the rough who shined a little brighter because of their surroundings. In particular, I'd been enjoying the posts of a local massage girl, whose ads frequently referenced The Ramones, tattoos, and Andy Warhol while putting forth requirements for grammatically correct propositions.

One Friday evening I saw one of those distinctive craigslist posts and I composed an email. I launched into the peculiar story about being a fellow traveler and suggested that we have coffee sometime the next week. I signed off with my working name and the digits of my ho phone.

The phone trilled almost immediately. When I answered, I heard a woman laughing open-mouthed and manic. I was smitten. She introduced herself as Lily and told me that she was hanging out at home waiting for calls from potential clients, and I should come over and do doubles with her. I didn't have to think twice. I grabbed my always-on-the-ready work bag (stocked with heels and lingerie in separate Ziploc bags, condoms, lube, gloves, and baby wipes) and headed to her place in the East Village.

Lily answered the door in a T-shirt and panties, colorful synthetic dreads piled high atop her head, her tattooed arms cradling a black cat. She was stunning in a messy East Village artist kind of way, and she immediately pulled me into a one-armed hug—the cat stayed securely in her other arm. Her studio apartment was almost entirely occupied by her queen-sized bed, her bong, and her writing desk; some of her belongings spilled out onto a small balcony. Her computer had two browser windows open: one to her email and one pointed at craigslist Erotic Services.

Lily was a full-body sensual massage provider—a.k.a. FBSM, the coded and polite way of saying "rub and tug" or "happy ending." She billed her sessions as being focused on relaxing the client, which meant that she always kept her panties on and didn't get sweaty and entangled with strange men. Though I had been commanding rates more than twice what she was making for an hour, I was running around the city and doing full-service sessions with executives for whom I had a hard time concealing my loathing. Though I had no confidence whatsoever in my ability to do a fifty-minute massage—it seemed like difficult and tiring work that I wasn't at all trained for—the notion of keeping my underwear on was pretty compelling. Lily marketed herself as herself while I'd been marketing myself as what I imagined a successful escort to be. She seemed much freer, and her client base tended to be graphic designers instead of corporate lawyers.

We spent that first night sitting on her bed, watching bad TV, smoking pot, ordering takeout, getting to know each other, and waiting for the phone to ring. The phone didn't ring. But the evening made me think about the ways that maybe I could change my business model a little bit so that I could be more myself while working instead of compartmentalizing so severely. It seemed to be working well for Lily—well, in theory at least.

Lily and I struck up a business arrangement. We planned to do massage girl doubles from her apartment one night a week, and she'd teach me the ways of FBSM. It would be my first experience doing incalls; my work so far had involved running around the city to hotels and private apartments. Incalls had never been an option for me because the thought of inviting clients into my home gave me the heebie-jeebies, and I didn't know anyone who I could share space with. As a sign of goodwill, Lily even offered to give my boyfriend a discount, though that rather unnerved me. Although he took her up on her offer once, they didn't see each other again on a professional basis—or at least, not that I knew of.

Lily dictated our scheduled doubles evenings; since it was her space and her business that she was letting me in on, I let her run the show. Because I wanted to work with her and be around her, I let some other unnerving things slide. While I used craigslist sparingly to drum up extra business on a slow week while I focused most of my energy on other advertising outlets, Lily's business was entirely conducted through craigslist. This meant that her clients wouldn't settle for scheduling appointments in advance—her guys weren't just same-day appointments but often same-hour. In the tradition of conservative and well-mannered escorts, I was accustomed to booking days in advance. In my independent work, I wasn't game for seeing clients past eight o'clock at night; Lily answered the phone whenever it rang, no matter what hour it was. More exhausting than this was the fact that Lily didn't screen her clients at all. If a guy called, his phone number wasn't blocked, and he gave his first name and agreed to a time, she gave him her address.

I kept my mouth shut about these things, and Lily never seemed to have any problems, except for the occasional incoherent drunk or high dude who didn't want to leave when his time was up. Though I could count on our two-girl sessions to make a few hundred a week, it wasn't the bulk of my income by any means. I retooled my vision of myself and where I fit in the sex industry and started doing massage sessions full time, completely dropping the escorting on account of not being very good at it and hating my clients. Younger guys with more artistic professions suited me, and the reduction in stress and physical intimacy more than made up for the lower hourly rates.

Though she was pretty focused on making money and would answer the phone anytime and anywhere, Lily and I also spent a hell of a lot of downtime in her apartment. This looked a lot like our first night together: lounging around in our underwear, eating takeout, and watching VH1. These idle hours quickly turned into something less innocuous—if there's anything innocuous to begin with about sex workers hanging out and waiting for men to pay them for orgasms. The intimacy of being each other's confidante about weird experiences in the sex business gave way to an acknowledgement of our mutual attraction, and that gave way to hot and heavy making out.

The heat between us, however, was dutifully managed. Neither of us could justify ignoring clients while we were on the clock, so our personal time consisted of stolen moments between clients. Because of scheduling issues, it wasn't until a client paid to watch us that we finally got around to having sex. Paid sex for a voyeur seemed like a logical use of our time and energy. The sex was fantastic—we got each other's bodies almost instinctively. Sure, it was a little annoying to have a dude sitting by the bed and trying to talk dirty to us and coach us on positions, but we pretty much ignored him and did our thing, and the money helped to make up for the awkwardness. Afterward, when we had gotten rid of our client, we laughed about how awesome it was to get paid for something we'd be doing anyway. We vowed to fuck each other's brains out and decided to officially commence dating and girlfriendhood.

We often expounded about our mutual erotic interests, but in reality the interest we were most focused on was making money. Money got us hot and bothered in practice, while we were reserving our attraction to each other for a theoretically less complicated time. When I think of her in an aroused state, I remember one day most clearly. Upon my arrival at her apartment, she was flushed with excitement and very grabby as I came in the door, all mouth and hands. She explained that she'd filed for disability a few years prior because of mental health issues, and seemingly out of the blue had just received a check from the U.S. government for ten thousand dollars. She of course had gone right to the nearest check-cashing place, since she didn't have a bank account, and stuffed the cash—in mostly twenty dollar bills—into her messenger bag. She had a sexy idea for our evening's entertainment: We were going to shut off our work phones, take a bath together and get very, very high, and then we would roll around naked in the cash on her bed. Even now, when I think of the hottest sex we had, I think about currency stuck to her flesh.

Over the next few months, we really only had sex when someone paid us for it. I tied Lily up and abused the hell out of her tits at a photo shoot, and we fucked each other with strap-ons for delighted paying onlookers. In those other moments, when no one was watching, the sexless gulf between us grew. We still talked animatedly about sex and lay in bed watching many a late-night porno, but by the time we'd finished our respective days of sex work, often spent touching strangers' penises together, I'd pretty much lost my appetite for fucking. I just couldn't cheerfully switch gears from professional sexual caretaker to recreational sexual dynamo, especially when this great range of fun and work was supposed to take place within the walls of her tiny apartment.

Inside the bubble of our relationship, I felt bonded to and secure with Lily, though there were plenty of things about the ways she managed her life and business that I found unsettling. I clung to her because she could understand what I was going through, my experiences in the sex industry, better than anyone else. No one else could ever understand the good, the bad, and the peculiar mess of working in the sex business. But the bubble popped on Valentine's Day.

In early February, Lily and I received an email from two women who were our massage doppelgangers. They had been working together for a few years and had an incall space in Gramercy Park, and they were very curious about us. I was enthusiastic about meeting other women in the business and expanding my support circle. Lily was less excited. We decided to meet up and swap stories at a quiet café about halfway between our locations, but as Lily and I were preparing to head out the door, she got panicky. She had a client in a few hours and was afraid that she wouldn't have enough time to prepare. She was anxious about leaving her cat alone in the apartment. She had plenty of excuses that just seemed crazy to me, but I picked up the phone and convinced our doppelgangers to come to us. They did, and we got along famously. At least, I got along famously with them. Lily had a hard time relating. She kept pacing around, going out the balcony and taking huge hits from her bong. I had never seen her act like this. But then, I had never seen her interact with anyone other than our clients. After our doppelgangers departed, Lily went on a rant about how suspicious she was about them, and she was afraid they were trying to run us out of business, and that she thought one of them had taken a book of hers. The two women followed up with me but conspicuously left Lily out of the loop. They wanted to know if I'd be interested in sharing rent with them in their incall space.

On the afternoon of Valentine's Day, I went to see the location and it felt like home. Stepping into their workspace where they had rules and structure made me realize in a big hot rush how toxic and bizarre my romantic and business relationships with Lily were.

Sex, money, and madness quickly unraveled my relationship with Lily, and that trinity of downfall is probably the most normal thing about the whole relationship. Non-monogamous relationships between sex workers are a far cry from the typical romance, but in the end, we faced and were defeated by the same stuff that affects every couple.

AUDACIA RAY is a new media professional whose medium is sex. She has worked as a curator, blogger, writer, magazine editor, adjunct professor, public speaker, video producer, and video editor. Presently, Audacia is the program officer for online communications and campaigns at the International Women's Health Coalition and an adjunct professor of human sexuality at Rutgers University. Audacia has a BA in Cultural Studies from Eugene Lang College at the New School and an MA in American Studies from Columbia University.

LAURI SHAW

MOTHER-DAUGHTER DAY

THE BUZZER RINGS and she's early. I kick a bag of stiletto shoes into the closet, then dash into the bathroom to hide the menagerie of brightly colored g-string underwear that's been hanging in there to dry.

I haven't seen her in months. I'm also nervous. We've never gotten along well. But the last time she was here, the fight we had was epic. She was livid when I told her I'd dropped out of school. Thanks to her, all my neighbors know, too.

I don't have a problem with the decision I made. I'm doing well right now, and school or no school, I'm proud of the way I've put my life together. Soon I'm going to diversify my portfolio, which is exciting, because how many twenty-two-year-olds can even say they *have* a portfolio? I wish I could just level with her about everything.

But I can't even imagine what would happen if she found out I'm a stripper. To say she would lose her mind is putting it far too mildly. I've hidden everything in the house that might tip off a normal person.

Since my mother is not a normal person, I run around one last time like a maniac, making sure there's not a single thing left to give me away. When I go to let her in, I'm panting.

"Where should I leave these bags I *schlepped* up here from the car?" my mother wants to know as I open the door to my apartment.

"Jeez, Mom, you should've said something. I'd have come down and helped you."

She rolls her shoulders heavenward in a dramatic gesture that means exactly the opposite of what she's saying to me. "No bother." Then she exhales harshly. That's her signal for me to take the grocery bags. So I do. They actually are pretty heavy.

"What is all this, anyway? You know we have supermarkets in Queens, too, right?"

"I just thought you could use some food in the house, that's all."

I peer into one of the bags. She's stacked cans in there, the way she used to help me do for the homeless food drives on Thanksgiving when I was in grade school. Most of it is stuff I don't even eat, and I suspect she doesn't, either. It looks like she emptied a shelf in her pantry to make room for something better.

It's the thought that counts, though, right? So I thank her and change the subject. "How's Grandma?"

"Oh!" she sighs. "I've been over there almost every day this week. The doctor changed her medication again." She runs down an encyclopedic list of symptoms and illnesses so long that I wish I'd never asked. "The doctor thinks she needs to be on Zoloft," she concludes. "He says her lack of energy is from depression."

"She's old, Mom," I say, taking a pack of cigarettes out of my pocket. "Lack of energy is part of the package. He shouldn't put her on an antidepressant."

When she sees the cigarettes, my mother begins clearing her throat, even though I haven't lit one yet. "Don't smoke that in the house," she says. "I can't stand it."

But it's my house.

Still, it's only one cigarette. I can wait until we're outside. "Fine," I acquiesce, jamming the Marlboros back into my jeans. "We should go soon anyway. The appointment's in an hour." I smile at her. "You know, I really think you'll like this place."

I've never understood how I could be afraid of such a tiny woman. She's five feet two inches to my five feet six, and despite her thunderous bosom—the one I unfortunately didn't inherit—she's relatively slender. Her short brown hair and endless supply of beige sweaters makes her resemble nothing so much as a cuddly little Yorkshire terrier.

But you know how they say that with those dogs, the bark is worse than the bite? Well, my mother's bark *is* her bite. And she's got our whole family convinced that it's lethal.

She sniffs. "They won't be able to do anything with my hair. Just look at this nightmare on my head. What a disaster."

"It looks fine," I contradict her. This is how I'm supposed to respond. I'll never hear the end of it otherwise. "But hey, we should get going. I want to stop for gas on the way."

"You're going to drive into the city during the day?" My mother is incredulous, as if I've just told her I'm going to sprout wings and fly us into Manhattan. "Are you crazy? Parking will cost you an arm and a leg. I thought we were taking the subway."

"I thought, since we're getting our hair done," I begin. "And it looks like it might rain—"

"Fine," she interrupts. "We'll take my car."

"Didn't you hear me say I want to stop for gas?"

"OK, then we'll take your car. I'll drive it."

I start to laugh. "You want to drive my car? Why?"

"I just feel more comfortable if I'm the one driving, that's all," she says, her face tightening.

Because you're not capable of delivering us there safely, say her eyes. Never mind that she knows I drive every day and that I've never had an accident.

"You know, maybe we should just take your car," I say.

"If you think that's best," she says. Her voice is demure, but she squares her shoulders before walking out of the apartment ahead of me.

I wish I could teach her how to relax.

• • •

"HEY, IT'S ALWAYS a good omen to find parking this easily, right?" I say as my mother pulls into a spot on First Avenue. She reaches over and begins rooting around under my seat. "Mom, what do you need? I'll get it for you."

She ignores me and keeps on fumbling until she finds her steering wheel lock. "I always use the Club when I park on the street," she says, fitting it to the wheel and giving it a good yank. "Especially in Manhattan. I hope you've been using the one I gave you." She purses her lips. "Since you drive into the city all the time."

"No one wants to steal my car, I can promise you that," I reply.

She's limping a touch as we walk down the road. I feel a twinge—usually her gait is strong and maybe even fierce. But every now and then she gets a touch of arthritis in her legs, and then she looks old to me. It's in these moments that I remember I can lose her. That she won't live forever. That our time together is precious, and that, gruff as she is, she's my mother and I do love her.

I try to take her arm. She doesn't notice. Instead she brushes past me to march ahead.

"Hey, slow down," I call. We turn onto 57th Street. "We're here."

"Oh, no." She shakes her head in dismay as the sign over the front door catches her eye. "Honey, this is a day spa."

"Yes," I say. "I know that—I'm a regular customer here. Now come on. We're going to be late for our massage appointments."

The door opens and a woman in a fur coat emerges onto the sidewalk. "You can't afford this," my mother announces. The woman gives us a dirty look before crossing to the curb and hailing a cab.

"Sure I can." I hold the door open for my mother. "There's a special today."

She sighs and follows me. Inside the spa's lobby, she elects not to sit down, instead pressing herself against the wall while I check us in.

"After the massages, I've got you booked for Ali. Your mother is with Philippa," the receptionist is saying to me. "Will that work?"

The door chimes. A hairdressers' assistant carrying several large boxes sticks her foot through to hold it open. My mother, standing right next to her, has her arms folded.

"Mom," I mouth at her, gesturing discreetly toward the girl.

My mother shrugs, and mouths in reply, "What?"

I hurry over to hold the door for the girl, who shoots me a grateful smile. She lugs the boxes into a closet and disappears behind them.

"Why didn't you help her?" I whisper to my mother.

"What are you talking about? That's her job," my mother replies. She forgets to whisper. When I return to the desk, the receptionist finishes reading me our appointments in a tone of voice that has just grown considerably more formal. And she doesn't look me in the eye.

• • •

"My massage was exactly what the doctor ordered," I announce, sliding into the hairdresser's chair. My mother's in the chair next to me with several pieces of foil crushed up against her scalp. "And how was yours?" I ask her.

"Eh," she replies. She makes a funny face to accompany the grunt.

"I'm glad you've got Philippa doing your root job," I say. "She's really good. That color will match so well when she's done, you'll forget it didn't grow out of your head."

My mother nods, a faraway look in her eye. She doesn't seem to feel like chatting, so I stop trying to make small talk with her. Philippa comes back into the room to check on my mother.

"Ali's gonna be right with you, hon," she says when she sees me. "Here. Have a *Cosmo*. It's the new issue." She passes me the glossy magazine. I thank her and spread it in my lap.

"'Sex Tips from Guys,'" I read out loud. "'Their all-time favorite mattress moves, revealed.'"

I always find *Cosmopolitan*'s headlines astonishingly funny. Who actually reads this stuff and expects to learn anything worthwhile? I'd love to write in about sex some time. I'd give them the stripper's perspective.

Philippa starts removing the foil from my mother's head. "So is there a man in your life these days?" she asks me.

"Actually, I just started seeing someone a few weeks ago," I grin.

"Is he white this time I hope?" my mother pipes up.

Philippa sucks in her breath. She doesn't say anything, but her chest rises, her shoulders tighten, and she blushes with anger. The blush spreads evenly under her own Kahlúa-and-crème colored skin.

"Philippa," I cut in quickly. "I'm going to need a root job myself in about two weeks. What do you think? Should we stick with the current color? Or should I redo all of it and go darker this time?"

"I don't know, hon," Philippa says. Her voice is hard. Staccato. "But you're gonna have to get someone else to do it for you. I'm booked solid for a long time."

"I guess I can wait a few more weeks if I have to," I say. "When do you think you're available again?"

Philippa, who has been my colorist since the very first appointment I had here, takes another long breath and shakes her head. "Don't know. It'll be a while. Like I said, you're really better off booking someone else."

• • •

"WELL, I'LL BET that wound up costing you a thousand dollars or more," my mother says. We turn a corner. "I don't think you should go back there. It's too expensive."

The dark gray clouds overhead have grown thicker. They loom in the sky, menacing and poised to strike.

"I don't think I *can* go back," I mutter. I gaze at my mother carefully, searching for even the smallest sign of regret. But her face is completely impassive.

From across the street, I notice a man staring at my legs. I see him lick his lips, a tiny and involuntary gesture of which he probably isn't even aware.

I know that look. He's a plain man, maybe even twice my age. But I get a secret little thrill because it's obvious to me that he appreciates what he sees. And when he realizes I've caught him, he looks away shyly, like a high school boy.

I'm used to this dynamic with men. It's how I make a living. I remember last night, catching someone's eye the same way from across the room. I slowly moved my hips onstage for him, a stream of sweat pouring discreetly down between my shoulder blades. A mating call rising from my groin to caress him with possibility. He bought a dance with me as soon as I got off the stage. We were on our way into the champagne room before he even asked my name.

All my mother ever told me about sex when I was growing up was that "nice girls don't." Sometimes I think her woefully old-fashioned attitude in this department is simply a red herring, and that she's jealous of my sexuality.

When she is looking away, I gaze across the street once again, and I give my admirer a small, secret smile before turning in the other direction.

"And here we are," my mother says, stopping at a storefront. "Now, I found this restaurant in the Hadassah newsletter. They raved about the food—out of this world, they said, and a bargain, too. I hope you're hungry."

The restaurant looks dingy to me. There is no one at the front to seat us. We sit down in an ugly orange booth. We're the only ones here aside from a bored-looking waitress, and—I assume—the chef. The waitress brings us paper menus.

"Order whatever you want," my mother tells me. "They're glatt kosher."

"Mom, you know I don't keep kosher."

"You do when you're on my dime," she says.

An odor wafts our way from the kitchen. It's greasy. Stale. Not particularly appetizing. I think that for my mother, the appeal of this place lies in the six-dollar main dishes I've noticed on the menu.

"How about I'll pay, and we can go somewhere else?"

"Nonsense." She holds up her palms in a magnanimous gesture. "You paid for the spa. It's my turn to treat."

The waitress wanders over, her pen poised. "What'll it be?"

I order a large matzoh ball soup, imagining that it probably comes in a can and will therefore be difficult to ruin. We both glance expectantly at my mother.

"Just some water for me," she says, fanning herself with the menu.

"You're not eating, Mom?"

"I'm not very hungry. You go ahead. I want to buy you a nice meal."

I bite my lip. As tempting as it is, I'm not even going to touch that one.

A couple walks in and takes the booth next to the window. She's wearing an ankle-length, denim skirt and an old pair of sneakers. He's got a black yarmulke pinned to his head with a barrette. My mother watches them and then turns back to look at me.

"So I talked to your aunt Sylvia yesterday."

"How is she?" I ask.

"Ugh," she snorts. "You know how I love it when she calls. It's all about her, all the time. No one else can get a word in edgewise. And she has an opinion about everything!"

"What a trait," I remark, stifling a snicker.

"Tell me about it." My mother rolls her eyes. "Anyway, your cousin Rhonda just got her degree in business management. So capable, that one, and I wish her all the very best, of course. But does Sylvia ever miss an opportunity to gloat? Of course not."

"She's proud of her daughter, Mom. There's nothing wrong with that."

My mother stares meaningfully at me. "She also wanted to know when you were planning on finishing college."

"Did you tell her I haven't decided if I want to finish?" I ask.

"Are you kidding? I didn't even tell her you took last semester off. She thinks you're delayed because you're taking too many classes."

"Oh, Mom, I wish you wouldn't do that."

"And what am I supposed to say to people instead? That you're a bartender? Her son is an architect!"

"What does one have to do with the other?"

She scowls. "Never mind. Forget that I mentioned it."

"I'll try."

The waitress appears and plonks my soup down in front of me. It splashes over the edge of the bowl onto the table. "Careful. It's hot," she mumbles, before sidling back over to the counter and picking up a dog-eared romance novel. I scald my lower lip trying to taste the soup. I wince.

"The girl said it was hot," my mother admonishes. "Oh! I almost forgot. I have some mail for you."

She slides an envelope across the table, inadvertently pushing it into the spilled mess. I hurriedly retrieve it.

"Thanks," I murmur. It's a bank statement. "I don't know why they're sending these things to you. Someone must have made a mistake." I turn over the envelope. It's already been opened. "Mom, did you read this?"

My mother looks away. "I must have opened it by accident."

"Oh, come on!" I exclaim. I've been bottling it up all day. Now I'm growing exasperated. "This isn't the first time, and I've asked you not to open my mail."

"They sent it to my house."

"Yes, and it's got my name on it. Mom, it's not appropriate for you to open mail that's addressed to me."

"You know what's not appropriate?" She fixes me with a glare. "How could you possibly have twenty-five thousand dollars in the bank? Where did you get that kind of money?"

The couple next to the window pauses their conversation to frown at us.

"I work for tips, Mom. You know that."

"Well, I've never heard of a bartender doing as well as you are." Her eyes glimmer ominously.

"Bartending is a skilled trade," I say. "And a cash business."

"I want to know just how you can afford to go to that spa all the time. Why are you so flush?"

Suddenly I'm really tired. Tired of lying to her, of protecting her. Tired of always taking the high road.

What's the point? She'll find a way to be dissatisfied with me no matter what I do. It's a whole lot of work that never seems to pay off. It's exhausting for me, upsetting for her. If nothing else, she senses that I'm lying and it pushes us farther apart.

In fact, how can I blame her for not trusting me when I'm not giving her any reason to?

She has no idea who I really am. Maybe if she knew the truth, we'd be able to put everything else into some kind of perspective. Maybe I'm doing us both more harm than good by continuing to lie to her.

Maybe the best thing would be for me to just come clean. I'm not ashamed of who I am. I haven't done anything wrong. I make a lot of money because I'm good at my job. A job that basically consists of me comforting people who are lonely and boosting their confidence. How can that possibly be a bad thing?

Maybe if I show my mother that I trust her, she'll feel more able to trust me in return.

"You really want to know?"

She doesn't answer. But she continues to glare.

Here goes nothing.

"Mom, I'm a stripper."

She doesn't miss a beat. "Very funny."

I sit back in my chair, my appetite forgotten, and quietly return my mother's gaze. We stare at each other that way until it finally dawns on her that I'm not joking. Her lower lip begins to tremble.

"Oh, no, Mom. Don't."

"Don't what?" she wails. "My daughter tells me she's a whore! And then she says 'don't.'"

I feel like she's just kicked me right in the stomach. "Stop it," I hiss.

"You think I don't know what kind of filth goes and spends money in those places?" Her voice rises. "What kind of trash you're meeting every night? What those men all think of you? I've got news for you, sweetie. I wasn't born yesterday." A fat tear departs from the corner of her eye and starts to make its way down her face. "And for this, you drop out of school?"

The waitress has put down her bodice-ripper and is staring at us. So is the couple by the window. But my mother is oblivious. She keeps on going.

"Your father would beat you within an inch of your life if he knew!"

"You say that like you'd be proud of him if he did." She's no longer the only one raising her voice. I don't know what sort of reaction I expected, but this definitely wasn't it.

The waitress hurries over. "Look, I'm very sorry. But the soup is four dollars. I'm going to have to ask you to settle up and leave," she says to us. "You're upsetting the other customers."

"Now look what you did!" says my mother.

"What I did? Me?" I cry out.

"Please," says the waitress.

We both get up. My mother holds up a five-dollar bill. "I hope you have change," she snaps.

The woman escorts us to the door and hands my mother a dollar. "I'd appreciate it if you didn't come back."

The storm that's been looming over us all day has now begun. It's absolutely pouring out here.

My mother shrieks when she feels the rain coming down. "My umbrella is in the car!" she gasps, and makes a mad dash down the block. I follow her.

When she gets to her parking spot, she pulls the keys out of her purse and turns off her car alarm. Then she jumps into the car, slams her door, and starts the engine. I run around to the passenger's side. The door is locked.

"This is ridiculous, Mom!" I yell, pounding on the window. "Let me in!"

The interior light switches off and I can no longer see her face.

My heart pounds and I fight back tears.

Come on. You're my mother! We have the same nose and the same crooked smile. Both of us are cursed with the same flimsy fingernails, the ones that break off the moment we have them painted. You're not perfect, and neither am I. But I don't expect you to be perfect. And I still need you.

"Mom!" I smack the window again with the back of my hand.

She rolls the window down a couple of inches on my side.

"Let me in," I repeat. "Please."

My mother shakes her head at me. Her face is shadowed and her voice is grim. "I can't."

"What are you talking about?" I say. I'm getting soaked. "Of course you can!"

"No," she says. "And I've got news for you, kiddo. If one of those men ever rapes you, it'll be your own damned fault."

My mouth falls open and I take a step back.

I'm stunned by how completely my mother is able to cut me away from her. With just one sentence, delivered so matter-of-factly that it leaves my lungs feeling empty, she has illustrated the boundaries of conditional love.

She rolls the window up once again and drives away. Her tires squeal as she rounds the corner.

I turn from the spot where her car was, my shoulders drooping, and start to trudge down the sidewalk. I don't look up from the pavement for several blocks. But I don't bump into anyone, because everyone else has gone inside. Everyone else is warm. Everyone else is safe from the rain.

As I walk toward the subway, underneath rolling clouds and rumbling thunder, I stop in front of a store window, where I see my face reflected. I watch as my hairdo flattens into a stringy wet mop.

The rain makes a paste of my makeup, slides it down my cheeks, rolls it over my chin and away. I look like I'm melting.

LAURI SHAW was born in Forest Hills, New York, and raised in West Egg, Long Island. Lauri remembers West Egg as an idyllic pastiche of bulimia, Prozac, nose jobs, and nose candy. Lauri was an insufferable problem child. She left home at fifteen, disappeared into the New York nightlife shortly thereafter, and emerged in her twenties with a terrible hangover. Lauri has written articles and web copy for lifestyle magazines, fitness publications, and various clients, including Warner Bros. Television. Lauri's hobbies include torturing well-meaning, innocent men.

MY DAUGHTER IS A PROSTITUTE

"MY DAUGHTER IS a prostitute," my mother announces flatly in her thick Russian accent as she enters my bedroom and sinks slowly down to the floor, glass of wine shaking in her hand.

Damn. I had hoped to avoid this. I had been working at the dungeon for a few months now as a submissive and was about to take the test to become a switch. In a week I was to become one, one week! I was planning to tell her then. I was going to tell her I was a Mistress: She wouldn't have known the difference. I tried to salvage the situation.

"No, Mum, I'm a dominatrix, it's different. I beat men, like with sticks and floggers."

"Oh? That is not what the website says."

Fuck. It's worse than I thought; she found my profile. It reads like a smutty novel, all full of perky nipples and firm, round bottoms. I use terms such as "writhe" and "nubile." It's the last thing I want my father to see, but if my mother knows, he will too, soon.

Father and I used to run about in our knickers all the time, but a few years back he began to see me as his adult daughter and was uncomfortable if I so much as donned tight pants around him. My body was no longer that of the child he used to put diapers on, but was now that of a sexual woman, who, by her blood relation to him, made him squirm and avert his eyes at the mere sight of a collarbone.

They knew, and from the way she said it, it was even worse: They knew and misunderstood.

"You are a prostitute," my mother repeats, tears in her eyes.

Shit. I hate making Mum cry. In my twenty years, I have seen it happen half a dozen times—when our cats ran away, when her father died. She never weeps.

"I'm sorry I didn't tell you, Mum, I meant to. I'm not a prostitute, I'm a BDSM player, it's different." I speak the way one would to a distressed child.

"How? How are you not a prostitute?"

"Well," I reply, slowly, "they have sex with their clients. I do not."

She knows that I aspire to open up a brothel in Japan one day, but this is not the time to defend the World's Oldest Profession; it's time to distance myself from it as much as I can.

Why did it have to be my submissive profile? Why? I had felt my IQ drop as wrote the stupid thing.

"It's not what it looks like," I hear myself say.

"Oh? That is not you naked on that website, with your tits for the world to see, like a prostitute?"

"It is," I concede, "but that is not what I am. I don't have sex with my clients, ever. I'm not even nude around them, I always keep my underwear on."

"It does not matter," she retorts. "You are a prostitute."

I wish she'd vary the terminology. Slut, whore, skank, hooker, hussy, tramp, harlot, trollop, strumpet, tart, painted Jezebel, streetwalker, lady of the night. She doesn't, though, just keeps throwing that word at me, spitting the three syllables at me like an exorcism, a magic spell that would drive away the evil in me. Proz tee tuit. It smarts like a verbal slap, and I'm trying to explain to her the gray area I inhabit, but she speaks only in black and white right now, and I am far from pure in her eyes.

"We have a girl who is a virgin working there! How can you be a prostitute and a virgin?" She doesn't respond, but she is far from convinced. "Look," I say, trying a different approach, "would you call a stripper a prostitute?" We hate being compared to strippers, but I am getting desperate, and I need to make my point.

"Yes!" she responds vehemently.

Crap. That approach will clearly not help. I try another.

"I like my job," I say. "What I do is legal, we have a panic button that will call the police and fire department, and we have a security guard and John takes very good care of the place—"

"John?" she cuts in. "Is that your pimp?"

"Yes," I snap. "He feeds me cocaine and beats me, Mum." I do not abide insults toward those I care about, not even from my own mother, not when they are not around to defend themselves. I immediately regret my sarcasm; it was uncalled for, and not conducive to my attempts to pacify her. "I'm sorry, I shouldn't have said that. He's not my pimp, Mum, he's a businessman who is on good terms with the police and runs nightclubs out of the dungeon on Saturday nights." I explain to her that what I do is safe, legal, and I enjoy it. It is the best reassurance I can give her right now, and she continues shaking her head and calling me a prostitute, in that sad, dead voice, too tired to be angry, too disappointed to believe it. She wishes me a good night and informs me that I may no longer live at her house. She will forgive the rent I owe her for this month, but I must leave.

The next day, she calls me at work and tells me that she cannot understand why I chose this for myself, she will not allow me to move back in, but most importantly, I must not, under any circumstances, drop out of school. So long as I am still attending college and studying, I may do whatever I wish with my life. She and I still see each other, and she loves me, of course. Once the initial shock wore off, she could cope with it, but it will always be something between us that we cannot agree upon.

ANASTASIA KRYLOV was born in Moscow and left when the Soviet Union fell. She spent five years in Jerusalem and then moved to Oakland, California. She now lives and works in Los Angeles and is looking forward to her next move. She is a graduate of the Sushi Chef Institute and currently attends community college. She is working on her transfer to UC Santa Cruz, where she hopes to major in Astrophysics and Linguistics. In her free time, she paints, sews, models, slacklines, writes, performs, stalks midnight movie theaters, and lurks on the Internet.

SURGEON

I first met the writer using the name Surgeon at the Sex Worker Art Festival in Tucson, Arizona. We ate dinner at one of those nouveau faux-diners that've sprung up like mushrooms in a field of cow shit when the sun suddenly bursts through the clouds and shines. She was so welcoming to me. Introducing me all around. Gregarious. Funny. Big easy laugh. Someone it would be difficult not to like. I had heard she worked in the field of domination. Apparently she was very good at it. She looked strong. Like maybe she could kick my ass. But as with so many people in the business of sex, when you meet them socially you'd never guess in a million years that they make money with sex, unless you already knew.

Of course as I sat across from Surgeon at the hipster faux-diner in Tucson, I tried to picture her torturing people. Going over the "safe word" beforehand. Making them scream and cry and quiver. She described to those present the project she was working on. She was asking citizens to write down stuff about their sex lives. Things they felt ashamed of. Stuff they wanted to confess. I knew exactly what my sexual confession should be, so I wrote it all down, every bit of it. I'd been in my late twenties. It was about ten years after I retired from being a rent boy. By that time, I had devolved into a dedicated sex addict. Sitting there in a diner in Tucson fifteen years later, the torrent of words pouring out of me, I realized I hadn't thought about this shit basically since it happened. I had never told anyone about this. Naturally. That's how I was trained. I wrote and I wrote and I wrote. And, of course, when I was finished I felt oh so much better. Black cloud lifted, weight of the world removed, dangerously swollen lactating bosom milked. I stuffed my sexual confession into the little box of Surgeon's, strolled out of the faux-diner in Tucson with a sparkle and a spring in my eye and my step, whistling a happy tune.

Surgeon had some people record all of these sexual confessions and put them together in a stream of consciousness aural collage. The night of her performance, the lights came down and the soundtrack of sexual confessions floated over us, and Surgeon began to play the cello so beautifully, that mournful sound so like the human voice. And then she took hold of a hook that was attached by heavy metal wire to a giant wooden frame constructed by her crew, and Surgeon pierced her flesh with the sharp pointy tip of the hook. Hooks pierced skin, sharp metal sliding through flesh, one hook after another hook coming through the other side of the skin. You could not look. You could not look away. Surgeon was piercing her flesh with metal hooks, until finally she had so many hooks in so much flesh that she was able to hang suspended from the wires, flesh stretching around metal, dangling miraculously there in midair.

Then all of a sudden, *shazam!* There was my story being read by some guy, piped in loud over the speakers. It was my confession. I was taking my girlfriend, a woman who later became my wife for some time, to an abortion clinic, because I had gotten her pregnant, and we knew we couldn't have this baby. First we had to walk past an angry rabid clan of anti-abortion fanatics chanting hate, spewing venom all over us. Which made me mad and sad and bad and disgusted and alienated and freaked out all at the same time. And then the waiting room full of all those women—it was the worst place on Earth, the saddest room that ever was. So by the time my girlfriend's name was called, I was having a meltdown breakdown of epic proportion. And I had no tools for expressing this at the time. I just had an overpowering feeling that I had to get out of there or I would start pounding my head into a wall until I split open my skull. So I sprinted out of that place of death, and while my girlfriend was having my child sucked out of her, I went and had sex with a prostitute in Alphabet City.

Listening to my story being told by someone else's voice, but using all my words, I was struck by the fact that I had, and still have, a belief that what I did was a bad thing. It just seems wrong by some arbitrary moral standard. Like if you were instructing someone on how to act in this circumstance, in a video, or a book, I don't think you would suggest that while your girlfriend was having an abortion, you should go and have crazy whacked-out sex with a mad hot crack addict industrial sex technician. But it was such a relief and release for me. The only thing that kept it from being a complete success was the fact that the sex worker I paid to have sex with me was a sad person, detached, someone who had clearly been torn apart, probably several times. But one part of my mind always says, "Hey, I gave her some money, bought her some food, treated her nice, gave her a good tip." I don't know, the whole thing is so confusing to me.

But as I was sitting there that night in that black theater with my words flowing over me, while Surgeon was hanging suspended in the air by wires attached to sharp metal hooks pierced through her flesh, I was overcome by wave after wave of deep wet sadness washing over me, flooding out of me, baptizing me. The confession, the music, the blood, the flesh, the spirit: It was religious in the true sense of the word. It was cathartic art, and it touched me so deep that it changed me.

And that's Surgeon.

A ROOM WHERE A THOUSAND WOMEN HAVE GIVEN BIRTH

I WORKED LAST night for the first time since I left Chicago, since Mexico, since I learned a new language and got lost in the desert. I left with that envelope of cash burning away the sickness. I walked down the late-night street in Russian Hill, the cold-ass air of San Francisco summer creeping in, discreetly slipped my fingers in to touch the money . . . oh God, it is so, so good. This is what I've been missing, this is what I need. Work. Give it to me, this sweet breath of fresh air.

I slept pregnant in a new lover's bed, dreaming of lions.

Sleeping on brightly striped sheets I dreamt of a lion who offered me his claws, one by one.

Later, napping still un-showered and oversexed, I dream I am in prison. We are reconditioned as patriots. I am standing on a mountain of plastic bottles, while a procession of old ladies drags heavy trash bags past me. I am turned into trash. I sit in my new shape, wondering what to do. A man comes in; he's been turned into trash too. He's built himself a new body from pillowcases, and I can see the shadow shape of the man around them. He looks at me seriously.

"You know, you can buy yourself a new body," he says. "You can buy your freedom as well."

But no, I would never. I belong here. He looks at me again.

"Our child has been planted in the pupils of your eyes."

In the half light of late afternoon, John tells me about his early years. He came to the desert to escape drugs and bad living, got married, had kids, and spent five years as a fundamentalist Baptist. He had to move to get away from it. "It's hard to leave it, once you're in that far," he says. Now, he has a large tattoo on his ass.

He says he explored all kinds of religions, read about everything, and then became a Baptist. I ask what made him leave the faith . . . He tells me that he realized he had begun oppressing his children.

The fetus in my belly steers me faster into stunning intimacy with the grave. I've spent my time there, with a dead girl's words and her last pair of bloody panties in my freezer, with my hands buried deep in a delivered urn, with my face smashed and swollen, with a needle stuck in my arm and friends no longer breathing and the xenophobic murder of my country and the potency of tragedy from outside or within.

I am not a mother yet, I am a pregnant daughter, one who remembers suddenly the way my father sucked the snot out of my brother's nose as a baby, his mouth locked. I recall the way he held out his hands to catch my vomit, the way he cradled me in his arms and ran down the stairs, blood pouring from my knees.

I remember all the things he did other than try to break us. All the nice moments before the drunken disasters, before the abuses of power, how he could love and deal with the child, but not the person. What is this need to force, control, tame, and inflict damage? How do we break the cycle?

Post-teenager, I have manufactured forgiveness, ready to pour over everything, to smooth out the rough edges. I have learned to speak softly, but not to ask the right questions. Not yet. Someday, he says, he'll write me a letter that will explain everything. But he's running out of time. His body is being consumed by the ravages of war. Agent Orange, bad blood transfusions, post-traumatic stress disorder, internalized oppression. But we don't talk about death yet. We're not there, yet.

I wonder if I'm strong enough, if I've worked hard enough, if my trespasses are just too great. I wonder at the consistency of miracles and if this is just another instance of choosing the experience over the story, stubbornly learning it all over again because I cannot hear wisdom.

I am bringing a child into this messy monstrosity, a child to whom I cannot promise safety or sanity or a mother whose choices she'll be able to understand maybe ever.

But, I will give her a life worth writing about, and I will etch my face with glee, may she remember me smiling if never young, passionate if always embarrassing, older and smarter than I will ever be until I am resurrected in the poetry of a distant daughter. Son. Whatever.

• • •

April 2006.

In a room where a thousand women have given birth, I have a child surrounded by whores.

She is a girl.

For now.

"If you want to reach the ocean of your soul, then die to all your old life, and then be silent."—from the *Mantiq al-Tayr*

SURGEON is an acclaimed multimedia performance artist, writer, musician, chef, and mother. She has worked in many facets of the sex industry since 1999 and currently focuses on purposeful BDSM and Tantra. Her work is experimental in nature and centers around themes of raceclassgender, family, tradition, sex workers' rights, science, borderlands, and liminal space. Recent exploits include a residency at the Tucson Museum of Contemporary Art with La Pocha Nostra and Guillermo Gómez-Peña. Surgeon is a radical hapa who loves all things organic, medical, mechanical, yogic, and sacrilegious.

I HOPE SHE ISN'T DEAD

I DID BECOME good friends with many women who I paid for sex. One woman was a friend of mine for many years. Every Thursday I would go to her squat in Alphabet City in Lower Manhattan, where you could satisfy all your crack needs, and she would have a different girl for me every week. Junie was her name and she was a lesbian, so she always had beautiful girls who she wanted to have sex with herself. Ahhh, good times . . . Junie liked a certain element of punishment with her sex and at the time I enjoyed inflicting a little pain on people because I was carrying so much pain inside me and couldn't get it out. So we made a good match, Junie and I. I wonder where she is now. I really hope she isn't dead.

I AM OFFICIALLY . . . A SLUT

Yeah . . .
I'm done.
It's official
I'm a slut.
Not just any slut
The Slut.
I'm writing the manual as we speak.
I'm a dirty
fucking
whore.
I'm hot kitty on a rainy nite
I'm two fingers deep
knees to elbow
lips to ear
fuck me
while I
whisper in
your ear . . .
Play tug of war with my head
as your dicks slide in and out of my rear . . .
Tell him that I'm your whore
your bitch
your girl
that this ring
my neck wears
means I belong to you
Your property
Your Sinn.

Order me to try my best
to do as told
to be loaned
but never sold.
I belong to you
your property
Your Sinn.
Thank you . . .
You light my sky
make my moon glow
my stars shine . . .
I never been so in love
in lust
impassioned
enthralled
in awe . . .
You gave me the best part of you
in giving me . . . away
knowing
that I'm stationary.
My comfort lies in that you loaned me
you trust me
with that closest to you.
I am forever in your honor
As long as you desire
I am in your service.
You are . . .
truly
myLove
myHeart
myKing

SINNAMON LOVE is an African American pornographic actress, fetish model, and glamour model. She was raised in Flint, Michigan, and moved to Los Angeles at the age of sixteen. While attending Santa Monica College she was married, but later divorced, leaving her a single mother of two children. She has since had one more child. Love began performing in adult films in the early 1990s and has since appeared in around two hundred movies. She directed the movie *My Black Ass 4*, which received nominations at the 2001 AVN Awards for Best Ethnic-Themed Video and Best Anal Sex Scene (Video). Love appeared on the *Jerry Springer Show* in 1995, and in 2003 she was on the cover of the first issue of the hip-hop and pornography magazine *Fish 'N Grits* with hip-hop star Redman. She also appeared on *The Tyra Banks Show*. She has survived a bout with ovarian cancer, but lost an ovary and a fallopian tube.

LORELEI LEE

I first met Lorelei Lee at the Center for Sex and Culture on Mission Street in San Francisco, two blocks away from SAGE, where the ovum of this book was inseminated in the basement years earlier. Lorelei Lee is everything you'd want in a porn starlet/college coed. Which is exactly what she is. For a sex addict, Miss Lorelei Lee is what we call a trigger. Certain key synapses in my brain went crazy when I met her. I kept having all these pictures in my head that involved me sexing her up ferociously. Does this make me a bad person? A caricature of a modern American caveman? At one point in my life, I would've tried really really really really really really really really really really really hard to have sex with Lorelei Lee.

Lorelei Lee, named after the character made famous by the tragic heroine of all tragic modern heroines, Miss Marilyn Monroe, is undeniably delicious to look at, all that blonde hair, white skin over cheekbones, a deep well of melancholy wrapped up in a body that just won't quit, with this Scandihoovian icy fire radiating cool and hot out of her. She looks like someone who might have been awarded both the youngARTS Scholarship and the Bishop Award for Best Tit-Tortured Model 2005.

The reading that night was a raucous affair, with lots of laughs and madness. Lorelei Lee was something completely different. When she came up on stage, the whole room changed. Sometimes on a night like this, with many readers and lots of naughty, bawdy, wild and crazy sexiness, it's difficult for quiet intensity to work. People fidget, fuss, and shuffle in their seats. Not at the Center for Sex and Culture that night. When she was reading, it was so quiet you could hear a nipple stiffen.

It was then I realized how much animal magnetism, charisma, star quality, whatever the fuck you want to call it, radiates off Lorelei Lee. I had already read her stuff, so I knew what a talented wordsmith she is, what a big brain she has. But that night she read a piece of dark, dark erotica. Brittle and sticky, nasty and nihilistic, bohemian and existential, her piece was populated by beautiful people desperately, debaucherously trying to fill the hollow places inside themselves with drugs and sex and alcohol.

Just about everyone who works in the sex business gets asked this question, "So! How did you get started?" One of the things I liked about this piece from the first time I read it is that Lorelei Lee answers that unanswerable question. And she doesn't. See what you think.

BEGINNING

IT BEGINS HERE, maybe:

When I'm twelve years old, my mother sinks into her depression. While she sleeps and drinks and gets hospitalized, I line my eyes and paint my mouth dark. I want to offer my face and skin, repainted, for recognition. A new breast, a hip thrust. For Rayid and John and Armando and Shannon to notice me, to teach me to shoplift lip gloss and cigarettes. To take me into the wash and hold hands, smoke, tongue each other's mouths, tell all the secrets, cry drunk, and feel a safety there.

Or, I could tell it this way:

Rayid Aman's big brown eyes look me in the face in the apartment complex parking lot. He holds the lip of his skateboard in his left hand, lets its weight rest on the cement. He's older, thirteen. With his right hand, he smoothes back his dark hair, the tiny dreadlocks damp, the Arizona sun bringing drops of sweat to bead in the silky fuzz above his lips. Because I've given up eating, my stomach feels tight and empty as it pitches; I can smell his skin and T-shirt and the boy-deodorant smell and I could chew my nerves they are so thick in my throat. I stare back at him and then his hand is on my face and I don't breathe and his hand, too, is a little damp, his fingers sticking lightly to my cheek and we have been staring at each other for an hour maybe. He's just walked me home.

Inside my apartment, behind the brown, chipped-paint door that is behind where Rayid and I are standing, my mother is lying on the futon on the living room floor, her face blank in the TV light. Or she's not there. She's at Greg's house, and she'll come home later and she'll perch on the arm of a chair, twenty minutes of cat smiles. Or she's at Greg's house and she's fighting with him, shouting maybe, throwing our things into boxes. Breaking the plates and my china doll in the continual stop-and-start of moving us out. It is our eleventh move and I'm used to it.

When Rayid finally leans in, finally kisses me, I think I'm a star burning out, too much heat and his mouth soft, his big lips taking mine in. I wonder if this is how it feels to be eaten. And even as he pulls his face away, flips his skateboard with his heels and rides off, fast, just turning back for one second and then gone around the corner, up past the fence of our school, I know that I have something new, that this will be my own, that it can make me need less.

Or maybe it begins here:

I'm eighteen. I have a boyfriend. This is a real thing. At eighteen, I believe it is the most real thing possible. Daniel is twenty-seven, a bass player from Philadelphia with dark hair and pale eyes who pours me glasses of rum and lifts me over his shoulder and throws me down in his wide white bed.

I move into his house across the highway from the airport. I work two jobs. Mornings at the coffee shop, steaming silver pitchers of milk with a machine that collects brown skins of burned milk-fat that must be soaked and scrubbed from the steam arms. Nights at the diner, where I stave my hunger with plastic cups of lemony diet soda and lay down ceramic plates of gravy-drowned potatoes and pot roast, all-you-can-eat spaghetti, and chef's salad thick with chunky orange dressing on the counter that is lined with single men who lean over their daily specials and fork the food into their mouths as if eating is its own kind of work. When they are finished they look up at me. They say, *hey Blondie, you sure look good tonight.* I'm wearing my uniform—black skirt, red T-shirt, nylons. I smile. I blush and giggle a shorthand evasive flirt, anticipating their tip dollars. Adding them in my head.

I have plans to move to San Francisco, to start college. I've won a poetry scholarship: two thousand dollars. But Daniel is short on rent. Then he needs his car fixed. He needs help with the electric bill. I pay for these things with my scholarship money and with my tips I buy us groceries. I cook us enchiladas; use a dishtowel to pull the glass pans from the oven. Before my nineteenth birthday, I've given all of the money to him.

This happens some time just before or after I turn nineteen: It's March or May, and we're in bed. I'm straddling him. He reaches up to touch my breast and he says, *you're so beautiful, people would pay to look at you.* Then he tells me about Ricky, his friend who is looking for young girls to pose nude for a "college co-eds" website.

I know you need money, Daniel says, *for school.* He pauses for a moment. The window is open above the bed and we're lying next to each other now. It's spring in San Diego and there's a breeze and the white cotton comforter feels like a net, something holding us. I'm sleepy and flushed and Daniel's voice lifts above me, into the dim air between the bed and the ceiling. *Ricky says he'll pay me a finder's fee. Fifty dollars. But I wouldn't even keep it. I'd give it to you, to pay you back.*

Or I can tell it like this:

I'm eighteen and I'm in love with Olivia Poverelli. She is Daniel's ex-girlfriend and we meet, first, at one of the pressed-in house parties full of spilled beer and red-shaded light where Daniel and his band play so loud and beat-heavy and everyone is dancing in a way that makes me nervous, makes me want to dance with them and also hide, so I just walk through the rooms to sit on the couch or the front steps. I wear my shirts cut low and swallow more rum. Olivia is in there among the bodies. She's dressed in a slip-dress and a fake-fur coat and her hair and lips are the same color red.

Later, another night, she'll stop by alone, and I'll watch her at the kitchen table, sitting in one of the old metal chairs, shading her lips with a red pencil before smoking a cigarette, drinking a beer, and then we'll be in Daniel's bed together—I'll be kissing her mouth and then between her legs where I don't know what I'm doing but I want the taste of her, metallic and wet and the stubble of her shaved labia and her breasts that are soft, softer than mine. Daniel will be there too, in bed with us, but I'll ignore him. I'll watch her body move and listen to her caught breath and in the morning—the way she pulls up her skirt. The way the thin fabric slides up her thighs. It will be Thanksgiving morning and she'll leave, she'll say, *I gotta go to Tina's. We're gonna cook a turkey if it kills us. Today, it's me and Tina against the world.*

Later still it will be December and another party and Olivia in a black dress, holding a red cup and sitting on the floor, leaning against the end of the bed. Her hair behind her and her dress fanned across the carpet. We have the door closed. On the other side of the door there's all the noise, but in here it's just us. I want to kiss her but I'm too scared. Instead, I listen while she tells me about the disciplinary camp she was sent to at fifteen and the time she was living in Los Angeles and she pawned her gold bracelet to buy toilet paper. She pulls a bottle of silver glitter nail polish from her purse. *My mother sent me this*, she says, *the color is called "psycho" so I guess it made her think of me.*

And another time at her house in Mission Beach, in her cluttered bedroom, her white tank top and no bra and a mason jar of vodka and ice, us sitting cross-legged, facing each other on her bed and she shows me a picture of herself at the strip club where she used to work. In the picture she is wearing a tall boot and the flash glares against the vinyl and against the white of her eyes and teeth. I'm looking at the shadows that demarcate her shoulder and thigh muscles, her breasts and collarbone, and the way she grins lazy at the camera, her gaze somewhere outside of the frame, her face sweet and distant like no one could touch her ever. *Onstage I could be anyone*, she says, *I'd just dance however I felt that day. If I felt crazy, I'd just dance crazy.*

When I agree to pose for Ricky, it's Olivia I'm thinking of. Of course the money is part of it—I've never before made two hundred dollars in one day—but more than the money, I want to be as beautiful as that photograph. I want to be as tough as she is.

Or it begins here:

I'm twenty and I work at Peet's Coffee in San Francisco. At 7 A.M. in the Castro, there is a line of people waiting for their coffee drinks and I'm standing behind the espresso machine, mass-producing lattes and cappuccinos while the little squares representing drink orders on the computer screen above my head change from gray to blue to red to black. Each color change signifies the amount of time that has elapsed between the order being taken and the drink being produced. This is a way of testing us; at the end of the day, our manager can check the computer to see how many black squares we had. Too many black squares means we get written up. Too many write-ups and we get fired. When I finish an order I shout across the store: *Small double soy latte for Eric! Medium dry cappuccino for Lynn!* I push a button to erase the order from the screen, just as a new one pops up to replace it.

Each full milk pitcher weighs about four pounds. I steam the milk with one hand, holding the pitcher by its metal handle, and pull espresso shots with the other hand, working the heavy portafilter like a hammer, knocking out the old grinds and tamping the new ones. In barista training, they tell us to use "proper body mechanics"—to keep our wrists straight, use the weight of our bodies rather than the muscle of our arms—but after six months, anyone who's been working there full time ends up in physical therapy, trying to undo the chronic pain of tendonitis and carpal tunnel.

The physical therapists all know we're from Peet's before they even look at our paperwork. I run into my co-workers at the downtown clinic. Jasamyn is just finishing up the wrist-strengthening play-dough-squeeze exercises as I'm being hooked up to the muscle-relaxing electrical unit—low volt pads that make my arm muscles pulse and jump in waves of current. After three months of therapy, the worker's comp insurance runs out and we are given the option of quitting our jobs, ignoring the injury and continuing to work, or going on disability. Regardless of what we choose, they tell us, our arms will never stop hurting.

I quit.

I put in my two weeks notice and sit in the break room at Peet's, reading the back page ads in the *SF Weekly* and the *Bay Guardian*. I begin to answer them. At home, I use the Internet. I make penciled lists, copy posts from craigslist into a notebook, then carefully reply to each. I take the bus, take the train to Hayward, to Oakland, to Marin, to Palo Alto, to downtown San Francisco. I pack a bag with high-heeled shoes and a robe, makeup and wet wipes and a library book. In condominiums, suburban homes, apartments, and studios, in living rooms, basements, and garages I begin to take my clothes off. This is how it starts.

And you want to know more about that first time. What was it like, really? Then later, in Los Angeles, where the money is more and the factory is bigger and everything is fast and brightly lit. And the sex. Tell me, what is the sex like? What really happens and how does it work and is it real? How real is it? Does it hurt? How much does it pay? And does your family know? And do you have a boyfriend, a girlfriend? Do you think you'll ever get married? Would you let your children do what you've done?

And here it is now:

My mother and I argue about bodies. I'm twenty-seven and I think I'm so old, so very grown. I go home to visit her and she looks at my short dress and shivers, grimaces, worries over too much bare leg. She wants to buy me leggings, wants me to wear my little sister's leggings and I turn away from her when I change my shirt, not wanting her to see the clothespin bruises on my breasts and stomach. I hope she doesn't notice the scattering of marks, remainder of last week's paycheck, on my thigh. Not because I'm embarrassed or ashamed or afraid my mother will find out about my job, but because she knows about it already, has known for years, and she doesn't like it and I can predict the argument before it happens.

But last year on the phone she said to me: *We all whore ourselves. We're all whores in some way.* When I was eleven, she said: *You have to be financially independent. Don't make the mistake of relying on a man.*

Here it is now:

My sister cries in her bed at the beginning of a day she feels responsible for. At ten years old, she already wears a bra and has sparse dark hair between her legs. She knows nothing about my job. During the weekend when I visit her, she wants to sing and run fast and watch crabs on the rocks and audition for TV commercials and make her own hot cocoa with the recipe on the back of the cocoa container. She wants to buy the coin-machine gumball with her own quarter. She looks away from my offered change and says *I don't want to owe anyone. I will pay for it myself.*

Here it is:

After Monday's shoot for Donna, her directing me in a gang bang with ten sweet amateur boys, so polite and uncertain fumbling with their woodshop props, stacked two-by-fours, playing blue-collar to my cuffed submissive. After Tuesday night at the strip club, me and Donna talking over the details like we always do—what worked and what was fun and what was awkward or badly positioned and what should be different next time. Jake listening, next to us in the bar booth, getting more and more silently uncomfortable. The resulting argument. Him not speaking to me. Me crying and then calling in sick to work and writing poems and mourning in the park sun with my legs outstretched, paper coffee cup leaving pale rings on the concrete next to my journal. Me thinking, *I'm losing him*, as if it means, *I'm lost*, and him not responding on the other end of the telephone and his jealousy over my job like a big shield between us.

After me calling Jake, tearful and scared and offering to quit, and meaning it for a whole day. And then remembering my tuition—the cost of things.

After all of it, I'm in the San Diego airport with the Stanford rowing team and they are six feet tall and young, wearing ties and white shirts and sun-bleached and tan and teeth like jewels all gleaming clean and their jackets and duffel bags embroidered red S-T-A-N-F-O-R-D like weapons in the class war only I know we're having.

Always this: this body and where it belongs and what should be revealed and how I should be touched. Always: my body and its abilities, its capabilities. And what is the trade for all of it: rent, tuition, printer ink and paper cup coffee and tomatoes and eggs and toilet paper and deodorant.

Here is something else:

My stepfather has a long scar, a poured swathe of red and pale, textured in swirls and depressions down the inside of his right calf. The year that we moved into his house, he slipped at work on the slant of someone's roof, spilled a bucket of tar, melting the skin of his own leg. He sat in his bedroom for weeks, healing, out of work, while my mother moved back and forth between the kitchen and the bedroom, fixing him sandwiches and uncapping bottles of beer and changing the stained strips of gauze. No money coming in. After the first week, the tension in our small house became like strings that we could bow or break.

And maybe this is where it begins.

LORELEI LEE is a student, writer, and porn performer. Her writing has appeared in *Transfer*, *$pread Magazine*, *Animal Shelter*, and *Denver Quarterly*. She has toured nationally with the Sex Workers' Art Show, and has been featured in the Queer Arts Festival, LitQuake, and the Bay Area Poetry Marathon.

JULIANA PICCILLO

I first met Juliana Piccillo when I was looking for someone to appear on a panel with me about people who took money for sex when they were underage. When we emailed and talked on the phone, she was always so thoughtful, honest, and funny. It's strange how, when you meet someone who's worked in the sex business at a young age, it's like you are part of the same club. The Teen Ho Club. Kind of like the Mickey Mouse Club without the funny ears. Juliana has a totally MILF voice and frankly, I must admit, before I even laid eyes on her, I had a major crush on Juliana Piccillo.

I finally got to meet her when she invited me to perform at the Tucson Sex Worker Arts Festival, and she was every bit as spicy in the flesh as she was on the phone. And she was so warm and welcoming even though she had a billion things to do organizing and running the festival, wrangling a dozen sex workers, trying to locate nipple clamps, death masks, and butt plugs. The festival generated a firestorm of controversy, and she handled it all with amazing grace. And while I was down there, I got to see her movie *I Was a Teenage Prostitute.* It's a fantastic film and I think it should be required viewing for anyone who has ever had or been a child.

When I asked Juliana to contribute to this anthology, she sent me this beautiful piece, which I think really illustrates how twisted relationships can get in the world of sex for money.

VICE

YOUTH DIDN'T SEEM to be much of an obstacle to my success as a masseuse after all. In fact, my less-than-legal status ensured I would be successful no matter what I did, so long as I simply showed up and touched penises on cue.

At seventeen, I was six years younger than the next youngest girl there, but she'd already had a baby and the accompanying stretch marks and had a tired depth to her voice. I imagine I looked like I was scarcely out of childhood, hips straight, full ripe breasts buoyant as if they were floating in salt water, looking like they were blossoming in a series of time-lapse pictures taken especially for each customer. Odd now, for me to understand the lure. I look at young girls and there's a way in which their bodies lack the softness their faces promise. Tautly wound muscles and skin hug tightly to their bones. There is nothing that gives, nothing to fall into. And I was like this, too—as if something had not been unclasped in me, not freed from the corset of childhood. And I was numb from its strictures. I couldn't offer a customer passion, nor sensuality, not even feigned because I had no idea what they looked like. And I wonder still why anyone would pay for a numb body of angles and sinew. But pay they did, even though I didn't dress or behave as provocatively and flirtatiously as the other girls. And there was one who loved me even more for my lack of development.

Bob hated that he was just one more john. He wanted more than anything to be as special to me as I was to him.

He asked, *Your name's not Samantha. What's it really?*

Your name's not Bob, so what? I replied with a smirk.

He took his wallet out, flipped it open with his wrist, and handed me his identification. *Here, see for yourself.*

A badge. He was a cop.

And his name was Bob.

That he worked vice in New Jersey and we were in Pennsylvania, out of his jurisdiction, did little to console me. He explained that he was there as a customer, that he was in fact on leave from the police department. He asked questions about why I worked at Emily's and where my family was. He cautioned me to quit before I became hard like the other women he'd seen in his fifteen years working vice. He said whoring hardened a girl, wore her out. He said some man in my life must have done something very bad for me to wind up here. It was so like a movie script, so predictable. Only in the movies, no one recited those sentiments as Bob did, lying buck-naked on a massage table. I again refused to tell him my real name when he asked.

I didn't like the johns as people. In fact, I hated them, but every time they showed up, like a Skinner rat both fed and shocked at the same nipple, I kept coming back for more. I loved them as customers, which was something akin to loving an ATM; I loved the part where they opened their wallets, handed me money, and left.

Their humanity wasn't necessary at Emily's. Neither was mine. It was better, easier this way. Touching another person's body is so intimate. My skin interacts with theirs, and sometimes at the place flesh meets a kind of alchemy can occur. I could see how much some of them wanted that merging of pheromones, intersection of chemistry, so I was careful to watch their eyes but never meet them. If on occasion I allowed them to touch me and my body betrayed my aversion by coming, I remained so utterly still they couldn't tell. I would give them nothing and they would leave with nothing.

Masturbation becomes sex when it's someone else's hand, though I could never quite understand how that was exciting. A hand-job was only a hand-job, and besides, in substituting another's hand for one's own, it was likely a less efficient hand-job—well, at least when it was my hand, I thought, it had to be. But no, I was starting to figure this out by then: The client was buying something else, not a technical improvement on the process but a witness to his orgasm, a breathing centerfold. Usually that was more than enough. Sometimes it wasn't. Some johns seemed to be unable to enjoy themselves if they felt I wasn't fully present and getting pleasure from the encounter. Bob was one of these clients, only more invasive, more needy.

What my clients failed to account for was how many orgasms I might bear witness to in any given shift, not to mention how un-erotic I found the whole thing. I might see ten men in six hours. Even if I had liked it, who has that kind emotional reserve, to give something of themselves—either thoughts or orgasms—to ten men a day, even ten men a week? And I didn't want or need to give it, even to one customer. They might as well have been donuts sliding down a conveyor belt and I some factory drone in an apron shaking powdered sugar on them as they rolled by. That's what I did anyway, I suppose: I shook something sweet on the penises that rolled by me. It wasn't so bad; in fact, it could be rather easy: I could do it in a state of half-attention.

In that I was willing to give only so much, I guessed I was merely adequate for the job, but my youth proved to be the great equalizer, and I still did a brisk business, getting chosen over and over again simply for my tender age. I couldn't stomach pretending I liked the work just to make the johns happy, just to eke a slightly larger tip out of them or to encourage their return business. I felt two minutes away from heaving into the wastebasket a lot of the time, so I simply endeavored to be pleasant and have as little conversation and interaction as possible. The girls always told me I was too prissy and squeamish. But it was such a perfect job in terms of the money. Nothing else paid seventeen-year-old high school girls as well. And in a way I was perfect for a certain type of customer—the ones who got off on youth, who had no need for theatrics and reciprocity. They only needed a young body to shower them with confectionary dust. Maybe other girls had larger menus of services and superior performance skills, but most of the men accepted the limits of my ability without question. And I made what to me was a lot of money. I could sleep at night without shooting up or drinking kamikaze shots. I walked the line between opportunism and self-destruction effortlessly.

On his third visit, Bob reached between my legs as I jerked him off. I squirmed a few inches to the right just out of his reach and pushed his hand aside.

Don't, I said.

But I want you to enjoy this too, he said.

I don't want to, I replied quietly.

Please, he persisted.

I don't know why, maybe because he was becoming a regular or maybe because the other girls thought he was dreamy, but I let him touch me. I was numb. My rare, involuntary orgasms with other johns probably happened because I was so relaxed, not aroused or engaged, just so off in my own world of daydreams that my body was able to sneak around my mind and do what it would do naturally. But I froze in Bob's hands, which just encouraged him to work harder.

It was as if I was anesthetized. I felt with him like I did with men from outside of the massage parlor—unsafe, unsure of what they might do next, what they might want, how they would bring me harm. And like with men from my real life, there was a way in which I feared disappointing him because, even if I didn't return his interest and desire, I wanted him to continue to want me, I told myself, so that he would pay me. But now I think it was so that he would continue to talk of rescue and innocence and I could imagine for a few minutes a week that I was someone else.

Thirty-six years old, the father of two small children (a boy and a girl both under five), and freshly left by his wife, Bob pried at me relentlessly with a caring urgency clearly out of place with how little we knew each other. I had seen him several times before this and told him little to nothing about myself—just the usual lies: that I was a community college student studying music, that I lived with a friend in a rented apartment in town.

With each meeting, Bob told me more—about his broken heart and his singular desire to be with his kids, but it all rang hollow. Men were always sad and pathetic, acting blindsided when they were finally left after years of bad behavior. If he was even a little like my father, I determined his wife must have had good reason to leave him. When Bob had worked across the Delaware River for the Trenton Police Department as a vice detective, before he was suspended, he'd acted on his intractable affection for whores. So he came under suspicion, more than once, for seeing the girls and tipping them off to approaching raids. The department suspended him when a girl ratted Bob out to another detective. Now he worked in some kind of food distribution business. And after all he'd lost—his wife and his career—he sought solace in the lair of the lion. Supposedly frantic to reunite with his wife and children, he blew hundreds of dollars every month, and increasingly every week, on me, a teenage girl in a massage parlor.

He was big—over six feet tall—and handsome, with dark, wavy hair and a mustache. He had a gentle, protective manner. But as he inched his way into the truth of my life, I noticed that he was also needy, in crisis, and what he needed was a girl down on her luck to rescue, as if saving me would redeem him. He made my stomach queasier than the ugliest, fattest, smelliest johns did. When I lied to him, he intuited it somehow. He wouldn't accept my standard, vague answers. And he said he knew that I was underage, so I admitted it. He wanted to hear it all: *What were my plans for the future? What was my family like? How had I gotten into Emily's? When would I leave?* Little by little, despite my qualms, I answered, uncovering pieces of myself for him.

Finally, I told him my name. I rationalized that he wasn't so awful, and in fact he was smarter and funnier than any of my other johns. He was different because he was an insider of sorts. Besides, I couldn't have put him off if I'd wanted too. And I wanted his business, I told myself. *I could always say no later, right?* But I knew I shouldn't have told him—not because I was afraid he would do anything with the information but because it represented an erosion of my boundaries. And the ability to have and hold my boundaries was what made working at Emily's OK, empowering even.

Bob quickly became my most lucrative john, paying more and visiting more often. Kimmie considered Bob very handsome, and I knew he was, although not for me, but for someone older like Kimmie, who was twenty-four. Both she and Raylene thought he was a perfect regular and that I was lucky to have him. And though they never said it, I imagine they wondered what the hell he saw in a dumb kid like me.

So I hung onto him. And hanging on meant talking to him honestly. I talked and talked and his wallet just opened wider and wider with each revelation. Telling him little details, what I thought and wanted, or who I dated, worked for him like stripping my shirt off or bending over to adjust the radio worked for the others. But it had to be the truth with Bob. He saw through any attempts at deception. Since I really couldn't lie successfully, I gave myself over to spilling my guts, at least to a degree. I wouldn't talk about anything that truly mattered to me. And though I wouldn't have admitted it then, it felt good to tell someone the truth—to be able to stop keeping track of lies—to stop stiffly posing as a human being, sucking in the fullness of my being.

I told myself that the truth could be a lie too. Even though I traded him facts, he would never actually experience me. He would never know the way I truly felt, and that was the only lie he never called me on. Maybe he chose to ignore it. When I said that I liked him or faked an orgasm—if he knew I was pretending he didn't say a word.

After I'd exhausted the details of my family, I disclosed my plans for after I graduated from high school—leaving Emily's to attend a music school, either the Musicians Institute in California or the Philadelphia Conservatory of Music. I don't remember what I was thinking that day, but he'd worn me down with accusations that I wasn't really going to be able to give up the money. I needed him, someone, to understand that I did have a plan, a real plan that I was capable of executing, that I wasn't going to become one of the drugged-up lifers he knew so well.

He liked my plan and I liked that he kept track of my auditions and applications. Though he grew more attractive to me, I didn't become any more interested in him romantically, and he annoyed me when he inquired about my savings—how much money I would need, how far off I was from accumulating it.

I let so much of myself show, and sometimes I felt cared for, and other times I felt like I did with my father and other men from my life outside: cornered but suppressing my fear and disgust because I needed something he had. I had to tough out an uncomfortable interaction, one that I wanted to run from but couldn't, or something terrible would happen. Even if the terrible thing was that I'd regret not hustling him, I couldn't let that happen. It was as if I was watching a girl in a massage parlor babbling to a john from a million miles away. She looked like such a stupid, scared girl.

I knew the bad that came from crossing men in my real life—a beating or a slap or a touch forced against my will, but what bad would come of rebuffing Bob? I wasn't afraid of him physically, but then maybe I was, because I had come to believe that any man was capable of violence if pushed to his individual edge. Most of all I feared regret, regret for not taking him and every john for all I could. If I was going to risk being a prostitute, I ought to be mercenary about it. Besides, it was meaningless. Bob wasn't a person. Our relationship only imitated a relationship, feebly. Even he must have understood this deep down. Whatever fairytale collection of facts I narrated, it wasn't me. It was only a story. He didn't even know my last name.

The worst part of our sessions followed all of the talking. It was when the time arrived for sex, when quiet stilled the room, when we returned to what he truly wanted from me. For a moment, I had slipped into myself in front of him, something I never let happen with other johns, and it was a slick, impossible trick—one that I had only a tiny bit of control over. I felt my two lives—the one I told him and the one I thought was real—tearing against each other. I was the one who had been tricked. He got everything he wanted. I compromised. His fatherly concern coexisted with his hard-on. He left me to reconcile this. He had not come in to talk after all. I felt foolish, utterly unequal to the manipulations of a grown man. Now, as an adult woman, I know that people can be a confusing heap of good and bad, of lousy decisions and altruistic intentions, but as a teenager I was not equipped for this. I comprehended little of myself and less of Bob, so all I could do was hate him and myself for the sticky corner I'd ended up in.

Bob carefully printed his phone number on a rectangular torn piece of paper and handed it to me. *Call me—anytime you need to talk or need anything.*

I took the paper and locked my eyes on the characters to avoid his intense gaze.

I have grown very attached. I think I'm falling in love with you, he said.

I knew I should look up at him now, to acknowledge him. This was a gift of some sort, for someone to profess love. But I was terrified and repelled. How incongruous: love and Emily's. People don't grow attached in rooms of vinyl tables, synthetic carpet, and windowless walls. There isn't anything to attach to. Nothing grows there. That was the point. Every surface in that place was built to repel fecundity, designed to be wiped clean for the next drops of semen or sweat. My skin was plastic too, covered in a perfectly fitted sheath, invisible and impenetrable. Endlessly, he picked at the fused, ductile edges. And I wanted him to stop. I would not be uncovered for him. He peeled at the protective barrier, to take it off of me. If he thought he could touch something raw and have me collapse sobbing in his arms, he had misread me. I had no need for penance, not from a vice cop or a john or anyone else.

I raised my eyes like a good girl and he pulled me to his chest, petting my hair and holding me for a long while. I stiffened and drew backwards, equally revolted with myself and him.

Later, he apologized for what he'd said, for causing discomfort, but it was too late for me. And it was more than what he'd said; it was that he could push me to places I'd promised myself I wouldn't visit inside of Emily's. He was on a crusade to persuade me to leave prostitution, even though I didn't want to leave, not because I loved jerking off penises and administering fake massages but because I was taking care of myself for the first time and successfully. I was saving money and learning all kinds of things from the girls, from dealing with the clients. Still, the intensity of Bob's concern compelled me because I didn't understand how I could prefer to stay there to being rescued. Again I felt wrong.

Bob's investment in saving me loomed over all of us at Emily's. The other girls were caught up in our drama, encouraging me to take his help, to try to love him. If I would quit, he would support me and pay my tuition for college, he said. Looking back, maybe I should've taken it, but then I would've been indebted to someone I only wanted to get far, far away from. No one had ever offered me so much and it frightened me.

Lord knows what he'd ask for in exchange, though he professed to want nothing. I didn't hate Emily's like he thought I should have—but how do you hate something that gives you so much?

At seventeen years old, I only wanted to earn my money without entangling myself with any johns. I needed the transaction to be clean, without residue. I was not looking for a daddy, I'd had enough of that, I wanted to scream at Bob. They only loved you when they wanted to use you, fuck you, hit you, or cry on your shoulder. No, I most definitely didn't want a daddy. Yet, I craved to hear the things Bob told me: that I was innocent and good, that I deserved a nice life. I just didn't want to hear them here, from a john. But maybe that was as good as it was going to get, maybe I needed to collect his clichés in case they never came my way again.

I thought I could put these things on hold. I even put thinking of these things on hold. Anyway, Bob was in no position to be trusted. He didn't mean what he said, even if he thought he did. He wasn't capable of honesty. I may have been young, but I could see that he needed to atone for whatever he'd done to his wife and kids or on the vice squad by playing the knight with a shining hard-on with me. And I knew that his, like all hard-ons, would subside, and his feelings along with it. I just wanted cash. Long over believing in daddies and white knights, I could barely stand to be near Bob.

Why was it getting so messy? There were lots of good johns—quick and easy, never wanting anything weird, paying well, and respecting the boundaries. All Bob had going for him was that he paid better and more frequently than anyone else. I was able to work less. I stopped picking up extra shifts for the other girls and actually began giving away some of mine. But he was long past easy and had pushed every boundary.

After he'd said he might be falling in love with me, he attempted to violate my most basic rule: He asked to kiss me. Sometimes other customers requested or simply attempted to kiss me, but this was rare and only happened with novice johns. Bob knew the rules, which made it all the more disconcerting when he asked. I balked and stuttered but was able to tell him, *I don't kiss customers.*

I felt set up. He knew better. In all the times I'd seen him I'd never ever kissed him, not even on the cheek, and he'd never kissed me. I don't even recall him trying to kiss me.

Wounded, he whimpered, *Is that all I am to you? A customer?* Of course he was. What did he think?

Again he had cornered me. Anxious for a way out, I lied, *No, no, you're not just a customer. You know, you're my friend.*

In truth I would rather have jerked off ten johns for free than feel one's lips on my mouth at any price. Even his. Especially his. But there I was. I'd gone down this road with him willingly.

I stomped out of the room. Soon after, he left, chin down, chest deflated, looking pathetic.

After that, I asked the girls to head him off for me—to tell him that I was busy with a customer or that I wasn't in when he came by. Sometimes he waited me out and I saw him. He refused to let other girls take him, though they offered. When I needed the money or when he was absolutely unavoidable, I gritted my teeth and endured him. But the tension between us frightened me, especially when he would go through the entire session without a lecture on why I ought to quit. Even without his mouth speaking the words, I knew what he was feeling. It was as if he was seeing me to irritate me, to rub my face in what I was.

One day, when I was hiding from him back in the printer's shop, he put a crisp, new hundred-dollar bill in an envelope with my name on it and gave it to Raylene. He did this again every time I didn't see him. And I looked forward to it, because every time that envelope lay in my hands, I could enjoy the feeling of value he gave me without having to stomach him in person. It was perfect really because I wasn't ready to let go of him. I would have to offer him some contact because I knew instinctively that he wouldn't continue to drop off money without a little in-person contact, so I budgeted my face time to what I could handle, and it worked for a while. He even dropped the kissing request for that time.

A few days before Christmas, Bob showed up at Emily's. The girls felt like family; a kind of normalcy and routine had descended like a blanket of suede and fur around me. I felt warm and unguarded. So when he led me outside to the parking lot, I went happily. He said he had something for me.

Close your eyes, he whispered, then he opened his trunk and pulled out what sounded like a crinkling plastic bag.

When he instructed, I opened my eyes to see he held a stuffed Santa doll in front of me.

Wait, he said, winding a little metal key in the back. The melody to "Sing a Song" pinged tinny, stilted notes into the frozen air. He hugged me and breathed hotly in my ear, like he had so many times. *You are so special to me.*

For an instant, he had me. I liked this present, this sensation of being precious to someone. I smiled a true smile, caught myself, and teased him, *Yeah, my tits are bigger.*

Wrapping his big hands around my arms, he pulled back and bore his eyes into mine earnestly. *I mean it. I care about you. I want to help you.*

I wriggled away, unease rising like bile from my gut. He ripped out his checkbook and said, *I will write you a check right now—do what you want with it.* I pushed it away, and after a few protestations, he relented.

Looking back, I wonder how I let it go so far, how I could reveal so much. I suppose I saw the chance to be understood. So I suspended disbelief, like one does at the movies. I let myself pretend that he mattered, that what he saw in me was real, that if he saw value then I had value. But it didn't matter, or at least it shouldn't have. Some john's affection should not matter, I told myself. And I shouldn't have pretended it did.

He dangled before me what I so needed and what he could not possibly give: friendship, fatherly love, and a sense of my own worth. That he managed to distract me with that made me feel both weak and stupid but also cruel for not accepting his kindness. I had strung him along, hadn't I?

He offered me money that would have enabled me to stop working an illegal job, and yet I couldn't take it. If I was selling myself to many men for twenty dollars each, why not sell myself to one for three thousand? Wouldn't that have been more expedient? Wouldn't that have ended it all sooner? Maybe I didn't want Emily's to end. Maybe I couldn't risk being pulled into a new world of sickness with Bob, one that I didn't want to know about. The thought of letting him love me in his fucked-up way, or letting him believe I might love him back when I knew I never could, disgusted me much more than the idea of six more months at the massage parlor and however many johns came with it.

Though I might once have said otherwise, I liked Bob, and even then I believed he cared, if in a perverse way. And knowing this made taking his money, taking his kindness, selling sex to him, not kissing him . . . all of it a maze and a maelstrom. I can't say I'd had much experience with people giving a shit, but when he said, *You're too sweet to be in a place like this* ten minutes after trying to put his hands between my thighs, I knew enough to maintain some distance. No way was I going to take three thousand dollars from him. He would want to phone me in college, maybe visit. He'd never let go and I would be dragging him with me forever, I feared.

One day it was done for me. I couldn't see him anymore. I just couldn't. It made me sick in my belly in a way I couldn't fight back down. I begged

Raylene to go into the room where he was waiting for me. She convinced him to let her jerk him off, but he couldn't get it up. He asked her to get me. When she told him I wouldn't come, that I was uncomfortable with seeing him, he cried. Raylene stayed a few minutes to comfort him and then came out for me.

He's really upset. He cares about you. Just go talk to him, she said.

When I heard that he'd cried about me, I wanted to spit on him. He was trying to control me with his tears, to manipulate sympathy just like my father. First they use you and then when you finally walk away, they play the victim. If this had worked for Bob before, it wasn't going to now, I thought. My resolve strengthened. But Bob wasn't my father and he hadn't abused me. He asked for and paid for what he took and he was kind, but he should have known better. What did he expect? I was seventeen years old. He was thirty-six.

The girls unanimously felt sorry for him and they told me so repeatedly. Which of course caused me to doubt my feelings and instincts. They were older and wiser and I looked up to them. I knew that they understood men far better than I did. So I went to him because perhaps, I thought, I owed him that. In some ridiculous outfit, a velvet bustier and red hot-pants, I stood before him earnestly explaining in my inarticulate, seventeen-year-old voice what I didn't understand at all: why I couldn't see him anymore, even though I didn't know why, but that I only knew that I couldn't, and that I was sorry.

After he dressed, as he was leaving, he met me in the hall and said that he would not come back or call if that was what I wanted. I said I did.

Then he said, *I'll give you one hundred dollars for a kiss.*

Bob, no, I whined weakly. But unlike the times before, I knew I would give in and he did too. It was the last time he'd ask.

He pleaded quietly, *Please, just one kiss, that's all I want.*

I don't know whose voice implored more, his or mine. I needed him to get away from me at least as much as he thought he needed to hold on.

I felt then as if I might burst open from all of it. I could take everything but this. I don't know that I understand it even now. Was he asking me to love him or was he only asking me to let him love me? Maybe that's it: He was asking me to let him be in love with me, to use him if I wanted to, whatever it took to let him help me because somehow to rescue me would save him, give him back something he'd lost somewhere. But I couldn't. He wanted me to do something for him, not the other way around, and I could not afford it.

Both of my parents walked away from me, and I was their flesh and blood, so I would never trust Bob. He would care until something better to care about came along, or until he didn't need to save little girls anymore. And where would I be if I'd succumbed to his fantasy? I was so tired of being used like this. He was a stranger. He was only a stranger fooling himself, trying to fool me too. My throat grew thick, my chest wall shrunk and shivered. I could have vomited or hit him with a brick. My body felt poised on the track, waiting for the gunshot so that I could run.

I drew a breath and tightened my throat. I asked, *One kiss and you're going to give me one hundred dollars?* I would never let him close enough to ask me for anything again, I promised myself. I would say *no* later.

He nodded.

I asked to see the money.

He took out a bill and held it up to me. It was new and thick, a hundred-dollar bill.

I paused to steel myself, close my throat, and lie to my stomach so as not to retch in his face. When I felt ready, I reached up on my toes and gave him a dry peck on his lips as hurriedly as I could. I snapped the bill from his hand as my mouth left his and turned away in one unbroken motion.

He called and came by after that, though he'd promised he wouldn't. Although I never again took him into a room, he continued to leave money every week. I looked at these hundred-dollar bills that I hadn't worked for as found money. I spent it taking Kenny out to dinner. We'd order chicken parmesan and clams casino with Italian cheesecake for dessert. It made the money disappear. Spending it would make Bob disappear, I hoped. And eventually he did. I don't remember the exact moment but over time the space between his visits became greater, until he stopped coming altogether.

Some months later, when I had completely forgotten him, going into a drugstore near my house with Kenny, I faced Bob coming out with a lady. He looked happy, relaxed in a way I had never seen, and she didn't look like any kind of masseuse. Pretty, in her twenties, with blonde hair, she seemed secretarial, like a receptionist in a lawyer's office. Bob and I stood in front of each other, maybe four feet apart in the parking lot. I froze.

C'mon, what are you doing? Ken asked.

I didn't answer.

Seeing any john on the outside rattled me, but this one especially. I had abandoned him a million miles from here and there he was, where he was never supposed to be, in my real life. I was wearing jeans and a sweatshirt, my hair tied up in a haphazard mess of barrettes, no makeup. I wished I looked sophisticated and womanly. Bob's eyes widened, while his body continued walking casually. His worlds had collided. His eyes begged me not to speak. It was so clear that he wanted, needed, to pretend he didn't recognize me. He was not only over me, I thought, he was ashamed of knowing me. And it made me ashamed and hateful and heartbroken. He might as well have punched me in the chest it hurt so much.

He could have said hello. He could have invented something, that I was a babysitter or a neighbor. But he didn't. He didn't even acknowledge me, and it made me believe every bad thing I'd ever suspected of him, and it made me feel dirtier than ever before. Bitterly, I gloated over every penny I'd ever taken from him and I wished, I wished desperately, that I had taken more.

The funny thing is, I still have the stuffed Santa doll. It's twenty years old. I've carried it from the massage parlor to music school in Los Angeles, to Boston, to Tucson. I take it out every Christmas. I put it on a shelf. I let my kids play with it. Sometimes I pretend I was wrong about him, sometimes I can't. By keeping that stuffed Santa, I am choosing to keep what I liked in him. It is commemorative. It marks someone caring about me. Even though his concern came with a hard-on, it was a hell of a lot more than any of the other hard-ons ever came with. Decency can exist with dysfunction, I learned.

We had shared a forbidden landscape, shared ourselves there, however incongruous that was. There were pieces that shone in that field of debris. I could pick them up or I could leave them there. Some of them, like Bob and his Santa, still mystify me as to their worth, their usefulness in my life. I will most likely hold onto the Santa doll for another twenty years, wind him up, listen to the stiff plink, plink of his aging music box, and let the notes fill me with that strange, familiar mix of shame and gratitude. It will be a quiet afternoon when alone I unpack the Christmas boxes, organizing garlands, icicles, and tiny lights so they'll be ready for the kids to help me decorate the house when they return from school. Always in that moment, it's as if I never worked at Emily's, as if I always lived in the orange flush of this cozy living room until I unearth Bob's Santa, always unexpected, and my stomach stiffens, my breath halts, and I feel fully everything good and bad, ugly and pretty that I have ever felt about my past. And for some reason I can't put it away or throw it away or ignore it because I want so to reconcile my past and present lives. I don't want to leave my seventeen-year-old self back there.

Bob treated me like a little girl when I'd never, ever felt like one. Though I knew what one looked like, and I longed to be her so often, I had to wait seventeen years to feel what that felt like. I will never forget when he took me out to the parking lot. Cold in my little skirt, shivering expectantly. Standing at the fender of his big dark Lincoln, he put his long wool coat over my shoulders, and I closed my eyes bathed in the heaviness of his cologne and thick fabric as he opened the trunk. When he put the Santa in my arms and I opened my eyes, I was changed, made innocent and clean. I acted as I'd only seen girls act in movies. I took a deep breath, looked at the Santa, smiled with my lips closed, blinked wet eyes and said, *Thank you so much. You got this for me?*

Perhaps he'd happened upon it for free somehow, or he'd picked it out for someone else who didn't like it, I thought. But I pretended that he chose it in a store just for me, and that giving it to me mattered to him. I couldn't remember anyone ever making me believe I was special before that night. I cherished that instance. I still do. For as hurt and lost as I was back then, he noticed that I was a child. Well, maybe he didn't. Maybe he was playing to the little girl in me to get what he wanted. I don't know if it matters. I was willing to pretend. I am still willing to pretend.

JULIANA PICCILLO is a soccer mom, filmmaker, writer, and sex workers' rights activist. She has an MFA in creative writing. She is the driving force behind the Tucson Sex Worker Arts Festival and has been teaching filmmaking as an adjunct faculty member of the University of Arizona in Tucson for four years.

JODI SH. DOFF AKA SCARLETT FEVER

LELE

I GOT TIME to kill. I'm not scheduled to work anywhere tonight and I don't know what to do with myself. There's no reason to be home—it's filthy and me being here sure isn't gonna make it any cleaner. It's night, but not night enough to go to bed, at least not alone. I got no weed, no wine, no dope, and no blow, but I got money, boy-oh-boy. I got money and a nervous itch so bad I can't sit still. Can't sit and watch television. That's what people do, right, sit and watch TV at night, curled up together all cute and cuddly on the couch? When was the last time I sat and watched television? It's on all the time, but I can't remember watching something, except the porno Junior brings home with the girls sucking off the horses. It's my nightlight, it keeps me company, keeps me from losing my mind, from feeling alone, feeling empty. It's white noise—something to quiet the voices. It cost me fifteen bucks. Worth every penny.

I've got time to kill and I don't know what to do with myself. I could go to Patti's but she's working or she's out with the Fat Man or somewhere else, but she's nowhere for me. If it was later I could hit the after-hours. I could call someone, if there was someone to call, who wanted to hear from me, who could say, it's OK, let's go do this or that. I could go to the liquor store and buy a gallon of wine and settle in for the night, go see what I could cop, but I don't like copping alone in Alphabet City—too close to home, too far to walk, too lonely, too many abandoned buildings, so copping means going uptown. I could take a cab up to Hell's Kitchen and cop there, come home, settle in with that gallon of rosé and a bundle. I could call Panama and have him deliver a bundle, ten lovely little bags of top-grade white heroin, but that means I'm stuck with Panama all night, him feeding me from his stash and dragging me around places, me puking every twenty minutes. I hate it when he takes me to the movies after snorting all that dope. I hafta buy a tub of popcorn I never get to eat just so's I have the bucket to puke into. Popcorn all over the floor, under my feet, under my seat. Everybody turning around, staring at me and shushing me, then moving away 'cause of the sounds and stink of all the puke. I could do that. Or I could hit Canal Street and Diamond Lil's, someone down there'll be holding, and the drinks are fast and free.

Diamond Lil's wins, less complicated. I can't handle complicated, I just need to get out of the house, out of my skin, out of myself, fast. I need to stop the screaming in my head.

Ten minutes and four cigarettes later I'm walking down Canal Street in my white cowboy boots, the ones with the red suede stars, the ones Fat Paul doesn't want me wearing on stage, the ones I wear anyway cause I wear them *all* the time. Canal Street stinks of rotting fish as I'm pushing in the door to Diamond Lil's. Lil's stinks of stale beer, cheap whiskey, smoke, and cunt. Unidentifiable disco crackles out of cheap speakers, reverberates off empty chairs, tables, the bare stage, dirty mirrors, wobbling unused barstools, the red pleather seats torn, then patched with silver duct tape. The linoleum checkerboard floor is filthy and sticky. Bottles of top-shelf booze collect dust behind the bar—it's a beer-and-a-shot joint at best; men come here for cunt, not cocktails. The fluorescent lighting gives everything a hard edge. Three of the tubes have colored cellophane sleeves, an attempt at atmosphere, but really it has enough atmosphere of its own. Two of the cellophane sleeves are torn and hanging off and not all the lights work, leaving patches of dark, damp, and sticky up against patches of too bright, cold, why don't we take this into the shadows, baby, baby. I'd rather be here than home any day.

The joint is empty, well, almost. There are five of us here. Fat Debbie, New York City's lone fat junkie, is behind the bar in a sweatshirt and jeans, working the old-fashioned cash register, which at any given time holds only enough money to satisfy the cops when they bust the joint. The rest is in one of Fat Debbie's pockets: one pocket for Lil's, one for tips, one for her stash (*she's holding, I know she is, she's always holding*), and one pocket for what she's skimming off the top. There's no register tape, no records of what comes in or goes out—just distribution of wealth at the basic street level.

Viva's sitting on stage, legs spread wide, a drink in one hand, cash and a cigarette in the other. The dozen or so round tables cluttering up the joint are empty, with the exception of the two middle-aged Japanese suits sitting right up next to the stage. One of the suits is buried up to his ears in Viva's snatch. His head bobs furiously up and down and up and down as he burrows deeper and deeper, his face slick with cunt juice. Every two minutes or so Viva taps him on the head and he hands her a twenty from a stack of bills he's holding, never looking up, never breaking his lick, lick, lick, rhythm—he's trying to fucking crawl right into her. The other Jap suit is right there with him, watching the whole thing, eyes glazed over, right cheek resting on Viva's left thigh to get a good view. Viva sees me, smiles, takes a drag of her cigarette, and waves me over, "jayJAY!"—a stack of twenties folded lengthwise in her cigarette hand. He's been at her snatch for a while by the look of the stack she's holding already. The Jap doesn't bother to come up for air to see who she's talking to.

I drop my shit on a table near the stage, my bag and my purple bomber jacket. Debbie's got a vodka and Seven waiting on the bar for me before my bag hits the chair. Just enough Seven-Up for color, that's the way I like it. I suck it down at the bar, light a cigarette, and wait for her to make another, precisely the same way. Looking at me over her shoulder as she reaches for the vodka, Debbie says, "You on your way to the Chink's?"

I could've called the Chink, made a left on Canal Street into Chinatown instead of a right into Lil's. Paulie the Chink was all tied up with the Tong. In New York's Chinatown Paulie was top Tong dog, he was *the* Chink to know. I loved the idea of being his round-eyed girlfriend, and he loved round-eyed girls, but being out with the Chink means strictly underground Chinatown—and Chinatown is already all shadows and secrets. With Paulie it's Chinese gambling clubs and Chinese gangsters. No one speaks to me, no one speaks English, women hate me, and men act as if I'm invisible. So, where's the payoff if I'm still no one? I don't even get to keep the full-length minks he brings over to fuck me on. No, it was fun for a while, but he was just filler, and Paulie the Chink is currently off the list.

I settle in at my table, lean back and prop my feet up on the stage. Still, the snatch puppy doesn't break stride. Men like that are invisible money machines—we're just faceless, nameless snatch to them, and you'd think that'd be hurtful or bothersome. Maybe, but tonight it's like we have the place to ourselves—me, Viva, and Debbie—and that's okay. We shoot the shit; the suit goes on with what he's doing.

"Susie's teaching me that thing she does, putting condoms on with her mouth; she says the tricks never even know."

"The Fundsalow brothers, they got some nice earrings, like the ones you got last time, cheap. You were fuckin' the older one, Barrio?"

"Till he wound up in Cabrini all stabbed up over something, yeah. I liked him though. Gimme another drink, OK? Speaking of stabbed up, I heard Wella was gonna try and get her baby back."

"You think?"

"They gonna give her the baby with her killing that guy and all, chopping him up?"

"You think?"

"Who's got a blow, Debbie, you got?"

"Gia came by, wanted to work the stage here, but she's still waiting for the bottom surgery. You can't have dick shit like that going on in a bottomless joint."

"Gia's still got a dick? Shit, you know she looks better than half the real girls out there."

"I was at the Silver Dollar last night. It was empty, since that shooting—Margo and what's his name—there's no money there. Hey, you heard? Genie's going home, saved up, gonna go back home, somewhere west of the Hudson, America."

"Good for her, this shit makes you old. Gimme another taste."

"She *is* old, she been here forever."

"Speaking of, anyone seen Lele around?"

Lele was the one that broke my heart. She was a cliché, she was all clichés. A sparkling kewpie doll face with apple cheeks, big round blue eyes, rosebud mouth, all framed with short dark blonde curls sitting on top of soft white shoulders and breasts that implants envied. Large, full, and erect, they were home grown and hadn't even heard of gravity; they took your breath away. The rest of Lele was just as flawless, her perfectly round, milky white bottom, her long gently curving legs, her giggle. Lele's giggle was absolutely musical. It tinkled and twinkled and she giggled all the time, onstage and off. Onstage, all eyes followed her. She never really learned to dance or to hustle, she never needed to. She was perfection and standing on stage, naked except for clear plastic sling backs and a gold g-string, Lele was a god-damned phenomenon.

Most of us were already broken when we showed up. Patched up here or there, held together with duct tape and sheer willpower. We came with scars invisible to the outside world, scars we saw clearly reflected in each others' eyes. You become part of the machine and hang on till the ride is over—you knew when you signed on that this ride couldn't last forever, but none of us were counting on getting old anyway. You throw the dice, you take your chances. The better ones crash and burn, going out big and leaving something for the rest of us to talk about.

Did you hear, Bonnie blew Vincent's head off last night? She was still sittin' on the bed holding the gun and staring at him when the cops showed up.

Beatrice's husband was in yesterday, ran right up onstage and cut her belly open! It was bad, blood all over the stage and shit. Rita was working bar, she just turned around, mopped up whatever'd dripped on the bottles, and went back to what she was doing.

They found Crystal and Angie, sliced up like a bloody roast beef, Angie's kids screaming in the other room—Crystal was trying to leave her pimp, ya know.

And then some of us hung on year after year, the business wearing us down like water on stone, turning us into human caverns, carving deep crevices in our faces and our arms, until we were nothing but vast empty chasms, and one day we simply imploded.

But Lele wasn't one of us. She was fresh, clean. You could see that the day she showed up—a pure white lotus blossom dropped by an errant wind into the abandoned, litter-choked city lot that was Times Square: dog shit, broken bottles, neon, used condoms, freaks, vermin, predators. But she was pure white light, a perfect porcelain doll, and we let the machine crush her. Like a jackhammer on a soft-boiled egg, it ripped her open and destroyed her while we stood by and watched. She was fifteen when she showed up. She was still just fifteen when she disappeared.

I was behind the bar the first time she got a big tip. Running back and forth onstage, showing the dancers, the barmaids, waving the bill at everyone. And giggling, always giggling. A hundred-dollar bill, she'd never actually touched one before. It came from a middle-aged couple sitting in the shadows against the wall. No one'd noticed them come in. No one'd seen them before. Couples aren't encouraged, they're unpredictable. Once you threw another woman into the mix, you lost control of the situation—and it was all about control.

They watched her dance and bounce and giggle and sent the money up. A crisp new hundred-dollar bill. Lele didn't care about the cash per se, not about what it could buy, but what it represented. Years before Sally Field, it was Lele who squealed, "They like me, they really like me."

I tried to warn her. Mouse tried to explain. Even Ugly Gina took her head out of the glue bag and gave it a shot. Lele couldn't believe anybody meant her any harm; she just wanted to be loved, by someone. And none of us tried that hard, really, to school her. Flesh ain't a stupid girl's game, and there's no room for innocence. Or maybe we just didn't believe in it anymore. Couldn't believe that someone could be so clean and still wind up here. Didn't want to see what we looked like standing next to all that trust and sweetness. We'd warn you once; if you didn't listen it was on you. It's not my job to save your ass, I'm too busy saving my own, thank you very much. Keeping my head above water, scamming for the next fix, the next trick, the next whatever. Hell, no one looked after me when I showed up. I was named after a pimp. No one told me it would take me ten years to leave. No one told me I was gonna become a dope fiend in the process. No one told me not to trust. No one told me how to take care of myself. No one helped when I was hurt. Or scared. Or broke. So we just shook our collective heads, took a drink, and thought, "Bitch'll never last."

Lele went back and sat in the shadows, the man and woman closed ranks around her, and she drank their champagne as they stroked her, petted her soft skin, toyed with her curls. She sucked in their attentions, and they fed off her. They folded in on her in the dark and digested her. And for Lele, I guess it felt like family. For her the trinity was mother father child, the fantasy of home, love, and safety. For them it was another dynamic entirely, one where being a child is not about being cared for, but about being the weakest, where children are a means to an end, where they are faceless, interchangeable, and disposable.

Fast-forward, not very far, Lele wasn't around very long. I'd managed to avoid dancing and just work the floor. When I timed it right, after sniffing a couple of bags of dope and taking just a pinch more than I could handle, I managed to throw up on someone's shoes. That'd get me off the stage for the night. Didn't get me the night off, you had to be dead to get the whole night off, and even then they docked you. The floor manager sent me into the bathroom to get Lele onstage for the next set. She was late and it was her or me, and I had no interest in dancing that night when I could stay high and work my hustle on the floor.

Inside the bathroom, Lele sat in a corner crying on the cold tiled floor. Those magnificent legs straight out in front of her, shoeless.

"Whassamatter Lele?"

She pointed a perfectly manicured fifteen-year-old milk-white finger to her delicate feet and continued crying. In between the toes of both feet were open sores. Abscesses. Open, crusty, and oozing pus. I don't know when she learned the junkie trick of shooting dope between your toes. I don't know whether it was to keep her habit a secret, or she'd just learned not to mar the merchandise.

She couldn't get her shoes on, the pain was too much. We tried powdering her shoes, so her feet could just slide in. She cried more. She couldn't dance barefoot and risk customers seeing the sores. As if I were some bizarre version of Prince Charming, it was my job to figure out how to get Cinderella into her shoes. There was a new batch of cheap cocaine circulating, cheap because someone was cutting it with lidocaine, an anesthetic. As it happened, I just happened to have a healthy supply on hand. The Mouse held her tight from behind, rocking her like a baby, while I spread the lidocaine/cocaine concoction on the raw pink flesh between her toes. She screamed and thrashed, legs recoiling. I waited and Mouse held her tight. Then Lele relaxed a little as the lido started to work and her feet began to numb. We fed her the rest, holding it up to her delicate nose as she got up and slipped tenderly into her dancing shoes. A few more lines and her mind was no longer on her toes or her pain, the pain she had tried so hard to hide, the pain she had tried to stop. Me and Mouse did a few lines ourselves for good measure—shitty coke is still better than no coke at all—and went out to work the floor and get our hustle on while Lele danced under the lights. Business as usual.

Then Lele just stopped showing up. Disappeared. The machine never really got to take its toll on her looks. I don't have to think about it, we don't have to hear it from the cops or read it in the paper. I know she's dead—we all know, the streets know, but no one will say it. Like a porcelain doll crushed and shattered by a vicious child. A toy no longer found amusing, left in a heap. I picture her tossed across a filthy bed someplace, staring blankly up at the stains on the ceiling in some transient hotel, sunlight hungry to get through grimy windows, yearning to dance across her perfect body one more time, her throat slashed, her body broken, bruised, penetrated, and abused in ways you don't like to think about. What's left of her perfect lotus blossom body now just the trash freaks leave behind when they're done.

Not the first, or the last, but Lele was the one that broke my heart.

• • •

Time for Fat Debbie to close up, time to hit after-hours. Time for Georgie Brooklyn's or the Firehouse or Valentinos or 366 or the 220 Club or a dozen other joints. The pussy hounds left at some point. I never noticed them get up from between Viva's legs.

Invisible men. Faceless cunt. The cosmic yin yang of the cooch bars.

JODI SH. DOFF AKA SCARLETT FEVER has published in *Penthouse*, *Playgirl*, *Bust*, the *Olivetree Review*, and *Cosmopolitan*. Her work has been anthologized in *Best American Erotica 1995*, *Bearing Life*, *Penthouse: Between the Sheets*, and *The Bust Guide to the New Girl Order*. She has been active in prostitutes' rights, harm reduction, and outreach. Jodi is working on a memoir of her ten years in the pre-Disney Times Square topless business, which is excerpted here. Jodi grew up in the suburbs as someone else entirely.

BERTA AVILA

CYNTHIA

I REMEMBER THE call clear as yesterday. The phone rang, stopped for a minute, rang again. Hungover and stupefied, still way too intoxicated, I picked up the receiver. Eight o'clock. Who's calling at this godforsaken time of morning? The Texas sun was already piercing and crackling through my cracked blinds, but dammit, this is the middle of the night for me. In the topsy-turvy world of dancing, drinking, and drugging, nights are days, and days are night.

"Hello, who is this?" DD's voice was stricken with grief. Erma was her real name and she was the oldest of us girls, mother hen to us chicks. We all thought she was so very old at thirty-five. In that life, it's dog years—thirty-five is like 107 years old. But she carried her age. Especially with the early-bird-special crowd, she milked those DD's like a real cash cow.

"My baby, my baby is gone . . ." DD broke down sobbing, gasping. And this was somebody who made nails look soft. Slowly emerging from the quagmire of my alcohol-saturated brain I asked, "What do you mean she's gone? Who's gone?" She had five daughters and called them all her babies. That made them all my babies, too. Just as my daughter was her baby. That's just the way it was. We girls not only shared the stage, the hootch, the dudes, the drugs, we shared our lives. Our tears, our joys, our triumphs, and yes, our tragedies. Like most big, dysfunctional, manic-depressive families, our bond was fierce.

"Cindy . . . it's Cindy," DD whispered a soft moan, "she's gone forever." She cried sorrowfully. My heart dropped into my guts and they plummeted to my feet, and I was instantly sober. The pain in my head was replaced by an ache starting in my heart and spreading everywhere. "Oh my God, DD, what happened?" I couldn't stop my voice from quivering, my whole body from shaking. All I could get out was, "No, no, no, it can't be . . ."

Cynthia was her oldest. Beautiful girl with long, chestnut-brown hair and a cute-as-pie baby face. She was developed beyond her years. As most of us had been. She was also definitely her mother's daughter. Cynthia reminded me of my six-year-old daughter. Only she was sixteen and packing DDs.

DD paused, exhausted. The she spoke softly, in a been-crying-for-hours shell-shocked monotone. The police found Cynthia's body by the railroad tracks. A pool of blood caked around her. She had shot herself through the heart with a gun. DD's gun.

We all kept some kind of protection. A switchblade. A thirty-two. These were as much a dancer's accessories as feathered boas and stilettos. A girl has to protect herself and her own. It's a dangerous playground, the land of grown-up fairy tales. One never knows when a dragon will need slaying. A thief, a scorned angry man, a scorned angry woman. It was sickening to think that the weapon we used as protection had pierced the heart of our most beloved baby. I fell to my knees sobbing. I sobbed for DD, for Cynthia, for all our children, for all of us.

Days passed in a dazed, misty, tear-drenched, slow-motion nightmare. The last time I'd seen Cynthia, she was following in DD's footsteps. This was her legacy. On my nights off, I would frequent the old Dollhouse, the first place I danced in, where Cynthia was dancing now. Old friends, old enemies, old customers. Old sights, old sounds, old smells. Like walking into an X-rated episode of *Cheers*, where everybody knew your motherfucking name. Seemed like such a long time ago when I was a baby, when I made my dancing debut. Now that I've reached the ripe old age of twenty-three, and feel at least twice that age, I am absolutely sure that I'm a woman of the world. But I soon found out that my heart was not so hard after all.

I remember thinking one night at the Dollhouse how Cindy was such a baby still. A puppy trying to run with the dogs. Or should I say, the wolves. Bizarre to think I was exactly the same age when I made my Dollhouse debut. And suddenly plunged into the playground, with all the players playing and getting played. So here I sat on my favorite bar stool watching this child-woman unknowingly making a choice that would forever change her life. I wondered if DD knew what Cynthia was doing. I was anguished. Of course I had no idea that I would be forever wondering if things would have been different if I had told DD. Wondering if Cynthia's death was on my head.

Guilt weighed my heart down, then rage and self-hatred, then despair, chased down with scotch on the rocks. This became my daily ritual, punishment for not having told DD what her baby Cynthia was doing, a fine tuning of my pain.

The funeral was beyond somber. We gathered, us girls, from trashy Alice to little Maria, all together, all falling apart. Only there wasn't a stage. No audience, no fans, no music and lights, just a quiet, ongoing hymn of inconsolable sorrow. Just poor baby girl Cynthia forever dead. One by one, we walked up to the open casket wracked with sadness and raw terror. As if our own mortality mocked us, naked, exposed, and palpable. Then came my turn. My feet felt anchored to the burgundy rug. I walked slow, breath labored, every step steeper. Finally, there I stood at the edge of the pearly white casket, and there she lay. Our baby Cindy.

"Why baby, why, please tell me why?" I'm not sure if I spoke the words or they were just bouncing around in my skull. All I know is my head was spinning, my heart imploding. She was so beautiful, so youthful, long hair gently lying on slender shoulders, hands neatly folded on her chest. Seemed like she was just sleeping. I could almost see mother's milk at the corner of her mouth. Her dress matched the outside of the coffin, pearly white. Same one she wore for her fifteenth birthday, her "quinceañera," an antiquated, absurd coming-of-age ritual for Latina girls that serves only to impose sexual expectations upon young girls and encourage unwanted and often grotesque advances from men who should know better. The irony that Cynthia had come of age in the same gown that she was making her final farewell in grabbed my heart and tugged so hard it broke all over again. I don't know how long I stood there, going back and forth from stoic to sobbing. The vision of this beautiful child dressed in her pearly white dress haunts me still and forever.

We aged that summer. The ache hardened our already hard hearts. I left El Paso, never to return. But the memory of Cynthia never fades. There are certain heartbreaks that never heal. They remain dormant, awaiting awakening at the least expected moment. On a hot summer night, when I hear a distant cricket, when I brush my child's long, chestnut-brown hair, or when I hear an old song, I remember Cynthia in her white gown. I whisper a prayer for her, for all the Cynthias of the world, for all of us who made, at some point, the choice to journey down the less traveled road. I'll hold my daughters just a little closer hoping and praying that they don't come of age too soon. Praying they're not blinded by the night lights or deafened by the loud music, or lured by the fast money. I pray that they don't get lost in that playground, get eaten by that fire-breathing dragon. No, there have been no quinceañeras for my girls. Instead, we celebrate every year the blessing of life, and say a little prayer for Cynthia.

Cynthia
R.I.P.

BERTA AVILA is a Chicana from El Segundo Barrio of El Paso, Texas. Some of her work can still be found splashed in loud colors on many an abandoned building in the barrio she grew up in. Graffiti, true, but there are some truths that must be said, especially when oppression, compression, and depression is the daily bread. Her present occupation as a translator pales in comparison to her past occupations, which include exotic dancer, escort service worker, brothel worker, waitress, medical-legal assistant, and instructional assistant for elementary school children. She considers herself a spiritual warrior, a survivor, who long ago found salvation by passionately expressing her rage, her despair, her resilience, and her hope through her poetry and her artwork.

3

Money

MOCHALUV

I first met mochaluv at one of those shitty little gas stations that is also a convenience store. Quicky Mart or Stop'n'Shop or Food'n'Fuel. She looks like Venus Williams, if Venus Williams were wearing six-inch fuck-me pumps, a plunging halter top, and a blingy micro mini. As soon as I saw her, my ho'dar went off. I have been developing the skill of spotting a prostitute for many years and I would've bet my Harley that Miss mochaluv was a Working Girl. Sure enough, she was purchasing two large packs of condoms. Trojans. Unlubricated. With some Diet Pepsi and Cheetos.

I made a point of catching her eye and holding it for a moment while nodding and grinning like I knew she was a playa. We slipped very easily into a conversation. Turns out she's from Oakland, or Oaktown as she called it. Like any good ho, she immediately began her hustle. Was I interested in a date? She had a hotel nearby. How much could I spend? She finished her pitch by touching me on the arm, nodding her head with blazing eye connectivity, and revealing that she was a Super Freak, the kind you don't take home to Mother. Back in my sex addict days, that's all it would have taken. I would have paid good American money to tap that repeatedly.

But at that moment I was more interested in seeing if I could get mochaluv to write me a little somethin' somethin.' After I told her I would have to take a rain check, she revealed to me that she had only been working a couple of years, so her time in the Life was all post-craigslist. She had never worked on the streets. She had never had a pimp. A client of hers helped construct and post ads and pictures in exchange for sex. She had a cell phone, a car, and now a couple boxes of condoms; that's basically all the overhead you need at this point.

I don't know how we got around to it, but suddenly we were talking about sex-positive intellectual activists. Apparently some of them, from Berkeley, had tried to recruit her to be their poster girl for decriminalization. At first she had been enthusiastic; she said it sucks not having any protection from thieves and violent perverts, and, yes, "the po-lice." But the more she was around these women, the more they got under her skin. They have a certain blank-eyed, evangelical, zealot naiveté which can drive you crazy. I've seen it myself. They want to make sex work into a political statement, use it as a shocking model for female empowerment. But most of them have never even done the work.

And the few who have done the work did it in the safest conditions imaginable at the highest end of the food chain, helping make ends meet in graduate school.

Mochaluv was so funny when she ranted, her hands with these long exquisite crazy painted nails waving all around, her head moving from side to side sistah-style, punctuating her tirade with profane poetry. I gave her my card, told her about the anthology, and asked her to write down what she just told me and send it to me. I honestly never thought I would hear from her again, but to my delighted surprise, a couple of days later, there she was in my inbox: mochaluv. I never did hook up with her, but here is what she sent me.

BEING A HO SUCKS

THE NEXT TIME I hear some rich white bitch tell me how great being a ho is, I'm gonna smack 'em upside they righteous head. I'm sorry, I kept my mouth shut too long, I can't keep it shut no more. This one chick she was from Berkeley she kept telling me what an honor it is for me to be a sexual healer, how it's important for me to tell everyone how proud I am to be a prostitute, how empowering it is to be a sex worker. Sex worker, I said, I ain't no sex worker, I'm a ho! You try getting fucked ten times a day by these nastyass motherfuckers, and you get your ass raped by the police, and the tricks, and the freaks, and then you gotta get high just to even do the shit, then it's like the chicken and the egg, do you suck Dick so you can suck on the glass Dick? Or is it the other way around? You tell me. You try goin' out in a little tiny pussy skirt when it's ten motherfucker degrees, and you can't come back till you got two Gs. You tell me how empowering that shit is! Well, I didn't say that out loud but that's what I was thinking. And if that offends anybody, well they can suck my Dick.

Peace out,
mochaluv

ALVIN ORLOFF (AL EROS)

I first met Alvin Orloff when I was thanking him profusely for his amazing reading. We were in the basement of City Lights bookstore, that living, breathing mecca/shrine to the importance of intelligent civil disobedience and the power of the word to change the world. It was a book release party for some outsider anthology: queers, trannies, dykes. The sort of literary event people move to San Francisco to be part of. Whereas a lot of readers that night were all hard glossy surface, often with a black hole in the middle where heart and soul should be, Alvin was a cut above. The words flowed so sweet and easy, like he was an old, beloved friend telling another of his crazy stories that you could listen to all night long.

I loved the piece he sent but I couldn't quite reconcile the picture of the go-go dancing boy with the writer guy I saw read. Where is Al Eros? I thought. Then I put together a Sex Worker Literati event in San Francisco, and I got to watch Alvin read this piece. So he gets to the part where he describes his go-go dancing, like Goldie Hawn or Ann-Margret. There were a bunch of baby dykes there, late teens/early twenties—I love these girls, they show up at lots of these sex worker events, I've noticed. But when Alvin referenced Goldie Hawn and Ann-Margret, it seemed like they had no idea who he was talking about. So Alvin put down his pages and demonstrated.

Al Eros was suddenly in the house. Doing this crazy zany sexy arm-pumping hip-swiveling head-bobbing *Viva Las Vegas* mad dance. People went berserk. Al Eros stopped the show dead in its tracks, stole it right out from under everyone else on the bill. And once again I was struck hard by what beautiful, surprising, and complex creatures we human beings are. Alvin Orloff taught me something very profound that night: We all have a little Al Eros in us. And I have been working very hard to embrace my inner Al Eros ever since.

THE STRANGE AND COMPELLING STORY OF A REAL LIVE NUDE BOY!

AT THE AGE of twenty-seven, I found myself unemployed with a useless college degree, no discernable job skills, and a spotty employment history. Worse, I suffered from an aversion to mornings that rendered most office and retail jobs out of the question. Whilst perusing the want ads of a gay free paper, I saw an ad for exotic dancers and, figuring what the heck, answered it. This involved making my way to a run-down movie theater in San Francisco's seedy Tenderloin district that alternated dirty movies with stage shows featuring (as the marquee bragged in two-foot-high lettering) "Live, Nude Boys!"

The shows, I discovered, consisted of little more than guys publicly masturbating and allowing themselves to be groped. A "dancer" (as the boys were so generously termed) would come out and strip, wank a bit, then move through the audience while men pawed him and shoved money in his socks or boots. The only real job requirement (beyond a rather minimal degree of sexiness) was not being shy. I did a trial show and was hired.

I found the work easy. The shows were all of twenty minutes long, and thus my job never impinged on my busy schedule of nightclubbing, creating absurd art projects, and sleeping late. I'd arrive fifteen minutes before my show and hand the man at the front desk my musical tape, then repair to the dressing room. There, I promptly changed into something both sexy and easily removed and proceeded to get in the mood by watching pornography. Soon I'd hear an announcement over the speakers informing the patrons that my show was about to begin, and that while the audience was welcome to get "intimate" with me, the city and county of San Francisco forbid them from touching my genitals and buttocks. Tipping was highly recommended. Then came my cue: "And here's Al for your enjoyment!" Show time!

I, for one, was never content with ostentatious onanism. I spent my time on stage dancing around like Ann Margaret or Goldie Hawn at their '60s swingingest. I didn't just remove my clothes, but flung them away with wild abandon. Even when transported into an erotic frenzy,

I kept myself grinding to the rhythm of whatever up-tempo music I'd chosen. I was going to give the crowd exotic dancing whether they liked it or not!

Of course, public masturbation is not scooping ice cream; there is a certain stigma attached. People routinely assume sex workers are junkies, prostitutes, uneducated, psychologically unbalanced, and/or promiscuous. I can happily report that in reality, few of us "dancers" were ever more than any one of those things at a time. Actually, I seldom had to confront the usual stereotypes since I live in San Francisco, and we don't have time for squares, daddy-o! The flak I got as a sex worker came from the sex industry itself. The clubs I stripped at (and the film companies I worked for when I later acted in dirty movies) often objected to my punky hair and clothing. People in the sex industry tended (perhaps still tend) to think gay men are turned on exclusively by the usual corny macho archetypes: jocks, military dudes, college boys, and so on. I had an upward battle convincing anyone that my hipster shtick would be appealing. It was, though. Plenty of patrons said they liked my red mohawk hairdo.

And while we're talking patrons, let me assure you that the customers were mostly ordinary guys getting a bit on in years, not creeps. There were always a few cuties in the crowd, and my chronically low self-esteem (I was a fat, ugly kid) was often lifted by the attentions they paid me. When patrons tried to touch my nether regions, a simple slap of the hand was generally enough to discourage them. When business at the clubs slowed, the prohibition against genital fondling fell away and I knew it was time to move on. Still, I look back fondly on my years as an exotic dancer.

Exotic dancing may be a little risqué now, but I fully expect that to change in my lifetime. Some day after the sexual revolution has been won, I will turn on my television. Sandwiched in between reruns will be a commercial for one of those job-training institutes. "Are you tired of your boring desk job? Do you want to earn big fast money with short hours? Are you good with your hands? The Exotic Dancers' Institute can train and place you in a glamorous position within days." (Well, it *could* happen!)

ALVIN ORLOFF began writing as a teenager in 1977 as a lyricist for the Blowdryers, a San Francisco punk band. After studying sociology at the University of California, Berkeley, he dabbled in underground theater with the Sick & Twisted Players, performance art with the Popstitutes, and deejaying at Baby Judy's neo new-wave nightclub, before wholly succumbing to his literary pretensions. His writing can be found in numerous 'zines as well as the anthologies *Beyond Definition*, *Tricks and Treats*, and *Pills, Chills, Thrills, and Heartache*. Orloff is the co-author of a transsexual showbiz memoir, *The Unsinkable Bambi Lake*, and a queer romance/alien invasion novel, *I Married An Earthling*. His latest novel is *Gutterboys*, a wryly twisted tale of unrequited love and debauchery set in gay Manhattan in the 1980s. Orloff lives in San Francisco's Mission District.

I first met Jennifer Blowdryer when I saw her read somewhere. I can't remember the venue, but I do recall that it was dingy, seedy, and smelly. Krazy fluorescent magenta hair, skin shining yet somehow translucent, she stumbled out onto the stage with a smile that seemed half hello and half fuck you. She kinda lunged at the microphone and sorta strangled it. She laughed to herself. Or rather, chortled with ironic mirth. Then she said some stuff about where we were, the room. People laughed. And in that moment I realized she was completely mesmerizing. You couldn't take your eyes off her. Then she started reading. Loud, rude, crude, in-your-face, up-your-ass, but still with this girly, almost sweet light shining through all that dark.

At some point later, we took a road trip—up to see Sam Formo in the wilds of Northern California, where he was being fabulous at the time. Spectacular hairpin roads winding through the mountains dwarfed by all these gigantic old-growth trees in the majesty of the redwood forests: It was America at its finest. Jennifer and me, we told each other our stories. As the layers peeled off the onion, I came to realize that waters run deep in Jennifer Blowdryer. I found out that she went to Columbia University. That she was the author of a couple of books. And when she told me she had been a singer in a punk band, the whole thing gelled: her performance style, her anarchy. But there's also a playful, silly side to Jennifer Blowdryer. A lot of people who graduated from the school of hard rock wouldn't know a sense of humor if it hit them in the head with a cricket bat while they were slipping on a banana peel.

So me and Sam and Jennifer Blowdryer, we went out to some hick bar in the redwood forest where they were having an open mike. It was basically just us, a buncha old sad ex-hippie singer/songwriters, and a guy who played the didgeridoo. And the locals, who drank heavily and played pool while talking loudly through the whole thing. And this is what I love about Jennifer Blowdryer: I was freaking out because I was sure no one would listen to what I was going to read. I was sure I was gonna crash burn bomb and die. But Jennifer Blowdryer was just her regular old Jennifer Blowdryer self. And when it was her turn to get up, she rocked the house. I love that. So, if you're ever in the position to take a road trip with Jennifer Blowdryer, do yourself a favor and just say yes.

LAP DANCING IS MY BUSINESS!

I PHONE IN an order for another pint of pork fried rice, noodles with sesame sauce, and of course a diet soda, sell tickets to a couple of tricks, and settle into a busy day managing a lap dancing salon. "Mardi Gras," the owner likes to call it. At our club, lap dancing doesn't just mean that the girls wiggle around on their customers' laps. It means open season on any kind of dry humping, groping, kneading, and cash return.

Customers pay twenty dollars for their first visit to Tempo and ten dollars every time after that, using a membership card just like those given out at arty movie houses, the kind that sell apple juice and brownies instead of popcorn. The girls either receive no pay and adhere to all of the myriad house rules, or they actually pay the house twenty dollars and more for an open season of protected hustling. In addition, the owner, a former stripper I'll call "Demonique," has several inventive and costly "fines" she extracts on a regular basis.

The lap dancing deal is similar to a "swing club" setup I once worked. Just a bunch of ghetto gals on the go, hustling tricks in a fun atmosphere of chips and colored light bulbs. Many girls prefer this protected environment to anything else and beg to be permitted back every time they get fired.

The clientele is the usual fun mix of New York City perverts: skin cancer victims, guidos, old men, ugly men, Japanese executives, and, most indigenous to New York City, Hasidim. Yes, Orthodox Jews—who aren't even supposed to have premarital sex—show up consistently at the hardcore joints. They won't sit around and sip a brewski while a go-go gal writhes a few feet away in a public bar, but they'll grope a fat, aging girl's cunt for a dollar a minute.

Strolling onto the swamp-like floor is a sublime experience. Up to thirty girls at a time could be either working or waiting to sit with someone. The tricks are either slamming a girl against themselves, groping a dangling tit, poking a displayed-for-easy-access twat, or trying to look casual while waiting for something they're interested in to come along.

It's funny to see a girl sitting on a Japanese guy who's violently clawing at her tits, as if he'll somehow get more for his consumer dollar, while he slams her up and down, and listen to her talk to a co-worker at the same time: "I have to be home at eight thirty now. I couldn't get the babysitter to stay . . . Uh huh. Uh huh. Well, I got caught in traffic last time . . ."

My agenda at the lap-dancing place is the same as at any job. I want to make money, but I also want to have long stretches of time when I can eat, read, do my makeup, make personal calls, or stare vacantly into space for hours. The girls, however, live in a state of low-key hysteria that demands attention.

One "oldie" called Sylvia has sagging cellulite-ridden hips, thighs spilling out from a lingerie leotard-type affair, and an indifferently stuck-on cheap wig. Every day she tells me she's not making any money, like she's surprised about it.

"It's really slow out there today. I've gotta make a hundred dollars before I go home. So what do you want to order for lunch so I can use this coupon? It has to come to six dollars . . ."

When I suggest she might find another line of work, something like my own cashier job, she sputters in outrage.

"Are you kidding? *Me?* Cashier? *Nevah!*"

There's a young, chubby white girl with farm-belt good looks, probably under eighteen. Her boyfriend, who's in porn, makes her work here. She seems to regard the whole thing as a kind of high school course she'd rather cut and lingers boringly in my cashier's booth for hours. She shares the same intense interest in ordering food as Sylvia and myself and tries to drag it out to a long ritual.

One day she claimed to have made $750 on an escort call, and the tired, washed-up whore hounded her for details.

"So what did you do for this $750?" Sylvia harped.

"Nothing, it was this guy, he wanted somebody young . . ." Cherry tried to put her off.

"Well, where is it? Why are you here today?"

"Spent it. I went shopping, paid back my boyfriend a bunch of money that I owed him anyway . . ."

This endless round continued all day. I believed Cherry, because she had sailed in wearing a bizarre idea of a business costume that looked new. Flashy black-person glasses, a power suit complete with a string tie, and a briefcase. Cherry had gone on some crazy shopping binge. All of a sudden three girls barged in at once, babbling in rapid-fire street Spanish in their low-rent bustier combos, and cut the tiring argument short. They had at least expended more purchasing effort than some of the white rock 'n' roll girls, who just wear ratty g-strings. (They actually found a place that sells *used g-strings* on 17th Street!)

A little Puerto Rican girl, Vera, had started that day, and they said she had a bad rash on her arms. Vera came barreling in, hot on their heels, and counterclaimed that she only had a little rash, and that the bitches were just jealous because she was stealing all of their customers.

I got a little suspicious when I noticed that, over the standard lingerie, Vera was wearing a satin warm-up jacket. She had visible chicken-pox-type scars on her chest. Her logic was the odd, pigheaded logic of the street whore: "They let me work at Show World like this. I have a son. He's fine; he never caught anything from me . . . I work at Show World, I work at Show World . . ."

She bounced out the door and tried to keep working, hustling customers while sporting bleeding, oozing sores all over her body. Soon, there was another ruckus. I'd only gotten through like two pages of my book during the whole day, but I knew I had to peek out the door. The tough older girls had formed a circle around Vera on the floor. Customers were scattering. They were all jabbering some kind of Nuyorican at each other, and Vera, whose face kind of looked like a girl at a beauty parlor who kind of looks like Madonna, was holding her ground and looking determined. She was going to get dry humped for cash until every pervert in New York had to catch whatever hideous disease she had. I dragged her in by her jacket, not wanting to touch her infested skin, even for free.

When my shift was over, I walked into the elevator and slipped on a condom, crashing into an exiting customer.

"How ya doin'?" he asked politely.

"Bored," I replied, my stock answer in those years.

"*I'm* bored, and I'm payin'!" he blurted, surprising both of us with his candor.

In 1978, at the age of seventeen, **JENNIFER BLOWDRYER** began to sing with her very own punk band, The Blowdryers. In 1983 and 1984, she put together her first book, *Modern English: A Photo Illustrated Trendy Slang Dictionary*. In 1984, she was singing in a party band, White Trash Debutantes, and got a fellowship to the writing division of Columbia University. At Columbia, she put together *White Trash Debutante*, a photo-illustrated lower-middle-class autobiography, and *The Laziest Secretary in the World*, an adventure novel about an overweight temp.

In the late 1980s, with the help of Annie Sprinkle and Veronica Vera, Blowdryer began to run shows called Smut Fests. The first were in a lap dancing parlor in New York City, and they expanded to Hamburg, Baltimore, San Francisco, and London. Eventually, HBO produced a half-hour special on them. In 2002 the first major production (well, perhaps major is a relative term) of her plays was produced at Theater Rhino in San Francisco: *White Trash Debutante* and *Behind the Candelabra*.

MISTRESS CHUN JAE-MIN

TOKYO

You call at 11 p.m., every Thursday.

When it's 11 p.m. PST Thursday, it's 5 p.m. Friday in Tokyo.

You are calling me from home. I have to count the hours of the time difference, because you are a liar.

The phone erupts with your ring tone. It's you calling. *Brrrring, brring, brring.* It's annoying and insistent. Maybe I hear it that way only because I know it's you. I associate that ring tone with your voice and your profile.

I look at the caller ID. It only shows the number of the relay service. It never shows your actual number. I always look out of habit. You could be calling me from anywhere, I'd never know. It keeps the fantasy real. At least, for you.

I don't have any fantasies. Well, at least not of you. I answer your call.

"Hell-oh."

"M-m-mistress Chun?"

"Yes, of course it is, who else would it be?"

"I don't know." Your voice is wheedling, whiny, and needy. "What are you doing?"

"I'm sitting here, impatiently waiting for your call. You're late." I keep my voice controlled, an undertone of menace. "Why do you insist on calling me incessantly?"

I know the answer; this is the same conversation we have once a week. I'm glad it's over the phone, because at this point I can no longer even pretend to be interested.

"Because you are a beautiful Asian mistress. And I live to serve you," you whine. Your voice spans the Pacific Ocean from your tiny apartment in some prefecture in Japan. Why can't some of the drilling nasal tonality of your voice be burnt away by the speed with which it travels across the world to my delicate ear?

"Well, then," I say, "let's get on with it. What are you wearing?"

"I'm wearing white stockings with garters and matching white lace bra and panties."

"And what else?" I am, after all, demanding.

"My CB-2000," you whisper with that tone of dark excitement. Your breathing gets more rapid as you wait for my response. CB-2000 is a locking male chastity device. The material is a highly durable plastic made of polycarbonate. The strength of this material exceeds that of acrylic and many other plastic blends. The device is designed to be worn for long periods and is almost unbreakable. It is also designed to break inwards upon shattering, to deter wearers from trying to break it off.

"I don't believe you. How can I be sure that you are obeying me, when you are on the phone, miles away?"

"I can tap the phone with my chastity belt and you can hear it," you offer.

"Please, you can tap the phone against anything and I would be none the wiser. Send me the keys to your CB-2000 and a Polaroid picture of yourself in lingerie and your chastity belt. Otherwise, there is no way I can believe you. You are duplicitous. You're whiny and a liar."

"I can't send you the keys; I can't wear this all the time."

"Yes you can and you will, if you want to continue speaking with me. I don't like you. I don't like talking to you. I think you're a lying, lazy idiot. I cannot believe that you have an Asian mistress fetish and actually *live* in Japan. You are so fucking lazy that you can't be bothered to learn the language and find a *real* Japanese mistress, so you bother me instead. And I'm not even Japanese. That is completely retarded."

"I'm sorry."

You are lame.

"On top of that, you fetishize your female coworkers. Forcing them, without their knowledge or consent, to play a part in your perversity, by having them boss you around at work. If you were in the States, you would be sued for sexual harassment. So, until you can send me the keys and the Polaroid, you are not allowed to talk to me."

I hang up on you. I'm still laughing when you call back.

I pick up the phone; hold it away from my ear. You whine, "Why did you hang up on me?"

I sigh, "Because I mean what I say, you have to send me the two things I asked for before I'll talk to you anymore."

"But I can't do it right now and I've already paid to talk to you."

You are whining again. I don't hear the words anymore; I feel a rising irritation. I know what you want. You know what you want. I simply don't think you deserve it.

I snap at you, "Quit whining. You are not a five-year-old asking his mommy for a cookie. Start talking like an adult."

Your tone goes lower and calmer.

"Sorry, I can't help it, I feel like I have to beg you for everything."

"Well, you do. But you don't have to whine to beg."

I'm feeling snappish. I want to be done talking to you. The service I work with wants me to keep you on the phone for as long as possible. I could drag this out for hours, but it's a balancing act, how long I can stand to speak with you versus how much money I'll make. It has to be enough to be worth the effort, so I can't let my disgust cut the call short.

"Where are you? Are you at home or at work?" I demand.

"I'm at home," you say, in your semi-normal voice.

"Good. And if you were to open your curtains, could people see you, in your lacy frilly things and your chastity belt?"

"Yes," you whisper.

"Open your curtains, drapes, blinds, whatever, turn on all the lights in your apartment, and stand in front of your window, now. I want to hear the light switches and the curtains being drawn back."

You do it. I can hear the click of the switch and the metallic slide of the drapes. I smirk, knowing that you are not actually wearing lingerie or a chastity belt.

"Oh, Mistress, my cock is hurting! It's trying to get hard but my CB-2000 won't let it. Please, can I take it off?" You are whining again.

My thoughts are so far away from you and your alleged penile discomfort that all I can do is say, "No. You will do as I have told you or, again, I will hang up. You may be suffering now, but you know how much shittier it is to suffer alone. Make your decision now."

You comply or at least say that you are complying. I fleetingly think, holy crap, have I become such a control freak that your little whining insubordination over the phone is getting under my skin? No, I enjoy the hell out of being mean to you. You can't get enough humiliation and berating.

"Mistress, can I tell you about the office ladies at my work?" you whimper, simper, hesitantly.

"Sure, what the hell, I've only heard it so many times I can probably recite it back to you verbatim and it's boring, but it's your dime."

I'm surfing the net, painting my toenails, reading a book. While you drone on.

"Well, today, one of the ladies I work with, the younger one, asked me to do some photocopying for her. She's not my boss and she's not supposed to ask me to do anything for her, but I think that the ladies I work with are onto me. I think they know I can't resist doing whatever they tell me to do. So I did it and she's so pretty, do you think she'd dominate me?" You continue on, do not wait for a reply. "Now all the other office ladies have me do their menial tasks, and I can never say no to them, they are so pretty and demanding. I'm starting to fall behind in my work. I am afraid my boss will notice. I like looking at them. They have such nice bodies. I like to imagine what they look like in leather and with stiletto boots on. I wore my CB-2000 to work the other day and one of the ladies accidentally ran into me and I think she felt it. I think she told the other office ladies and now they all know about me and my secret desires and they are going to use it against me to make me do their jobs and laugh at me."

"I'm sure they will." I am thoroughly peeved. Your fantasy is now involving innocent and unsuspecting people at work, no less. I also think you're completely full of crap. I laugh.

"Why would anyone care about you and your fetishes? Especially people you work with? No one cares about you. You have to call me and pay me to verbally abuse and humiliate you, and I don't care. Even when you tell me, in detail."

"You are so mean," you whisper.

"I am mean. That is why you call me. You don't deserve anyone to be nice to you," I snap. "Go get a ruler, a wooden spoon, or a spatula. I want to hear you rummaging around in your kitchen for it."

I hear you rummaging around. I'm shocked. You actually fetch a spatula.

"Now, sit in a chair, with your legs spread wide. Wider! Sit on your left hand. Hit your inner thigh with the spatula, hard enough so that I can hear it."

I hear a little *smeck*.

"You are not hitting hard enough. Really give yourself a good whack. It should sound like a slap."

You smack yourself harder. I can hear you whimper a bit. "Good, now do that twenty-five times on each inner thigh, count off, and thank me."

"One, thank you, Mistress. Two, thank you, Mistress. Three, thank you, Mistress." You are panting now, trying to keep your voice level and not whimper, whine, or cry. You start to hesitate on twenty-one.

"Do not stop. I did not tell you to stop."

"Oh Mistress, it hurts and my thighs are all red. It really stings."

"I do not care. I will add more if you do not start again immediately!"

You start again.

"Nah-ah, start from fifteen. You get a penalty for whining and for not taking your punishment like an adult."

"Fifteen, thank you, Mistress . . ." you drone on.

"You are the one who chose the spatula. What, did you think it would hurt less? Well, it doesn't. This will teach you when I ask you to make a decision the next time, won't it?"

I don't expect an answer. You're too far gone. Eyes closed, autopilot engaged, droning and counting off the fleshy smacks.

"See, your endorphins have kicked in, it doesn't hurt anymore. Now I can tell you to do it one hundred more times and you won't even notice. That's the whole reason for this humiliating process, to get you to this point."

I sigh as you repeat numbers into the phone. Finally, you've hit your adrenaline- and endorphin-fueled high. You don't notice your sad little nubbin of a penis, allegedly trapped in your chastity device. You don't notice the stinging of the spatula on your tender inner thighs. All you notice is the singing in your nerve endings, the pulse of your blood through your veins, and the trilling in your brain.

The slapping stops. I can hear you breathing, slowly and evenly, as you have been taught.

Two weeks later, I receive a package from the phone service. It contains two very small suitcase keys and no Polaroid.

MISTRESS CHUN JAE-MIN is a retired professional dominatrix, born in Seoul, adopted at nine months, and raised in the Midwest. She worked at the St. James Infirmary, a nonprofit human service organization serving sex workers, for four years, ending her tenure on the board of directors there in January 2007.

JUST FEED ME THE LINE

"So, WHY ARE you late? I need to write down something. So just give me a reason," inquired my supervisor, a full-out goth woman in her early twenties. She was wearing a black sexy slip dress and Doc Martens and had all these incredible tattoos and piercings. She looked more like what the callers probably thought a phone sex worker looked like than the rest of the workers in the downtown San Francisco office, who wore jeans and sweats and were women of all ages and body types (none of which matched the ones we gave on the phones). There were many mothers. All were great women, and talking with them during the slow periods was the best part of the job. Let's just say odd jobs collect odd characters to work at them, so the stories they had were great.

"Alien abduction," I said in my most cheerful 7 A.M., half-awake voice.

My supervisor rolled her eyes at me, so I countered with, "OK, would you accept bus problems?" She did, and I got myself all signed in, collected the calling record forms, and chose a cubicle.

The first call was on the one-nine-hundred number, which requires the workers to follow special rules. The one-eight-hundred number involves the use of a credit card to talk to a woman, so the age of the caller can often be verified, but many callers who use the nine-hundred line are under eighteen. We had a fiber optic Big Brother occasionally monitoring the phone calls to make sure we followed the rules. So we needed to make sure that we obeyed the rules and didn't verbally give any hard-ons to minors (without them really working for it).

In addition, the rules for phone sex lines out of California in the late '90s, as explained by my supervisors, specified that there could be no talk of bestiality, underage sex, or incest. This was taken so seriously that we couldn't even use phrases like "Daddy's little girl" or "Let me be your sex kitten" without verbally clarifying that we were over eighteen and not related to the callers, or that we weren't actually feline. Do you know what a cock block it is, during a naughty-high-school-cheerleader-being-disciplined-by-the-principal story, when you have to stop and explain twice that you are an eighteen-year-old high school cheerleader?

So, to make sure the callers were eighteen or older, we played the math game: We had to get the callers to give us not only their age, but year born and year graduated from high school. There was a chart of corresponding years so the phone sex workers wouldn't have to do the math. If callers messed up on the math, they failed, and not only did they not get any "Baby, give it to me, give it to me hard," but their coded phone numbers were put on a list. If any number appeared on the list more than three times, our supervisor would call the parents. Yes, the phone sex line would turn you in, junior.

Along with Minor Math, we had to play Feed Me the Line. We couldn't use any sexually explicit words or phrases till the caller used them first. We couldn't actually talk dirty to callers till they talked dirty to us, and strangely enough, getting a very horny man to talk dirty to you isn't as easy as it seems. Most of the callers are slightly socially retarded toward women. If they were able to talk to women about what they wanted, they would be getting laid without Ma Bell playing madam. The typical caller expected you to be an easy verbal lay: Just dial the number and instant orgasmic satisfaction. But I couldn't give them what I knew they wanted without them "feeding me the line." So it was a conversational tug-of-war: "Talk dirty to me." "Tell me about what you want me to do for you." "Talk dirty to me." "Come on, baby, tell me your fantasy." "I want you to talk dirty to me." "Tell me exactly what you want me to talk about." "Talk dirty to me." And so on and so on.

The best I could do, without hearing the right words from them, was say something like, "Baby, I would like to do something pleasurable with your penis." We could use the actual medical names for the body parts, but we couldn't say "cock" or "pussy" till they used the words first.

The callers would sometimes get frustrated and feel the female rejections that had led them down the phone sex path. They would be counting each minute and the cost of this cat and mouse game, the way they would count drinks bought at a bar while wondering if this too would lead only to lonely and quiet masturbation.

I couldn't tell them what I needed to hear first to bring forth the dirty little masturbation cheerleading. Much like in dating, we needed the guy to guess what he had to say or do to get in our pants (even if only in his fantasy tale). Some guys, out of frustration, anger, or enlightenment, would start the "dirty talk" conversation and get the proper words into play; then it was smooth sailing into a sea of smutty stories and perverse phrases. Eventually, the other guys would ask me just to moan and say their names while they jerked off. It wasn't a fantasy, but it got them off.

Did you know that if you moan for long enough you can become lightheaded and almost pass out? I know this because I sometimes had to moan for hours.

"So baby, use your dirty, dirty words and tell me your fantasy."

LILYCAT came to San Francisco from New Orleans in 1988 to study communications arts and broadcasting and fell in love with the arts scene she found. Since 1988, she has worked a bit in radio, television, theater, and publishing and has had a series of short and odd jobs. She has been a hostess for Popcorn Anti-Theater and has made a documentary film, *Why Should I Live?* She has written erotica, horoscopes, and dark and twisted tales. One of her true loves is event production, and she has produced and stage managed over one hundred events for the Sisters of Perpetual Indulgence, drag queen and drag king groups, burlesque troupes, sex workers, film screenings, and underground art. She has never met a creative person she didn't like.

SHAWNA KENNEY

I first met Shawna Kenney at an event she put together in L.A. She wrote a book called *I Was a Teenage Dominatrix.* I have actually seen people walk up to her at readings and ask, "What is your book about?" Maybe some of the disconnect is the fact that Shawna so does not look like the stereotype of a dominatrix. But this is another lesson I learned over and over again in the world of sex work: Don't judge a hooker by her cover. We had corresponded, and somehow I had the idea that Shawna would be six feet tall with huge stiletto heels, a sneer on her big red pouty lips, blood on her long red pointy nails, and handcuffs hanging off her belt. But Shawna Kenney is so not that. She presents as a cute, sweet, alternative, edgy rock chick. Which I suppose in some ways is what she is.

Shawna is sharp, but kind. Generous and hard working. Totally cutting edge. And a world-class networker. She doesn't seem to have a mean bone in her body, though. How could someone like that possibly be a dominatrix? But in the sex worker world, oftentimes we choose a persona, an alter ego that allows us to do this work behind a mask. Again and again when I talk to people who have sex for money, they tell me how they compartmentalize, remove themselves, watch themselves as they perform these acts for these people. (I had a name for the character I played when I was a rent boy: Loverstudguy. It was like I was creating and starring in my own movie; it even had a soundtrack, this basso profundo sleazebag voiceover from a porn movie: "Oh yeah baby, you love it, don't you baby, you want it, don't you baby, you need it, don't you baby."

Try as I might, I couldn't bridge the disconnect between the Shawna Kenney I met in L.A., and the teenage dominatrix. Then I did a Sex Worker Literati event with Shawna Kenney at the Hustler Store on Sunset Strip in Hollywood. The master of ceremonies, Stan Kent, asked the audience, "Hey, who wants to be humiliated by a dominatrix?" The crowd went quite wild, naturally. Shawna Kenney herself, she didn't really seem that anxious to humiliate anyone. But Stan was insistent. So a hand-picked submissive dude came up to the stage and Shawna got up from her chair. What happened next was nothing short of shocking. Shawna Kenney transformed utterly and instantly. This hard glowering filled her face and her eyes shot fire. She seemed magically to grow taller and harder. We were transfixed and hypnotized, me and the audience. When she ordered Mr. Submissive to his knees, he fell with a gasp of rapture.

Then it all made sense.

SEVEN MINUTES WITH STRIPPER #2

THIS TIME IT'S called a "passion party." An acquaintance is getting married and I've been invited to join in her pre-nuptial celebration. The pastel pink flyer covered in quarter-sized hearts promises that a "carefully selected" group of sensual products (creams, lotions, adult bedroom toys, books, and other novelties) will be introduced in a positive, supportive manner. It assures me that ordering is confidential, and I'll have the option of ordering gifts for the bride, as well.

Last time I attended something like this, it was a bachelorette party for a coworker. It began with a group of twenty women in a hotel banquet room. After chowing down on chicken wings, macaroni and cheese, and potato salad, we turned our attention to a thirty-something named Jasmine. In her red power suit and black bob, she could easily have been a member of the cast of *Melrose Place*, but she was there to sell us sex toys. I watched as she demonstrated the various French ticklers, silicone dildos, edible underwear, massage oils, nipple clamps, fuzzy handcuffs, glow-in-the-dark vagina replicas, rubber cock rings, warming lubricants, and bullet vibes. I tasted the chocolate, strawberry, and mint nipple creams. Having grown up in a repressed Catholic household, I found it inspiring to encounter such openness about sexuality in mainstream America (even if it was a bit disturbing to see what Mary in Finance was ordering, or witness Tricia in Billing trying on lingerie). After the sex toy party, we all moved to a second-story room in the hotel, where the bride and friends giggled, waiting for "the first male stripper" to arrive (they'd "ordered two").

Although the idea of a male stripper has never done a thing for me sexually, I stayed out of curiosity. Only one of my coworkers knew I'd worked in the sex industry briefly as a dancer and mostly as a dominatrix before working in film post-production. It wasn't as if I was ashamed of it—I mean, I'd written and published a memoir about the experience—but my "straight life" colleagues didn't even know I was a struggling writer, much less an ex-pro domme. It'd been about eight years since I'd been in the business, and five years since I'd written about it. Certainly, all of my friends knew—it just never came up in conversation around the water cooler at work.

Stripper #1 knocked on the door, and I moved to the kitchen section of our suite, trying to make myself invisible. "Ebony" barely had time to introduce himself before the maid of honor led him to the center of the living room, pointed out the bride-to-be, and put on the generic house music CD. He was a bald, mocha-skinned black man with well-defined muscles who stripped smoothly out of his tight black T-shirt and side-snapped jogging pants down to an electric blue shimmering thong. One by one the women waved dollar bills, and he danced over to them, touching himself lovingly, thrusting his growing package into their faces, allowing them to touch and kiss various body parts as the others screamed and took pictures. I'd only done a bachelor party once while in the business, and the men never got half as intimate or grabby as these women did. After most of the party had their way with him, Ebony reached into his duffle bag, covered his nipples in whipped cream, and finally shimmied his way to the bride. Lick after lick uncovered his nipples, then his butt, then his stomach. When the song ended, a tall redhead with long curly hair who'd been drooling at the bride's side (I think she was head of Human Resources) took Ebony by his hand to lead him away into a bedroom. The women fanned themselves, laughing about the performance and checking their watches for when "the other one was gonna get there."

"Maybe Ebony will do another dance—when Nanci's done with him," said one.

"Number two better hurry up because I told my husband I was shopping," said another.

"I got Ebony's number and don't *think* I won't be calling him for a private performance," said another. Others huddled around bowls of potato chips while talking about work. I said goodbye to the bride and left.

Outside of the hotel, I waited as the valet retrieved my car from some faraway lot. A young man with short wavy brown hair, green eyes, and a blue adidas tracksuit walked up next to me and threw down a dirty duffle bag. He squatted to unzip it, and then removed a small boom box, revealing a huge pile of crumpled bills underneath. One by one, he picked each up, straightening them meticulously into his hand.

"Long night?" I asked.

"Yeah," he sighed. "Just drove through horrible traffic from Malibu."

"Well you've got an eager crowd up there," I laughed. As if on cue, high-pitched screams escaped from a balcony above.

"Is that where you're coming from?" he asked.

"Yeah. And that's where you're going, right?"

"It's my fourth party today. Whatsa matter? Not having fun?"

"I used to be a dominatrix. And a phone girl. And a dancer."

"Ah," he said, nodding in empathy. "It's like knowing the magician's tricks."

"Yeah. That guy up there's probably gay, you're exhausted, and these women who are so uptight at work are blushing like little schoolgirls. I'm just . . . bored, I guess. I'd rather be watching a movie or something."

"Me too," he laughed. "I should go home. I've made enough today."

"At least you don't have to wear heels!"

The valet returned with my car.

"Have a nice night," I said, walking away.

"Wait," he said, stuffing the bills back into the bag. He walked to me and shook my hand. "What's your name?"

"Shawna. And yours?"

"Mike. But the agency calls me Maximus."

"Nice meeting you, Mike. Good luck."

"Thanks. Thanks for talking to me. Nice meeting you too."

The next day, the bride-to-be called to thank me for coming. I asked her how Stripper #2 was.

"Oh, he never showed up," she said. "But Ebony stayed another hour."

SHAWNA KENNEY is the author of *Imposters* and *I Was a Teenage Dominatrix* (Firecracker Alternative Book Award, 2000), as well as hundreds of articles, features, essays, and reviews. Her work has appeared in *American Writer*, *Juxtapoz*, *Transworld Skateboarding*, *Alternative Press*, *LA Weekly*, the *Underground Guide to Los Angeles*, *Etiquette for Outlaws*, *Let Fury Have the Hour: The Punk Rock Politics of Joe Strummer*, *Putting Your Passion Into Print*, and many other publications and anthologies.

In the late '80s she produced the D.C.-based music fanzine, *No Scene 'Zine* while booking weekly all-ages punk shows. She moved to the West Coast after receiving her BA in Film from American University in Washington D.C. and has since performed and been featured on panels at Cal State Fullerton, Cal State Long Beach, UCLA, Sarah Lawrence College, Goucher College, the *Los Angeles Times* Festival of Books, the West Hollywood Book Fair, the Hollywood public library, NC Ladyfest, and the D.I.Y. Convention. Kenney has hosted numerous literary events, including the Unhappy Hour, Lydia Lunch's popular monthly reading series. She received her MFA in Creative Writing from the University of North Carolina Wilmington.

TRISTON BREWER

THE CANDY HOUSE: TALES FROM THE BORDELLO

BACK TO THE heaux house. Take two.

After selling barely nothing at Mauerpark, I take a last-minute rideshare from Berlin to Frankfurt. And the driver and his lovely girlfriend say all of eight words to me. No, seriously. They are:

"Alex, where do we let you out at?"

Not that I care. Just get me the fuck there so I can make my money.

I am more than relieved to arrive at Casa de Heaux four hours later. The German Autobahn has its strong points. When I arrive, Micha is there, as loud as ever.

"Greet me, Foo Foo!" he says, tapping both his cheeks. I give him a quick peck on each side and then he's down to business.

"Theron, you have direct competition this time."

As he is finishing his sentence, into the office walks a big hunk of chocolate. As I scope out my competition, Micha continues . . .

"And he has a twenty-six-centimeter cock."

Because saying "he has a big massive cock" is not enough information for a madam. It's all about size, dimensions, positions.

"And," Micha continues again, "you have a high roller client scheduled for twelve, so get ready. How was the forest—teaching children? Molest any?" A madam with enough heart to remember my real job . . . or at least one of them. I can't help but laugh.

As I walk into the kitchen, I meet my co-workers, who are walking around in various states of undress. Not that I'm complaining. I enter Emile's room, the house caretaker, where he is lounging in barely there boxer briefs, Youtubing Brazilian pop music.

"Hey, you're back!" Kisses and then instructions. "This time you have the Canopy Dream room."

As I scurry to the room in the corner of the flat, I come across another hot Brazilian I wouldn't mind seeing in less.

"Hola," he says, smiling and adjusting his crotch. Hey, I can't help but notice!

As I unpack my bags, I decide to let the Wonder Heaux Nation know that I have arrived in one piece. Text message to Holly: "I have not been here even an hour and already work beckons. Cha-ching!"

Before the text message is validated as sent, the doorbell rings once (two rings means it's a fellow escort) and Herr MoneyBags comes in. So much for a disco coma to prepare for tonight's skankery. Instead, I decide to have a little hash to calm my nerves.

It seems Herr MoneyBags is an all-nighter, a client eager to devour every cock in the house. For his appetizer, he calls my fellow big black Brazilian and another hot Brazilian boy into the S&M room, which is adjacent to mine. I try to block out the grunts and porn DVD soundtrack, but it is difficult to do knowing what is happening on the other side of the skank sugar walls. Before you know it, Emile is introducing me to Herr MoneyBags.

"We have another black boy. I'll bring him to you."

I hear this through the walls and thirty seconds later I'm in the S&M room staring at a table filled with used condoms, beer, poppers, and a vat of coke, and accessorized with fifty-euro notes all around.

Yes, this is my life.

"Hello," Herr M says to me, as naked as the day he was born, stroking his glorified clitoris. "I like black boys," he says, gazing at porn.

I see that the reasons for his preference are two-fold. Big black man with big black penis versus little white man with an angry inch.

"Would you like some coke?"

You know me, heauxz. I don't do drugs. I do drug. However, since I'm "on the job," so to speak, I have to make an exception. Just a little dab'll do ya. I take his platinum Visa card, making a Karen Carpenter line for me and a Mama Cass line for him.

—snort—

"You have nice fingers," he says to me and he grabs three of them and they disappear into the abyss. This, dear heauxz, is when I make the heaux disconnect, separating mind from body as he re-positions me, pops me into his mouth, and I think of all the hot nations and territories I've conquered in the past. Condoleezza Rice and Kofi Annan never could or would envision this.

"Can you come?" he asks me, stroking his unit. Notice I said unit, not units.

"Of course." And of course I can. I'm a heauxfessional!

"I can if you do," he insists, eyes glossy and hazy from the crackery on the nightstand.

Two minutes later, I'm wasting ten million children and waiting for him to release his own bastard abortions onto his stomach. But, alas, he can't. Of course he can't. He's done enough coke to knock out Naomi, Kate, and Amy.

"That was hot. I go to the bank and get some more money. I want you and the black Brazilian boy together."

"Hot," I say. And I mean it.

He leaves. I clean the room, shower again, and re-moisturize my body to get ready for bed. Surely, he is not coming back for more. Are three cocks not enough?

Apparently not, for ten minutes later, he returns and calls the first two escorts from before back into the room. Somewhat relieved, I go to the kitchen for some light housekeeping.

There are plates everywhere, filled with white residue and then some. I consolidate them, make a pile and wait for MoneyBags to call me back.

And I wait and I wait.

An hour later. Nearly 4 A.M. to be exact, there is a major dilemma brewing in the heaux house.

Cocaine? Check.

Poppers? Check.

Cigarettes? Frantic, Emile asks me to go out and buy a pack.

"Sure," I say and head out for what I expect will be a five-minute foray.

Wrong.

All the stores are closed. None of the hotels has any. As I circle around Frankfurt's main station, heels clicking, I finally stumble across the only bar that is still open and grab a pack of Marlboro Lights. When I return, Emile has news for me.

"He wants you and me together in ten minutes." With that, Emile returns to the S&M room.

For a few minutes, I hesitate. A ménage e trio with Emile? Ordinarily, I'd be good to heaux, er, go, but in this moment, I am feeling very shy and not wanting to go through with it. Besides, after five hours and counting, I am just craving a disco coma. Nevertheless, I have only seconds to think about this conundrum, for Emile returns stark naked, grabs my hand, and ushers me into the S&M room. To conserve energy, Emile and I, without prior discussion, morph into tag-team skank partners.

As MoneyBags lies there and sucks on Little Brazil, I use my fingers to massage the client's cavernous man pussy.

The question is, will I be able to come after all this skankery?

A resounding "yes." With a visual aid like Emile within arm's reach, it is a given. Emile has also pledged to come, but he breathes a sigh of relief when MoneyBags requests a break.

"When are you going to bed?" he asks.

"I don't know," Emile responds and continues to offer his jewels to MoneyBags's mouth.

"If we have to go another round, I'm definitely going to need Viagra," I say to Emile as I sit in the kitchen, drinking my third cup of coffee—something I never do.

"I know him. He's a regular. He's almost finished."

"Well, that's good, because it's nearly 7 A.M. and no one else is up to fuck him but us!"

"I think he's done, so I will go in and send him off with a bang." Emile traipses back into the executive fuck suite, leaving me in the kitchen. An hour or so later, I have somehow managed to drift to sleep despite the abundance of caffeine in my system, but a bathroom trip is in order. As I walk through the hallway, I encounter Emile, who is shaking his head and pointing at the S&M room.

"He's still here?!" I yell with disbelief. "Who's in there with him now? Which boy did he wake up at the crack of dawn to invade his crack?!"

"I don't know. I don't know!" Emile proclaimed. "It's after 8 A.M. and I have not slept. No gym for me today." No gym for an escort is like no diuretics for a runway model. This is not to be taken lightly.

No gym for me either. Two hours later, hunger overtakes me, so I wake up and go grocery shopping. I already know I'll gain about five to ten pounds during this week, so I prepare. After running more errands, I return home to compare notes with all the other boys about our mutual client.

The tally? Two grams of coke. Seven beers. Two bottles of Ballantine's. Four packs of cigarettes. One value-pack bottle of Astroglide. Countless condoms.

He said "I love you" to each and every one of us.

It really pays to be a heaux.

Two hours later. A new day. Make that the same day and my entire day goes something like this: Eat. Sleep. Eat. Sleep. Eat. Sleep.

You get the picture . . . It is my night that gets all fandangoed.

At around ten, Micha screams my name as I am making my third ice cream smoothie, filled with three eggs, creatine, weight gainer, bananas, and strawberries. Ah, the essential nutrients for a heauxfessional.

"Theron! Ten-thirty, outcall. Get ready now!"

"Do I have enough time to get there? Where is this place?" I ask. I've never had an outcall before and maneuvering the trains at this hour is not something I am eager to do.

"Just get ready. We have a driver to take you!"

Classy.

Ten minutes later, I am whisked to the south side of Frankfurt, passing by the Rhine on the way. Joey, the driver, gives me instructions.

"I will drop you off and I will return fifteen minutes before 11:30. Call me if there are any problems." And with that, I am let out in front of a high-rise building. Since I am early, I take the time to roll a cigarette. Once my cell phone shows ten thirty, I ring the bell. I wait. I ring again. I wait again. I ring again. After five minutes, I call Micha back at the office.

"Just ring it again. He's a regular. He'll be there." And sure enough, two minutes later, the client is coming up the steps to let me in. As I enter his flat, I am waved in to the right, where there are dim lights, porn on the flat screen, poppers, grappa, and paper towels on the table. This is a prepared client if there ever was one.

"Make yourself comfortable," he says. I place my bag on the chair and undress.

Usually, I am not opposed to pauses in the action. That is, if there is enough action to justify pausing in the first place. In the middle of my massage, the client requests the first of what turns out to be many.

Although my job description includes having sex with my client, that never really happens. Nearing the hour mark and after the umpteenth pause, the client suggests that we can end the evening. Am I opposed? Not in the least. But at the very least, I can give him the money shot.

I do, and I am out the door.

Easy come, easy go. Easy dough. Out the door I go and back to the chauffeur.

"What took so long? It's 11:40. He should have paid you for the extra time."

"But it was only ten minutes," I proclaim. As I keep pleading my case, Micha calls and rips me a fresh one.

"Next time, he has to pay. We are not in the grant business!"

Click.

Well, at least I know he has my back.

The next day is supposed to be gym day. I want to go. Really, I do, but something keeps me back. I am the first one up, as usual. I have breakfast. I have my second breakfast, and slowly but surely, two of the Brazilians enter the kitchen with me, preparing their breakfasts of champions . . . in their underwear.

"You want some of my shake?" Do I ever.

"Sure," I say. And I watch as they make protein shakes filled with enough nutrients to rattle Schwarzenegger.

"Are you working out with us today?" he asks, smiling at me.

"Yes, of course," I say. And I mean it.

But not even two minutes later, they are out the door, leaving me there with no pass to enter the building, so I am forced into Plan B: breakfast number three. As I cook my egg and ham burrito, I try to gather my thoughts on what has transpired the past forty-eight hours. Definitely worth writing about, I think.

After a tall glass of milk, I decide to take a shower before the other boys wake up and force me to wait. Clad in a towel only, that is when I hear the front doorbell ring. It is one ring. A client this early? I panic. No one is here but me and two other boys. I answer and pray I can figure out how to handle this potential fiasco.

"I have an appointment with Diego," he says, smiling at me and simultaneously visually raping me all at once.

"Diego is not here. He is at the gym," I say. I motion him into the waiting room.

"Well, you are very nice as well. I would have a date with you too."

"Thank you. Maybe next time. Diego will be back soon."

This man is easily older than Methuselah. Thus far my dates have been on average only ten years older than me. Adding him to the mix would drastically alter my statistics. In a panic, I call Micha, who is at the gym, puffing away.

"Tell him that Diego will be there in five minutes."

Two minutes later, Diego returns and I am somewhat relieved. That is, until I realize Diego is not Diego. Ten minutes later, Emile bounds up the stairs with Micha in tow and runs toward the S&M room.

"That's Diego? I thought his name was Emile?" I say, feeling confused.

"Emile is just a joke. His name is Diego. You black people are so retarded," Micha jokes.

"Well, how was I supposed to know? He has three fuckin' names."

"Yes, he does. Literally!" Micha laughs and goes into the office.

"He said he had an appointment for earlier," I reply, following him in.

"He probably has Alzheimer's and can't even remember!" Micha responds.

"Well, you do have a point." And he does.

TRISTON BREWER is an American artist living in Europe.

SADIE LUNE

ENVELOPES

MAYBE I HAVEN'T had enough bad experiences and so I've gotten a little careless. It's a fucked-up thing to think, I know; a sour idea courtesy of a world that tells me my work is highly dangerous and that sooner or later I'll pay for the sins of my profession.

Well, I have had bad experiences, but they were long ago, several lifetimes at least, when I was greener and hungrier for it; less confident that I deserved to be treated well and compensated handsomely for my offerings. Before I had the luxury of taking it for granted. Before San Francisco.

These days mostly we've met before, and they know the deal and I'm not thinking about it. When they reach the top of the stairs, after the long ascent following my slowly swaying ass, I do notice if there is an aberration in the routine, if they fail to pause by the small green box on the curio cabinet, or if there is a question. I feel secure that for the most part, everything will go regularly; their hands have pre-counted the folded bills, have measured the worth properly and perhaps with excitement; they have anticipated the red of my lips and the silk of my touch as they pressed a touch screen outside some suburban bank. I'm not sure, but perhaps while I offer them the bathroom with a non-judgmental, flight-attendant-style face my eyes do a quick sharp dash to confirm with the green box in the lower left corner of my vision, like a spastic version of the eye yoga I used to do. It seems like I would, but these days I can't guarantee it.

It's a little different when I'm standing in a hotel hallway, double and triple checking the number next to the door with the one scrawled on either the back of my left hand or the scrap in my planner before knocking. Nothing worse than a whore at the wrong door. I'm alert; fingers tingling from the naughtiness of my mission, scalp prickled from the perverse satisfaction of living the lurid cliché, pussy stirring with my hotel fetish. I love this part of my job, the absurd luxury in which I get to dip a sloppily pedicured toe, the wonder and fear that I most likely look like a carnivalesque version of exactly what I am: a whore visiting a traveling john in his business-expense room. Perhaps I'm a business expense? The idea tickles me: my cunt or whip a write-off in a world I don't belong to or believe in. I always ponder whether the piercings and wonky drag adds to or detracts from the hotel staff and other guests' suspicion that soon I'll be a-straddle a dude I've yet to meet and totally unconcerned about my cab fare home.

So when it's an outcall I remember, I remember to ask within five minutes if it isn't offered. I will hug and give a light kiss and accept some sparkly water and then it's straight to: "Oh, and do you have something for me?" It's best when I don't have to ask, best when fewer words are said, best when they smile and indicate a full, pregnant envelope that will gestate in my purse and give birth to my rent. I do get off on the idea of receiving the evil corporate dollars donated by generally nice people who've bought into the system so I don't have to, and funneling them back down the economic hierarchy into queer-art-whore land. I feel like a slick pornographic money chute in a game of Chutes and Ladders.

On the other hand I get that feeling in my gut like a big store full of terrible crap and high warehouse ceilings and low heavy fluorescents; that icky, lost churn when they say things like, "I left the money in the envelope over there for you," or, "Wait, remind me again how much it is for two hours?" It's the feeling of overwhelming sickening ambivalence: Do I potentially entrap myself with a straightforward response or try to correct them with a verbal dance around our crime? Excuse me, my crime. If they are speaking so boldly then their delinquency is not the issue; and frankly, with the way that I usually work (inside, rich men, but not too rich or politically vulnerable) it never really is. These men may be afraid, may have concerns about their privacy or fear of arrest, and invariably they believe I'm more likely to infect them with some imagined cock-shriveler than they are to affect my oft-tested but un-insured body, but let's be frank: In any case it's my sentence to serve, not theirs.

If it all comes off as it should, he, or occasionally she or they, are glowing and grateful, and I've got the warm satisfaction of a job well done. Then my body seems to spill across the whole hallway with a vivid viscous redness, the surge of strength from my sex radiating around the corners of the long dim corridors. Once, after a romp in a suite in one of San Francisco's more opulent hotels, I leave my lovely client spent and smiling and as I enter the small elevator chamber my hips with the breadth of their swagger seem almost too wide for the brass-railed walls. I generally reapply lipstick in the room or the hall mirror, my one post-commercial attempt at maintaining appearances, but that day I flip open my hand mirror as I lean against the back of the elevator, legs crossed, toy-stuffed bag dropped carelessly, hair a bit tousled. A middle-aged man steps into the plush compartment and glances at me as he feels for the button of his stop. Himself looking just like a client and myself just like a strange, self-satisfied version of a whore, his head slowly swivels back to me as I execute the final stroke with the lipstick, and as I meet his gaze my eyes tell him, "I do not give a shit if you know." His eyebrow inches up his forehead and then the smile starts to spread like a slow leak across his creased face. When the elevator opens its arms to the lobby, I brush past him, full of the force of what I've managed to get away with, yet again. The gilt and marble reflects my luster, as with a lush look, I mutter, "Excuse me," which I know sounds to him just like, "You wish."

You can tell so much just from the way that they go about it. The classic for my line of business is a white envelope with the exact rate nestled inside, flap unsealed. In a home or hotel, the envelope should live on a bedside or end table, already awaiting my arrival. At the incall the envelope is placed within the green box, whose lid is then closed. At least it should be. But there are so many telling variations on protocol; for instance, straight cash placed atop the box, connoting a casual lack of care about the details of my instructions. Then there is the "I forgot to check your site" / "I didn't think to ask" guy, his wallet half out, ringing the alarms in both the cop-alert and severe annoyance sections of my brain. The last thing I want to do as a gray- to black-market peddler is have a conversation about money. I don't want to verbally outline my rate structure, I don't want to hear, "Well that's a bit high, can't we work something out?" as I'm preparing to undress, and I could die happy without ever again hearing that if I enjoy myself at work then maybe I should be paying them. I do not want to hear it. I lose both my boner and my patience very quickly when the money is not offered neatly, readily, and in the correct amount, served with no sauce except silent respect. Which is not to say that I won't accept it any other way; if the money is green and available, and the gentleperson about to hand it over not unbearable, then I will work it out. But the way that they handle this early part sets a tone for the rest of our time together, and clues me in to the levels of attentiveness, etiquette, and desire to please me that I can expect in our play.

There's a story I've heard from both colleagues and clients. A local lady saw a new trick, and everything went fine and he was nice and the session went well. When she went to collect from her envelope after he left, it was full of little green pieces of paper, but not the kind that works as legal tender. She retired from the business the next day. Of all service industry jobs, theft of services is probably felt most intensely by sex workers, especially since we often have no legal recourse and just have to sit with the gruesome feeling of being fucked and fucked. That's why money up front, pay before play, and the occasional quick count while he's washing up is a vital part of the learning curve for new hos. Personally, my envelopes get recycled into the ersatz filing tool of my budgeting system. Maybe I believe keeping the little envelopes partially full of cash will attract more full little envelopes to me. Perhaps I just hate to waste paper.

On the online domination boards, no one can stop talking about power. Where power comes from, which dominatrices wield "natural power," what a domme's powerful self has "made" a proud man do, blah blah power-strength blah. But what *we* talk about, often off the Internet and out of leather, is the power of money. We discuss the fallacy of the "ultimate control" we're attributed that in reality depends on the humiliation sluts for tuition and childcare payments. More often than not the money tops the scene. Money says it's strap-on time when we are tired of looking at asses. Money demands slow heavy bondage when all we feel like is smacking a grateful subject around. Money wants to be humiliated in a way that runs contrary to our well-crafted sex-positive communication skills. Money forces us to bring out our diaper-changing mommy personas when we have run dry of emotional presence and support for our friends. Money wrangles a hard-core top out of a squeamish, tired woman or man, and forces slow sensual tease and denial out of a stone sadist. Well, sometimes. Sometimes when somehow the bills didn't quite get covered or there's a recessionary panic or we are heartbroken and shaky or we're only two hundred dollars from our new ____. And then, sometimes, we love it. And often we put in the energy and the time and we get well compensated and have a little fun and it's just about right for a good job. But the biggest trick is really coming to terms with the fact that money is the boss's boss, and if you work it right and have enough resources you can work with the money and not at odds to it. You can attract the people who want what you look like and what you like to do, and you might have enough of them that you like or tolerate to be able to release those who drive you nuts. If you've got the privilege and the luck and the support and the boundaries, you can pull it off much of the time. Until a surprise police sting or a medical emergency, that is.

I find it more relaxing, though less satisfying to my inner power-hungry sadist, to take money for vanilla manifestations of sex. When I spread my legs for money I get a little high, a little aggrandized with the fantasy of it all. I know what the rules are, and since he's paying for the privilege he'll follow my sweet convincing lead if he wants to play. While I feel I'm in charge in either context, and relish both aspects of my work, BDSM layers so many veils of meaning and power around the dynamics that sometimes it feels like a vacation to lie back and happily take it, focusing on his pleasure and the latex barriers instead of the precarious Jenga tower of making sure *I* seem sufficiently pleasured by "forcing" him into whatever kink is his fetish.

I've gotten so much better at talking about sex, about safer sex, about what I want in bed and outside of it since prostitution pointed a slim red nail at me. Not that I always use these skills; there is still a lot of silent re-positioning and un-verbalized attention-shifting in my professional sex, but I have no fear of bringing words to my boundaries and preferences if my companion doesn't get it or seems open to talking. But either way the money gives me the right to say what I will and won't, to measure our time and give my attention some tangible value.

In the beginning, ten years ago now, I worried that my livelihood would suffer if I really kept to the agreements that my partner at the time and I made about my activities at work. The money held the weight of my worth: as a provider, as a fuck, as a looker. But somewhere along the way, with some age and experience, the leverage slid and balanced and the presence of money provided a container for practicing negotiation, alongside flogging and fellatio. I took the conversations from work into my personal life and started spreading seeds laden with condoms and communication amongst the lay-fucks. These days all cocks and pussies that aren't fluid bonded with me get a latex barrier, whether our interactions are professional or recreational. I learned how to enact my value of my partners' health as well as my own through the consistent polishing of my paid erotic limits.

So the bills themselves, well, they hit me either as hype or relief. Sometimes it's a straight exchange: difficult and draining, but the money is the product of the work and so it's all right and makes sense. Sometimes the money creates its own power in me: to be more seductive, sexier, stronger, entitled. Sometimes I look at the stack and see the price of the physical vanity that as a teenager I never believed I'd adopt; I couldn't conceive of an adulthood spent wrinkle scanning with a tawdry magazine at the manicurist. Often I'm cross-calculating the division of bills, groceries, snake food, and savings against my perception of his sense of satiation: Was I really worth it?

In the end, though, I know that I am extremely lucky: Not only do I enjoy my work, but I am privileged enough that I get a lot of choice in how I work and what I might do if I stopped enjoying it. The cash I garner affords me much intangible luxury; of time, of leisure, and of the space to sit and analyze the dynamics of power in the money/sex transaction in a way that many participants of this exchange never know. The money fills my stomach consistently and well, so I can open my mouth about what I do to make it and how I'd prefer the world to act toward people who trade in eroticism. After ten years the little white envelopes and I know each other intimately. We understand how we affect each other, who has what sway in our relationship. While I, personally, could most certainly survive without them, and they have never needed me, I stand by the agreement that we're pretty good for each other. And as far as trade-offs go, I'm still turning a good profit.

SADIE LUNE is a pleasure activist, bizarre and erotic absurdist, writer, and multi-media artist based in San Francisco. Sadie has been a sex worker of varied specialty for eleven years. She is also the co-creator of Paul Reubens' Day, an annual celebration of sexual expression and Pee-wee Herman. Sadie is a regular contributor to *$pread* magazine with her sex-work-centric comic, *Saturn Returns Komyx*. Her visual and performance work has appeared at venues such as Femina Potens Art Gallery and the SFMOMA. Sadie lives in San Francisco's Mission District and enjoys presenting at colleges on topics relating to sexuality and performance art.

DIANA MORGAINE

A LITTLE CRISPY AROUND THE EDGES

TWELVE YEARS OF hairy legs, crew cuts, and men's clothing are suddenly gone as I try on a black velvet brassiere with pads and sexy lace. Yasmine is with me, and we giggle and hoot inside the pink and gold striped Victoria's Secret dressing room. It has been so long, I need some coaching.

"OK, try this . . . lean over and scoop your boobs into it from the top, so they're just lightly sitting on top of the pads."

I do so, and it's amazing. "Wow!" I say. "Now I know what everyone has been talking about with the whole Wonderbra thing."

"Um hmm. It's the secret to cleavage, my friend."

Walking home, the power of my new secret identity is burning up the sidewalks of my smug Berkeley neighborhood. I stride toward my apartment with long steps, swinging a fuchsia shopping bag and humming to myself. I am bigger than the charming houses with their funky colored trims, surrounded by perfect little gardens.

• • •

THE NEXT DAY dawns wintry crisp and sunny, and I ride my bike six blocks up to the "massage parlor" location. The neighborhood around it is a busy shopping district, a mixture of the upscale and the mundane. Pricey boutiques with skinny dresses in the windows and expensive restaurants are side by side with discount drugstores and delis. The people in the neighborhood are predominantly white: mothers with jogging strollers, retirees, some old hippies in flowing clothing, and business people in suits. The manager, Elizabeth, has requested I arrive in casual clothing and no makeup. My femme gear is packed away. I lock my bike and look for the door.

It is beyond discreet. There is no street address, simply a dark green steel door in a long wall. I open it and go up the wooden steps. At the top of the steps is another doorway, and beside it is a buzzer. I ring the one marked "C," and the unmarked door buzzes open. The place is completely invisible to those who don't know what to look for. Having always been a sucker for strange initiations, I am enchanted. As I enter, Elizabeth greets me with a soft hello and a hug.

• • •

As part of my training, I get to do a double with Karesha. The studio is filled with plants and wood floors and skylights. It is airy; windows open to blue sky all around. There are two massage rooms; each one has plants, candles, and a massage table. They are decorated with shells and stones and driftwood from the beach, and images of bodies showing acupuncture meridians and reflexology charts. They smell like sage.

In our dressing room where the phones are, we are getting ready. Karesha strips absentmindedly, pulls on cream lace panties up to her waist that are cut high enough for the pearly globes of her ass to peek temptingly out, and a cream satin bra. Even the metallic chain around her waist seems only to add to her retro '40s look, a goddess of the film down on her luck and pulling in some extra cash until her next smash success. She sighs and sits briefly on a meditation cushion with closed eyes, breathing deeply. Then she gets up and dabs lavender on her forehead, chest, and belly.

Unsure if I feel more like a teenager playing dress-up or a drag queen, I follow Karesha through the sunny hallway and into the room. An Englishman in his forties is lying nervously on the table. I rest my hands lightly on his feet, and Karesha goes to his shoulders.

"I want you to relax and let yourself be taken care of," Karesha purrs. "This is Heather; she's just learning how to do this. I want you to touch her with the same kind of gentleness and respect that we're both touching you with now."

I watch what Karesha does and try to imitate it . . . long, smooth strokes, then silky fingertips barely touching his pale and goosebumped skin. Occasionally she leans over and allows her breasts to brush against him, and he quivers and gives a stifled moan.

By the end of the session, Karesha has him on all fours with a finger up his ass and her other hand sliding back and forth on his penis. I stand at the head of the table in confusion for several minutes before I go to one side and grab a foot. I rub it as sensually as I can. The client roars as he shoots semen two feet in front of him.

• • •

AT HOME THAT night I think of a phrase from a book, *el mundo malo*. Spanish for "the bad world," the idea seems to hinge upon a belief in two different worlds. Which one you inhabit depends on your choices and/or luck. In *el mundo bueno* relationships work out, creativity flowers, and your efforts are rewarded. But at any moment, you could fall into *el mundo malo*, where the benevolent laws of being are reversed. In *el mundo malo* disaster, death, and corruption are the norm.

As I beheld a total stranger's erect penis and watched him get fucked in the ass by a serenely smiling woman, I felt as if I had fallen into *el mundo malo*. It's a deeper world where the hidden is revealed, where the body and all its truths are routinely witnessed and acknowledged. A world that St. Matthew's Episcopal Church and the Girl Scouts and the Brady Bunch and white suburbia and Lakeside High had all denied. And yet here it was.

• • •

I AM ACQUIRING new skills. I become adept at phone screening, at the double-talk required at an illegal sex operation. Tone of voice: intimate and soft but not brazen. If anyone is so foolish as to ask, no, we do not do sexual massage here. I learn to make prospective clients jump through hoops; to place a high premium on their willingness to follow instructions. They must call back to confirm their appointments; only then do they get directions to the neighborhood. Any attitude or refusal to cooperate along the way, and my schedule is suddenly too full to see them.

The vast majority are the types we call "Joe Businessman," with cell phones and pagers, nervously peeling cash out of wallets and suit pockets. In my personal life I choose men out of blind passion. I am far safer here, where I choose them out of disinterested logic. A few are pushy, but most are simply grateful, thanking me profusely. In their eyes, I see that I hold the power of a goddess.

• • •

AND A GODDESS I become, with ever-changing faces. After six months, I have devoted regulars. Each day I light our ritual candle at the top of the stairway, and I am in the center of powerful magic. I am smooth, supremely confident as I greet them at the door. I am Persephone, spending my time as Queen of the Underworld. I have a newfound love for my own body, adoration even. As each man walks in, I hold some power over him, and he gladly gives cash in recognition.

One guy allegedly named "Bob" comes to see me every week for a while. I find him beautiful, and look forward to his visits. He is a Korean man in his forties who looks like he is in his twenties. He has beautiful skin. I fantasize myself as his mistress. If it weren't against the rules, I would happily fuck him. In his presence, I see myself through his eyes. I am the Earth Mother providing a feast of flesh, Gaia appeased by offerings and blessing my acolyte with transformative touch.

Other times I am a vengeful goddess, devouring the life energy of the men who bow before me. I have given love away to men freely as a young woman and been abused in return. One of them took my body against my will. Here I make them pay. I am the bait, and at the same time the fisher. I reel them in hand over fist, making more money than ever before. My closed heart is safe from the physical exchange, looking at my body from the satisfied distance of a successful merchant.

• • •

Sometimes when I arrive in the evenings, Maeve or Lorraine is strolling back and forth nude or in lingerie. They blow me a kiss as I walk in. Bella and I lounge around naked when it's hot, massaging each other's feet. She sits and trims her blonde pubic hair or informs me how her yoni is feeling that day. We all wink at each other, tell each other how gorgeous we are, and help each other with makeup and lingerie.

Almost everyone is an artist of some sort . . . lots of dancers, a few musicians and painters, and naturally some performance artists. Everyone is educated and from middle-class backgrounds; all but one of us are white. We easily blend with the neighborhood. I doubt that a group of black women doing the same thing would be able to operate here safely. Even in the underbelly realm of sex work, there are stark gradations. Our social status as nice white girls protects our illegal activities like a big umbrella.

• • •

I love that there are guys like Sam. He's a burly bearded man with lots of fur all over and a gravelly voice. He works as a psychologist at a prison, and is deeply troubled by his job. Like so many of my professional male clients he's not happy with his work, but can't figure out another life for himself. He's always kind, asking about my life and how my artwork is coming. Sometimes he brings me a rose, and it never feels like manipulation, but respect.

When I stroke him, it is a different kind of sexual experience. He does not turn me on, but I like him. He's a good person, and orgasms make him happy. I want him to be happy, so I give him orgasms. Simple logic. Maybe this is sexuality in the context of friendship, something deeper and more solid than my true love illusions. "Oh, Heather," he sighs afterward, as he hugs me. "You're so wonderful." I like the way I feel with him, like that I can give to him so freely. A feeling of abundance.

• • •

I AM CONSTANTLY pushing back the borders on forbidden territory. Slut, dyke, whore . . . three ways that women claim their sexuality for themselves and operate outside of socially ordained roles. This restless intellect in a female body refuses to carry a passport, refuses to stop at the borders. Each time I enter a forbidden zone I am afraid, half expecting legions of furies to descend upon me, a scarlet *A* to appear upon my breast, a darkening of the world as a shadow overtakes my soul. And each time the world has kept going just the same, with wars to resist and phases of the moon, with people loving and misunderstanding, just as before. There is no *el mundo malo*, there is only one world with infinite complexity. Everything changes, and nothing does. I am simply reclaiming territory.

• • •

SPRINGTIME, AND I'VE been doing "the work" for a year and a half now. I am, as they say, getting a little crispy around the edges. Getting involved with Steven has changed how I feel about doing erotic massage. Well fulfilled, I no longer need the vicarious sexual thrill. I find myself stepping back emotionally, distancing from the work. It requires more effort to simulate interest. It's too much. But I'm used to the money, and going back to housecleaning is unthinkable.

I've always placed a high value on authenticity; have always struggled to carve out falsity whenever I find it in myself. I was a dyke for twelve years because I refused to play the role of submissive heterosexual woman. Some of the clients were easy to appreciate, and most were innocuous. But very few was I attracted to. The longer I did it, the more of a strain it became to portray even mild interest. Sometimes I could justify it in terms of learning to love and accept all people. Other times it just felt like I was dishonoring my own reality, that I was shriveling behind the facade of a soft-voiced woman in lingerie.

• • •

AFTER A YEAR and a half, I can barely work. Only financial necessity forces me. Karesha is gone, saying that her body is hurting, her stomach upset after sessions. Her theory is that when we massage them, we sometimes absorb their emotional projections . . . fear, desperation, negativity about sex, rage disguised as lust. She thinks that in a culture where sexuality is so repressed and distorted, this work puts us in the trenches between the genders. I'm not sure about these theories, but I am feeling some form of shell shock. I have a literal sense of heaviness around my heart after sessions. A deep suppressed pain, connected to hours of tears, is pushing at my chest and throat. I can't quite excavate it, so it keeps building. It's not just the clients' emotions but also my own, pushed to some invisible limit.

Feeling underground in general is starting to wear thin, an act of rebellion I no longer need. I long to be part of the world, to use my mind and my education. But the money is so great . . . maybe if I learn Tantra and do it in a more conscious way I can continue?

• • •

AFTER A FEW sessions with a woman who teaches Tantric sexuality, I change the way I book clients. With new clients, I stress that I choose to work with men who want to learn how to receive. The type of clients who call me changes in response to my new parameters. My last client was the embodiment of my best attempt to maintain integrity and continue the work.

As always, I asked him what kind of massage he liked at the start of the session. He said, "Well, you're the expert here, so I'd like you to do what you think is best." He was lovely, open and willing. I moved into my Goddess of Abundance place, and the sweetness and compassion and power poured through me and into my hands, my touch playing him like an instrument. He almost bowed as he thanked me at the end.

Afterward in the dressing room, I sat on the meditation pillow and stared blankly into space. My heart felt more sodden than ever. I still needed to sob and couldn't. This was the way I wanted to work, the most conscious way to do it that was in my reach, and still the pain was too great. That's when I knew I had to find a way out.

DIANA MORGAINE is the pen name for a writer who prefers to remain anonymous. She came to the San Francisco Bay Area from the Deep South. Before becoming a writer, tarot reader, freelance editor, improv performer, and the editor-in-chief of a Bay Area arts and culture magazine, Diana worked in a "massage parlor." She holds a BA in Creative Writing from San Francisco State University and lives in a communal household in Oakland, California, with her cats Sweet Pea and Sasha.

TOD JACKSON

YOUNG, DUMB, AND FULL OF CUM

IT'S A BILLION dollar industry that broke my heart. I was a rent boy for about two years while I lived in Los Angeles. Only now, after I've escaped to Portland, Oregon, am I picking up the pieces.

It started as a joke. On the border of West Hollywood there's an all-night restaurant that serves God-awful Gold Rush–inspired food. The Yukon Mining Co., it was called. I think it got shut down not too long ago. Anyway, my friends and I would go there for kicks because it was a great hub for tranny prostitutes looking to make connections and money. Incidentally, I had just started taking hormones and was struggling with gender and finances. I'd joke, "Maybe I should just turn tricks." S. always humored me. "Yeah, why not? It'd be fun!" I guess there is some truth to every joke because a month after that I posted my first ad on craigslist. It's not like I was selling my soul or anything, I reasoned. Besides, I had no money and no job lined up. I've always hated the nine to five.

I didn't have much luck with that first ad. There were too many responses to wade through and my debilitating shyness made it more difficult. That shyness has never left me. I learned to ignore it, though, at least to survive. Every time I waited for a cab, or to be picked up, or on the subway, my stomach danced with violent butterflies. I turned to a popular gay chat website, gay.com, which my roommate, the aforementioned S., used for dating. I was sure I could find somebody to pay me for sex. I struck up a few conversations with former hustlers (conversations that I unfortunately don't remember too well because I usually had a bottle of Jack Daniel's next to my computer) by unabashedly posting in the main lobby, stating my dilemma. I got my account banned a few times, but eventually got some bites.

"I'm broke, anybody have any advice?" I asked. One guy recommended working through an agency; another insisted that I do things on my own terms. The latter seemed like less of a commitment, and was my original intention anyway. Right next to your name and thumbnail picture you could include a one-line comment about yourself, so I threw the words "seeking generou$" in there somewhere. I used the dollar sign for effect and, more importantly, because they censored "generous." The site was well aware of my ploy, apparently. They also censored "massage," but "ma$$age" would take and was more to the point anyway.

I started keeping email logs of conversations with potential and future clients. As part of my screening process, I always exchanged at least a few messages back and forth before I even got them on the phone. I am including some of the more poignant ones, with commentary supplied when I'm so inclined. Names and locations have been withheld, but I have left actual dialogue from email exchanges grammatically untouched.

[August 2008]
H: can i see pix, face pic please? laidback here in *.
Me: cool. i'm in * too. i attached a face pic, i took it today.
H: what would you be looking for? love to suck and rim you.
Me: that sounds fun. can you host? how about $140 donation? i got laid off last week . . .

Boohoo, right? I wasn't lying, though. I was working at the faggiest (and best) gelato bar in town. I became friends with its Korean owner and before he fired me, he had always enjoyed hearing stories about my sexual proclivities.

H: can do 100 later tonite, if sooner will let you know. i can host. let me know if that works.
Me: sounds good to me. later is fine, like about what time did you have in mind?

We settled on eight o'clock, but I still wasn't too sure about this guy. I talked to so many flakes. I was flaky myself if I found something more convenient or my intuition warned me not to be desperate. I wasn't intoxicated that evening, though, so my judgment wasn't impaired.

H: any naked pix i can see in the meantime?

I wasn't asked that nearly as often as one would expect. I always figured that the mystery of what I looked like naked was part of the fun. I didn't care either way what they looked like naked, so long as they didn't have missing limbs, or extra ones.

Me: all i have is this one from last year . . .
H: your hair is better now.

Fucker.

H: so are you straight or gay or bi? do you 420 or party at all?
Me: i'm bi. 420 can be fun but i try to stay away from other stuff these days. i drink once in a while. how about you?

Although I am bisexual, I always made a point to exchange sex for money with men I wasn't at all attracted to, to avoid conflicts of interest or something. I can count on one hand how many times I had anal sex with clients, and I was always the bottom because my dick often failed to cooperate.

H: i 420 and usually don't but have been partying today. that doesn't mean i expect you to. just wondering. so you seem like a laid back guy.
Me: i try. :) i don't judge either. parTying or just weed? i didn't ask you earlier, how old are you?

I added the capital T to specify meth. T is slang for Tina or Tweak, generally in gay circles.

H: been partying. i am 51. your other pic was pretty wild—wanted to make sure you weren't like real nellie. no offense. its just not what i like. so are you able to hang a while tonite?

I was young, so I can hardly be blamed for changing identity like underwear. If I hadn't been hurting for money I would have just called him the pot(head) calling the kettle black.

Me: that was over a year ago . . . was just experimenting with some different looks, or something. i dunno. i've got some time . . . might want to catch up with some friends later on, but yes.

I usually aimed for an hour or so with a client but if I was enjoying myself, which happened occasionally, I'd stay longer.

H: ok, sorry bout all the questions, just trying to make sure when we meet you aren't freaky. what time can you be in front of *?
Me: 15 minutes?

I didn't and still don't own a car. After an on-the-cusp DUI (0.09 percent) right after I turned twenty-one, I'm in no big hurry to get one. Nervously chain-smoking, I waited in the designated parking lot, trying to look inconspicuous. When I got into his car, he told me that he had been circling the lot for ten minutes. We hadn't noticed each other. He had a nice car, but it was missing the driver's side-view mirror. When I asked about it he said he'd side-swiped a parking meter in reverse. Loser! But at least he owned a car at all, unlike myself.

He was slightly overweight but had his hair, and was a former web designer turned pot dealer. Apparently the latter market was better. Before he drove me home that night he gave me some weed, which I shared with friends at a get-together later that night.

He told me to be discreet so we ran straight through the hallway to his room when we entered his apartment, avoiding roommates. After we smoked his meth, we watched straight porn as he gave me head. It took about an hour for me to get hard enough to cum. Tina Dick, I've heard it called. He was a nice guy, actually (or maybe he just had good drugs), but despite that, the impression I gave him that we'd meet again was false—but I'm glad I did it because he tipped me twenty dollars. His lifestyle seemed too poisonous, as I was identifying as a recovering addict by that point. I think more than getting my load in his mouth he enjoyed the company. Many of my clients seemed lonely. When I got home that night I saw that he'd messaged me with his number.

H: here you go with my phone * . . . hope you keep in touch!

A few months before that I had a very humorous dialogue with the following douche bag via email.

[June 2008]
J: okay, Im 46, in *. discreet and generous. so, what u have in mind?
Me: hey there. i'm 24, 5'11," 150ish lbs . . . i attached a face pic from a few minutes ago. i'm in * but can't host. where are you? basically i'm just

looking to get together for some oral, j/o, massage, that kind of thing. not into anal. i'd ask $100 donation. hit me back if you're still interested. :)–tod

J: Im in * . . . u cool with makin out? are u smooth? if so, cum on over and lets play . . . d/d free discreet here . . . ub2

I suppose I'd better explain some of his terminology. Smooth refers to body hair, so at the very least he wanted me to be less hairy than him. D/D is simple: drug and disease free, as if any hustler can promise that. Lying successfully was half the battle.

Me: yes and yes. no worries.

He gave a more specific location, which wasn't particularly close. The Valley, where I lived at the time, is a big place, especially for those without a car. Public transportation in Los Angeles is horribly unreliable.

Me: i know where that is. would you be willing to wait for me to take the subway? i should be there within an hour. driving is probably faster but my roommate is asleep and i don't want to ask to borrow the car if possible.

Actually, at that time, by roommate I meant live-in girlfriend and by car I meant hers. She was aware of how I made ends meet, but we avoided the truth whenever possible.

We exchanged cell numbers and he informed me that he could pick me up at the station. Then, he hit me with this gem:

J: thats fine . . . be wearing shorts and no shirt, so I will know you . . .

I didn't know what to say to that, and didn't respond for about ten minutes.

J: let me know when ur leaving . . . dont make it too long
Me: sorry, i'm not coming. your request was too ridiculous. good luck.

I met a lot of zany characters, including a Z-list director responsible for the third film in a feature-length trilogy that nobody saw, and one of the many Barney Rubble voice actors. The latter had convinced himself after ten minutes of knowing me that we were destined to fall in love and live happily ever after. The former is actually a sweet fellow who I saw many times.

This is hard stuff to write about. Since I started working on it, thus far in about four different sittings, I've been drunk every time. As I'm backtracking through old logs, I just rediscovered the week around Christmas 2007 when I was entirely alone and only entertained johns to make rent. One guy thought that I was supposed to pay him, and at the inevitable, awkward moment when we asked each other about money, I had to chase him out of the apartment with a forty-ounce bottle of King Cobra. Perusing our email conversation together after the act: "Dude! Look. I said $140 right there," he said. "I thought you meant that's what you'd pay me," I retorted.

There was one guy, "M," who I saw many times. I would take the subway, about once a week, to Long Beach. One time he gave me squid he'd caught. I ended up keeping the tote bag he loaned me to carry it home in and now my sister uses it as a book bag. I never told her where I got it, or that it carried a frozen slab of squid at one point. It's funny that that's what comes to mind first when I remember him. Here's how he responded to my craigslist ad for the first time.

[December 2006]
M: Hello—What a beautiful photo. I'm 49, wm, 6'4," 275. You, on other hand, are young and beautiful. Would love to know more about you. What have you in mind?
Me: i'm available this week in Korea town for some non-intercourse, easygoing fun . . . my stats: 22, 5'11," 140 lbs, white, 6" cut (;)) . . . I'm not into anything too wild. looking for $150 or so donation.
M: Hi Tod—Nice to hear from you. Do you by chance do massages? As well, do you do overnights? I also do not wish intercourse.

I agreed to an overnight but asked for $250. He ended up regularly giving me $300.

M: Hi again, I have attached a pic. I would like to do an overnight. I need to be held, and would like someone to hold/sleep with. How does tomorrow eve look for you? I have a nice place on the beach in Long

Beach w/10th floor balcony and sound of waves all night. Would you like dinner also?

Looking for love in the wrong places. I've gathered that it's hard to be old and unattractive as a gay male.

Because of transportation issues, we settled on the Sheraton in downtown Los Angeles. I was used to staying in dives so I was totally out of my element as I entered the place with all its golden gilt trim and transparent elevators. Naturally, the carpet was a terrible vomit color. He recognized me at the top of some stairs and snapped me out of my confusion. I must have looked lost. We exchanged an awkward handshake and hug, and he pointed me in the direction of an elevator. The room was somewhere near the top. The view was great. There was another hotel across the way, and its ceiling was a triangular, illuminated crystalline. I'm a sucker for that kind of crap.

For some reason he felt inclined to talk about his religion, Mormonism, and the associated guilt he felt about his homosexuality. It kind of bummed me out, so I asked if we could have dinner. We went to nearby Little Tokyo and had Japanese food. I ate too much and spoke bad German to him. His business was importing rare stones, so he was often in Switzerland, where German is the mother tongue.

I don't remember much about that particular evening because we met so many times and the sex always happened the same way. I do recall that I never got enough sleep: Every hour or so he'd wake me up by grinding his boner against my ass. We never had full-on anal, though. By the time the sun came up he'd be furiously jerking off as I sat on his face. That night we made plans to meet again the next night, at his place, but I flaked because I hadn't slept well.

We continued to meet, but at his place in Long Beach. I found that he was right about the waves of the ocean being audible through the balcony door, but it wasn't comforting. I'm actually more comforted by opening a window and hearing the neighbors screaming.

I rather miss him, maybe as a father figure. More than anything, though, he paid well and seemed to really like me. I don't know which was a more important quality in johns. Most guys I met didn't want to see me more than once or twice. I'd like to say I didn't care either way, but I'm not sure it's true.

TOD JACKSON was born in New Jersey but has spent his life wandering. After spending three years between Los Angeles and San Francisco doing sex work, he has retired to Portland, Oregon, where he takes classes at Portland Community College.

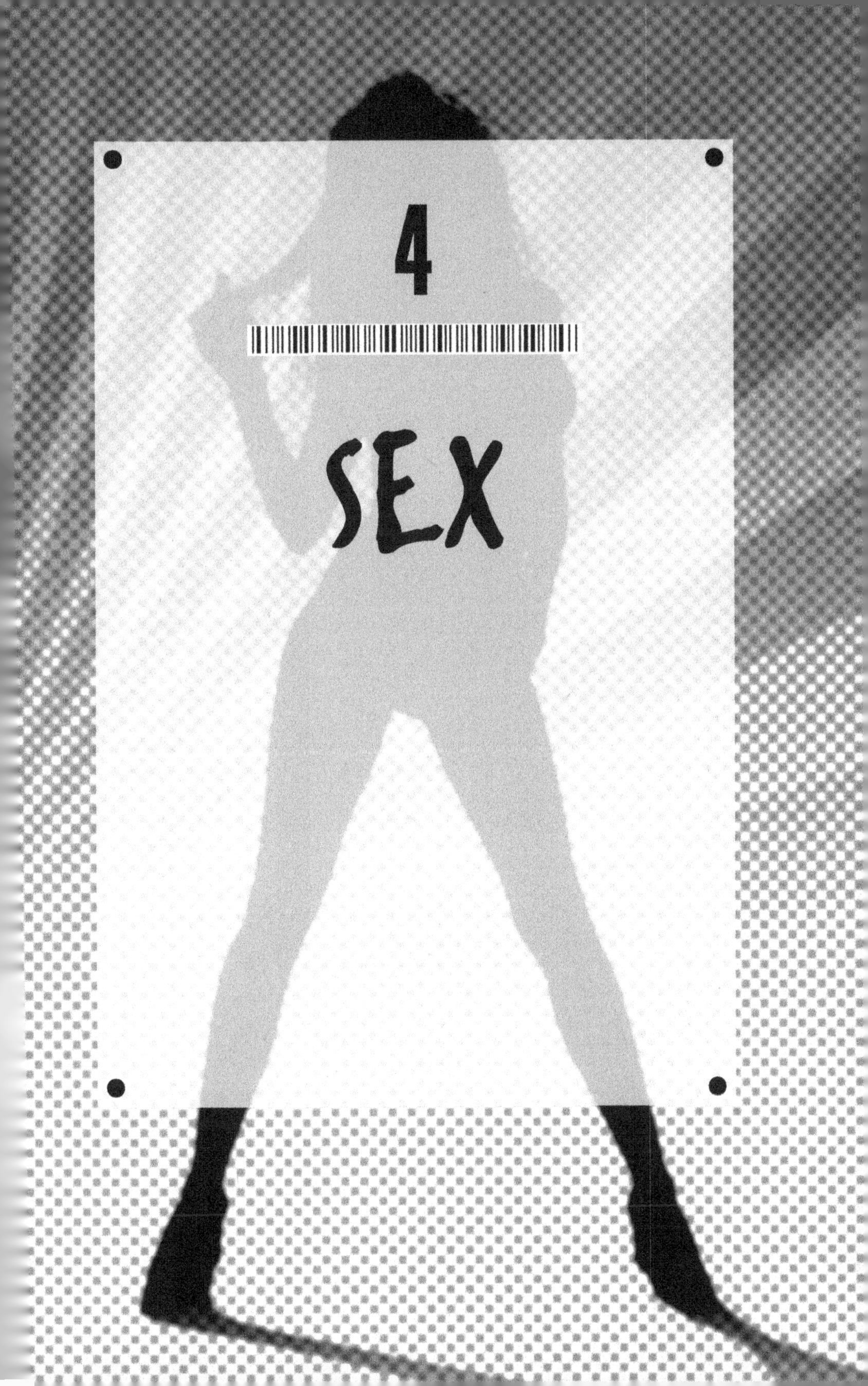

4

SEX

NINA HARTLEY

PLAYING IN THE SANDBOX

I LOVE THAT my job is sex. I like sex work. I like how cut and dried it is.

I'm a sex nurse. Our sexuality as a society is not well. It's sick. People so desperately need nursing around sex. I was trained as a nurse. I'm a registered nurse. Only now I nurse people's sexuality.

We are in pain and discomfort and misery sexually and it breaks my heart.

For me, the negative effects of sex work come from society's judgments and prejudices.

I've been a sex worker for a long time, a lot longer than the usual career trajectory in this business. I can tell you that despite what you will hear from many people, men are not pigs.

Being a sex worker has enabled me to explore sex without the encumbrance of traditional relationships. In our culture there's enormous pressure to conform to a very narrow view of what sexuality can be, of our own sexuality. So people lead stunted, stilted sex lives.

Men are scared, ignorant, and isolated. And our culture conspires to keep them so, to make money off the fear, the ignorance, and the isolation.

Men are victims of culture and patriarchy, as are women, obviously. Only the areas of damage are different.

It's not just girls who want to have fun. Boys want to have fun, too.

Some strippers are crazy.

I *love* helping turn on the sex light bulb, to relieve the fear and ignorance.

I became a sex worker for narcissism, for altruism, for voyeurism, for exhibitionism, and as a long-term field study.

I've been in jail for sex work. I feel terrible for the sex worker who doesn't have resources, who has to give forced blow jobs to cops.

I've been playing in the sandbox for twenty-five years and I've loved it.

An exhibitionist with a cause, **NINA HARTLEY** created an original persona that has become part of the broader cultural lexicon: "feminist porn star." Ms. Hartley, first as a dancer in San Francisco and then as a performer in adult videos, put her body on the line in support of her ideas about sexuality, feminism, personal liberation, and social responsibility. In the "porn wars" of the mid-1980s, she was a founding member of the Feminist Anti-Censorship Task Force, whose impact on mainstream feminist thinking gave rise to a younger generation of sex-positive writers and activists. Through her six-hundred-plus videos and films, her two decades of dance tours, and her thousands of personal appearances, she has become the most enduringly popular star in the history of the medium. She is known by a more mainstream audience for her casting in *Boogie Nights*. Ms. Hartley also co-produces her own line of instructional videos, Nina Hartley's Guides, the market-leader in adult sex-education video programming. Her writing has appeared in *Sex Work: Writings by Women in the Sex Industry*, *Whores and Other Feminists*, and *Tricks and Treats: Sex Workers Write About Their Clients*. She writes advice columns for the magazine *Hustler's Taboo* and is the author of *Nina Hartley's Guide to Total Sex*, a comprehensive book based on her video Sex Guide series. Nina lives in Los Angeles with her husband and collaborator, I. S. Levine.

KIRK READ

I first met Kirk Read at the South Carolina Book Festival. He was reading a steamy, hysterical, homo-erotic scene from his memoir *How I Learned to Snap*. He seemed to me clearly a boy of the South. A flaming boy of the South, to be exact.

After the reading, during the question and answer period, this gnarled, constricted, faux-Christian, stupid white man got up and started ranting about Jesus and Satan and how Kirk was going straight to hell, never mind the handbasket. I was appalled. I imagined myself up there taking the brunt of that barrage. I would've wilted like a weak wallflower.

Not Kirk Read. No way, no how. He stood right up to the fire and the brimstone with some fireworks of his own. As he was illuminating why it was important for people to tell their stories, especially Southern gay boys who get bullied from every which way, it was clear to me that Kirk had been down this road before. Having grown up in the dark heart of the post-Confederate nation, he had obviously learned how to defend himself against these attacks with style, wit, and grace.

I got up and said something lame about how brave he was and wasn't America built on tolerance and didn't Jesus talk about loving thy neighbor. It didn't seem to penetrate the faux-Christian's righteous shield of hate, but there at the South Carolina Book Festival, me and Kirk Read had our own little simpatico moment.

Kirk moved to San Francisco soon after our first meeting, and we kept running into each other at events; in fact, we shared the bill several times, sharing a bond that ex–rent boys do. He is a delightful blend of Old South charm and biting, witty, New Age Oscar Wildeness. Kirk is a natural born performer who has also honed his craft reading in a billion dingy bars and seedy cafés. If he is ever performing anywhere near you, do yourself a favor and go see him. If you are not completely satisfied, email me and I will fully refund your money.

IT'S A SHAME ABOUT RAY

I WAS LOOKING for size 12 heels, which is not an easy thing to find, even in San Francisco. There is the drag queen store, the Foxy Lady, but I was committed to finding the shoes at a discount store like Ross. All the queens call that place Cross Dress for Less. It's my favorite store. All my kitchen stuff is from there. And they have that section over by the underwear with miscellaneous items like yoga mats and headphones. My mother goes to the East Coast version of Ross, which is called T.J. Maxx. Our shared retail addiction is one way that we kindle our relationship.

Because of work, I go shopping at Ross about once a month. My clients have an appetite for new ideas. I love the guys who are exploring. About a year ago, I rewrote my Internet ad so that it specifically appealed to these kinds of guys. I thought of it as outreach. I used phrases like "non-judgmental" and "open to the fantasies that grip you." Remember that Burger King commercial? The one with the jingle "Hold the pickles, hold the lettuce; special orders don't upset us . . ." It was kind of like that. As a guy in this business, you're surrounded by thousands of ads in which the escorts reduce themselves to a handful of stock ad copy, passing their bodies off as fast cars worthy of worship and frequent waxing. I was never interested in being that kind of car. I always saw myself as a Toyota Camry: attractive but not showy; reliable and practical. This is an indication of how deeply entrenched I am in the capitalist machinery. I'm a Camry. I say this voluntarily, I am a Camry.

It's certainly better in the age of Internet advertising. In the old days, when guys ran print ads, each word was extra money. Those print ads were haiku. Three lines of text. Something along the lines of:

Swimmer's build, a body guys love to service,
Hung top, young and fun, clean,
No attitude.

In any given ad, a potential client could be triggered by a single word: "athletic" might mean that the escort would be willing to reenact a client's childhood trauma of nearly drowning and being resuscitated by a lifeguard's hour-long certification training in CPR. The word "service" might mean that the escort was straight and possibly married at some point, with small children in some other state. A man's children are sexy only when they reside elsewhere. The print ad format created a social dynamic wherein the escort became a projection screen for every fear and fantasy the client could possibly have. It was all so open-ended, the way someone's identity was compressed into fifteen words. *He sounds like an ex-con. Maybe he's a nice kid putting himself through college.* The whole enterprise was a giant guessing game.

The Internet has mitigated this situation somewhat. On the web, escorts have more room to spread out. Surprisingly few take advantage of this liberty. It's the sad dilemma of democracy: that we as a people have all this leeway and we do nothing with it. Even on a website where one is afforded five hundred words of text, you see the same clipped language, the same numbers and stats and meaningless phrases like "no attitude." Why would someone say they had no attitude? It's like saying you don't have an ego. You do. The question is not whether you have an attitude or an ego. The question is whether you're a conceited prick. Attitude and ego are conditions, not unlike the weather. Can you imagine the tourist bureau of a vacation spot bragging that the island has "no weather?"

I never had one of those ads, which seem to be written by people with no sentences at their disposal whatsoever. English as a third or fourth language. All of that said, I am reluctant to set down the exact text of my ad because I've built it up into this mythic, messianic sacred text. Like it's not on the god damn Internet at all; rather it's on a scroll that you unroll with the help of two clerics. At the risk of being overly simplistic, I'll say that all I did was use complete sentences. We live in an age of fission. All around us, the language is being split into tiny, marketable pieces. Three-second chunks of information—visual media is edited in such a way that we're all careening toward epilepsy. Meanwhile, the sentence is an old friend. The sentence is a familiar revolution. I trust the sentence.

Okay, I'll give you a few of the sentences, but I'm changing the text, because I'm still out there working. I am not writing about some quaint indiscretion of youth. This is how I make my living. Here's a short piece of my ad:

> *I have a rolling suitcase of toys and erotic clothes I can bring to your hotel room or home; if you want, we can play with what's there, or you can just look through it. I've seen or imagined damn near*

everything, so if you've got a fantasy that's particularly out there, it's only going to delight me. Why not? You might as well.

The new clients who came to me after I ran that ad were hungry men. They were a varied lot, but they had a few things in common. Many had been through unsatisfying experiences with other escorts who didn't accommodate their peculiar fantasies and in some cases shamed them for asking in the first place. Another thing these clients had in common was a sense of devotion. They'd carried these secrets for many years, enacting their fetish lives in private. They'd kept bags of lingerie hidden in a shoebox in the basement. They'd hidden porn videos under floorboards. They'd gotten ashamed and thrown everything away, only to re-gather a new set of taboo items. To me, they were heroic, like the people in *Fahrenheit 451* who memorize books to preserve literature. Erotic freedom by any means necessary.

I'm thinking of one client in particular—Ray. Most clients use their real names, I've found. You can tell when a client is using a made-up name because it's more generic than their actual name. For instance, when a client named Ethan picks a fake name, he picks Joe. When an escort named Joe picks a hooker name, he selects Ethan. That says it all.

Ray was staying at the St. Francis in this really big suite. Visiting from Texas, although I wouldn't find that out until several sessions later. You know that stereotype about how clients want to tell you all their problems, so much so that you don't spend very much time having sex? The sex worker as talk therapist? It's complete bullshit. It makes non sex workers feel less threatened by the concept of sex for pay. Like when the government invades a country and launches a media disinformation campaign so people think the troops are just there keeping the peace, when really they're carrying out midnight raids and razing apartment buildings and shooting civilians point blank. I grew up in a military family. I know that's what really happens because the men in my family are all emotionally unavailable. That's what happens when you murder small children in the name of God and country. Veterans are a trip as clients. I don't even want to go into that right now. I want to stay with Ray.

Ray and I communicated solely by email before meeting. He hired me for an overnight and often I like to confirm those sorts of appointments by phone, just to make sure the guy's for real. However, I got such an honest, gentle vibe from Ray's email that a phone call wasn't necessary. In addition, I really love the surprise of seeing who's behind the hotel room door. I know sex workers who require the clients to send them pictures and ask for stats and all of that. They don't like suspense. They want to know what they're getting into. For me it's a deeper practice to arrive with very little to go on. The clients who don't give you any hints at all—no phone voice, no age, nothing. Those are the guys I end up learning the most from. Especially if they're not traditionally handsome. Maybe they've got some extra weight, maybe their skin has red patches, maybe they have a micropenis. If there's some characteristic that renders them defective in the eyes of the culture, it makes me more excited to play with them. Like when a firefighter gets a call for a five-alarm blaze. It's exciting. It's a challenge. I feel like I'm being of service in a larger context, that I'm transmitting ancient sex wisdom to people who need it badly and are cut off from it. That's a grand assessment, certainly. No grander, I would argue, than saying you're a man of God. No grander than stepping forward to teach our nation's children. No grander than signing up to bear arms so that you can preserve civility itself. I take my job seriously.

When I arrived, Ray greeted me warmly, extending his hand to shake. Very few clients shake your hand. Some grab you and kiss you right away, but nobody shakes your hand. Every now and then a client will want to meet you in the lobby. Usually they want to make sure it's a match, or they feel safer meeting you in a public place. It makes it easier for them to back out at the last minute. Ray had none of these hang-ups. I'm just giving you a frame of reference. Ray was a hand shaker in world full of quick-to-kiss men.

I sat down on a loveseat in the living room area of his suite. He appeared to be around fifty years old, just a few years shy of the client median age.

"Can I offer you anything?" he asked.

"No, I'm fine," I said. This is my automatic Southern response. Then he's supposed to tell me what he actually has to offer. Then I refuse again. Then he tells me what he's having and would I care to join him. As a Southerner, that's when it's OK to accept a drink from a stranger.

"I've got wine and beer, soda and bottled water."

"I think I'm OK."

"I've got a bottle of white wine already open."

"That sounds lovely."

He poured me a glass of chardonnay. I'm sure it was expensive. The nuance of fine spirits is entirely lost on me. As an alcohol drinker, I cut my teeth on Sun Country wine cooler from two-liter bottles. We'd be lying on hillsides overlooking dirt roads out in the county, passing the bottle around. Just about everything tastes expensive to me.

Ray had these massive blue irises that were too big for his body. Babies have those sorts of eyes and then their faces catch up. He had a sweet Texas lilt—in the South, many men and women have the same gentle vocal mannerisms. The desire to please crosses gender lines. Ray was no exception. As we talked during that first visit, whenever I said something remotely agreeable, he'd say "Aren't you kind to say that" or "Bless your heart." I felt like I was ten years old, serving triangular finger sandwiches at my mother's luncheon. It's delicate when you first meet someone for sex. You want to ease into familiarity with them, but you don't want to be so chatty that you kill the mysterious sexual energy that exists between you.

After about half an hour of conversation, Ray abruptly pulled out a bag of nylon hose and Lycra shorts and dress socks. Via email, he'd said he wanted a witness, that he wanted to show me what he'd been doing over the years. It's tricky, when someone offers you the raw components of their desire. You ought to be supportive, but you don't want to be a cheerleading mom about it either. They're going to the underworld, for Christ's sake. Your job is not to gush over their watercolor and tape it to the refrigerator door. Your job is to go to the underworld with them.

Ray showed me the bag. "This is my passion, right here."

I could see both men's and women's stockings, tight athletic clothing and the like. He had a penchant for the enclosure offered by elastic fabric. It didn't seem like he wanted to kiss yet or interact physically, so I asked him to do a fashion show for me. I put it in more masculine terms. I asked him to show off for me. I told him I wanted to see him slowly take every single piece of clothing off, fold them neatly on a chair, then put on every single piece of clothing in that bag. I was just hazarding a guess, but as it turns out, this was precisely his fetish—the pileup of stretchable layers, one upon another. As he stripped down, I could see his hairy back and his short stocky legs. He had an enormous cock, the kind that doesn't grow too much in an erect state. I had a boyfriend with a cock like that once and he ruined me for getting fucked by anyone else for several years. It took will power for me not to jump Ray right then, grease him up and slide his cock into my ass. Ray needed me to suspend my interest in his penis and bring all my focus to his wardrobe. A cardinal rule of gay male escorting is Don't Give Them Bottom Energy Unless

They Specifically Ask For It. So I sat back and admired him in all his overgrown splendor.

He narrated his assemblage of clothing, which amused me and turned me on. I love a dirty talker more than anything. It's a skill I've never really developed. I've tried and I just feel silly. So when someone goes for it, assigning in-the-moment language to their behavior, I'm all for it. It seems like a huge blind spot in a sex healer's skill set, the gift of dirty gab, but I make up for it with other forms of fearlessness.

"These black stockings," Ray said, "I bought on sale at Bloomingdale's. The woman who helped me asked if I wanted to try them on. Didn't even assume they were for my wife. This was in New York. You know how they are in New York."

I nodded. I knew exactly how they are in New York.

"In the dressing room, they pushed my cock down so much that I leaked pre-cum right away. I was supposed to try them on over my underwear but I didn't. So I had to buy them. They're so thick that I've never had a run."

He turned his ass toward me, which the hose pushed up and out as if it was a shelf you could put drinks on. This was confusing the bottom part of me that was still fixated on his big floppy dick. Because now, more than anything, I wanted to fuck Ray.

"Hey Ray—I'd love to cut a hole in your stockings and fuck you right through them."

"No," he said, "I love these stockings too much. Maybe we can go shopping and find some that I wouldn't mind cutting. These are sacred to me."

Ray pulled on a pair of lacy pink panties over his pantyhose, then immediately followed that with a pair of white Lycra biker shorts. You could see the lace bunching under the shorts. His bulge looked artificial, like a lead singer from a hair metal band. Like a superhero. Ray was my little superhero.

He pulled on a bra and came over to me so I could help him fasten the back.

"I can do all of this myself but I thought you might like to help."

"Do you want to be my little girlfriend?" I asked.

"No," he said, "we're a couple of guys and I'm trying things on for you."

Leave it to this Texan to have a way more complicated gender identity than a professional San Franciscan could articulate.

"Good for you, Ray," I said. "You're fuckin' beautiful."

Ray pulled a spandex T-shirt, the classic circuit-party gay-boy kind, over his torso.

"I want you to lick me through the elastic," he said. "Lick me so hard I feel your spit sinking through the fabric."

"Sure thing," I said, standing up with my tongue at the ready.

"But not right now," Ray said. "I just got started."

Ray continued putting on every article of clothing in the bag. He pulled on a pair of gold gloves that reached up past his biceps. He tucked the ends under his T-shirt and then put on a black spandex hood with two eyeholes and an opening for his mouth. That did it. He was completely covered. He stood there, panting out the mouth hole in his mask. He turned and faced me, holding his hands up into the air like a victorious Mexican wrestler. Humble. Brave.

I lifted my wineglass in a toast, then took a gulp. Ray kept his arms up over his head. I wasn't sure if he was offering himself up to God or the Devil, but I think either way, it was a hell of a gesture. I wasn't sure what he wanted me to do. I wanted to clap or tie him up or something to make myself useful. I decided I would take my cock out and show him how hard I was looking at him in this purest of states. I unzipped and pulled my cock through my pants. I gripped my erection and grunted a little bit, not wanting to puncture this moment with useless words. Ray started making gurgling noises, like he was just about to wake up from a nightmare, the sort of sounds you can hear yourself making to jolt yourself out of sleep. I looked at his cock and saw his cum soaking through three layers of fabric. There must have been a lot of it. It created a wet spot that grew until finally he put his hands down by his side.

"Bless your heart," Ray said. "You can go home now." He gestured to the bedside table, where there was a stack of hundred dollar bills. He was paying me for an overnight, since that's what we'd booked. I'd been there a little over two hours.

He stood, motionless. I pushed my cock back into my pants, wishing I could have at least jerked off for him. My work ethic was kicking in and I really wanted to do something for all that money.

"Thank you," he said. The way he said it made me think he wanted me to leave faster, so I went into the other room, got my overnight bag and rolled it toward the door.

"I'll call you again," Ray said. I closed the door and stepped into the hall, trying to remember whether the elevator was to the left or right. I heard the door echo through the hallway as it closed, like a buzzer signaling the shift change on a factory floor. I was thinking that the only part of Ray he'd let me touch was his hand.

KIRK READ is a writer, performer, and event-maker based in San Francisco's Mission district. His books include *How I Learned to Snap* (American Library Association Honor), a memoir about being openly gay in a small Virginia high school, and *This is the Thing*, a collection of performance essays. Kirk received an MFA in Creative Writing from San Francisco State University and has been editor-in-chief at the longest running grassroots LGBT newspaper, Virginia's *Our Own Community Press*. He has toured the country twice with the Sex Workers' Art Show and has performed and lectured at over one hundred colleges and universities nationwide.

ALL THAT SHELTERING EMPTINESS

I ALWAYS LIKED hotel lobbies, the chandeliers and so much ceiling I'd yawn like I was oblivious but really I was trying not to go in the wrong direction. If I made a mistake then the key was to act as if it was the funniest thing—oh I'm so relaxed! I developed fantasies about what the front desk clerk did and did not know, fantasies that might involve mischief if our eyes met in a certain way—I wanted something like understanding. I'm not sure I would have called it that.

This particular hotel was the Hyatt or one of those chains, right on Central Park and the lobby wasn't on the ground level—more exclusive that way—the place was fancier than I'd expected. The mirrors sparkled and everything looked freshly designed—camel, auburn, amber—a little different from the standard beige. I imagined the views were spectacular since the hotel was right on Central Park but tricks always have their curtains drawn, they don't want anyone to see anything not even the trees.

This guy had the features of someone very popular in the '80s, swept-back hair and still a walled muscularity, disdain in his eyes, he wanted to give me a massage, sure. He rubbed the hotel lotion into my back, something awful and floral-scented—strong hands, I always needed a massage.

Of course, then he was grinding on top of me, dick teasing my asshole. This was no surprise. Then his dick slid in, so easy and dangerous, this was also familiar. I allowed a few thrusts so I could relax, then I said, "Oh I need you to put on a condom." I was thinking about the lotion, what good would the condom do with lotion—maybe I should get a washcloth. His dick remained in my ass, so different when it slides in smoothly like foreplay instead of that desperation, push push push. I started to push myself upright; he was heavy on top of me, still thrusting as I struggled to get onto my knees. I'll admit it was hot. Then he slammed me down on the bed, his weight on my back, holding me down. I'm not sure I can get him off me.

I thought about screaming but what would that do? Hotel security has ways of dealing with certain situations but nothing that would help me. Maybe no one would arrive at all, bruises or blood and more rage directed my way. At least I wasn't in pain, my asshole was relaxed I was still hard, he was fucking me faster and I didn't want him to come in my ass, that was the important thing. "Come on my face," I said. "Pull out and come on my face, I want your come on my face! I want to eat your come!" I wasn't sure if he was listening but then he did pull out and I rolled onto my back, he straddled me with shit on his dick in my face, jerking fast and moaning I could feel his come in between my chin and neck I closed my eyes.

The bathroom was always where I'd go to breathe; in the shower I was shaking, soft towel, just hurry up I need cocktails. Studying myself in the mirror before opening the door, do my eyes look OK? Back to the trick, he had his clothes on he wasn't smiling or frowning I wondered how often he did this. He handed me $250 in three crisp bills, I smiled and said thanks, I was glad for the money I wanted to think it was worth it.

Back into the elevator, then downstairs to the ground level past those spotless mirrors, glass doors and then I was outside. Walking fast through the wind like everything and nothing mattered I wanted safety; I hailed a cab.

If I say that cocktails cleared my head, then you know that all my analysis failed me: I didn't tell anyone, I felt stupid; I thought it was my fault. Yes, there was force; no, he didn't pull out when I asked him to, but otherwise, how was this trick different from every other guy who just slid it in? Every guy who assumed that if his dick was near my asshole and I was enjoying that gentle tease, the security of arousal, then forget about words: My consent had arrived.

New York is a lonely place; it was a lonely place for me eight years ago. I felt stupid because I couldn't use language to help. I was nervous that my friends would think I was someone to worry about. I thought maybe this was a trauma to push aside, with bigger issues in the picture, from a childhood of my father splitting me open to the overwhelm of the everyday. If consent was already assumed in the public sexual cultures where I searched for beauty amid the ruthlessness of objectification without appreciation, then what about the rooms where I swallowed cock for cash? I didn't want to call it rape because it felt so commonplace. Except for the shaking afterward, desperation mixed with a determination to escape.

MATTILDA BERNSTEIN SYCAMORE is the author of two dangerous novels in which the narrator is a hooker—imagine that: *So Many Ways to Sleep Badly* and *Pulling Taffy*. Mattilda is also the editor of four nonfiction anthologies, including *Nobody Passes: Rejecting the Rules of Gender and Conformity* and an expanded second edition of *That's Revolting! Queer Strategies for Resisting Assimilation*. She is currently working with Gina Carducci to make "All That Sheltering Emptiness" into a devastating short film.

DR. CAROL QUEEN

I first saw the good doctor performing on a gigantic stage in front of a huge crowd, which she held in the palm of her small hand. With her glasses and her bangs, she could pass for a Midwestern librarian. She is so earnest and good-natured that sometimes you feel she must be pulling your leg. And of course sometimes she is, because she has a total goofball side to her personality, and she loves yanking on people's chains. Because she is an educator, an entertainer, an intellectual, a comedienne, and a provocateur—she's able to put it out there so easy and large, and yet she's humble—she puts the crowd at ease instantly and leads them on this journey, into a world where she sat in a booth and stared through glass into another booth where a man masturbated while she chanted scriptures he gave her from the Bible. The crowd howled. Dr. Carol Queen bowed. She smiled this big huge goofball smile and they roared.

BLOWJOB CITY

FOR SOME REASON I am the one with the extrasensory ability to know whenever a blowjob is happening, anywhere in the city. I get a shiver, almost a small seizure, that rocks me for a few seconds—longer if the blowjob is really good. I don't tune in to anything else—I know there are clairsentients who go stiff or go limp when someone leaps off a bridge, or buys a weapon with murderous intent, or snatches a kid off a bench at the mall. I'm sure I'm not the only one with sexual powers, but blowjobs are all I get. No cunnilingus, even, though I would be curious about how the feeling does or does not differ. No fucking. Thank god, no jerking off—I would never be still if I could pick up jerk-offs, happy or furtive masturbators, because the one thing this blowjob thing has taught me is that someone is getting off *almost all the time*.

One out of a hundred, out of five hundred, I feel it almost like it's happening to me, and of course that can't be true. It's like how I imagine having a phantom limb would be . . . real sensation in an unreal, an absent place. Oh, I've given enough blowjobs to know what they feel like from the other end, mouth stretched out and teeth covered or scraping lightly over cock flesh, prick hitting soft palate or knocking at the tonsils, spit drooling or, if it goes on too long, drying up. It *does* go on too long sometimes, I'll tell you, especially if they jerked off first because they thought they'd cum too quick if they didn't, so unused to or undone by a hot mouth approaching that some of them can spurt even before you touch your lips to them. But those are the guys whose cocks are barely connected, who are so afraid of you that they have to get it over with, who really don't want to expose themselves to a mouth at all, a cunt either—these are the guys who *should* be masturbating instead of spending that extra twenty dollars or fifty dollars on a blowjob. I could never believe how many guys paid for them who really didn't want them, only thought they did, only thought they should be the kind of men who got 'em.

But I digress, huh? I was going to tell you about the feeling that suddenly my clit extends and grows and I can feel tongue and teeth and hot wet immersion six inches out, where my body doesn't even reach, and yet it's a feeling I know so completely, it's like I truly have a cock of my own. Maybe from a past life when I was a guy. I don't know if I believe in that, but if anything were going to convince me it'd be this cock-feel, this sense that if the unseen mouth on me sucks just once more, I'll burst, I'll shoot. Then I know somewhere in the city, some guy is coming good, somebody's about to pull off their prick wiping their mouth and smiling with pride. Not every blowjob leaves the cocksucker feeling that way, and I should know, but when the cock and the mouth fit right, or sometimes when there's love bathing the cock and not just spit, it turns into a song. Sure, I come when that happens, just like it was my own orgasm bubbling up although it's not, and I've been embarrassed in public a time or two. I've learned to keep it down. Plus I don't go out as much as I used to. When the lady at the SSI office heard my story she looked at me funny and then just signed the papers. So now for days at a time I lie in bed and feel the tremors of mediocre suck-offs and the rare good one that shakes me and my phantom dick into breathlessness.

The lady at SSI didn't even ask me how this started. You'd think she'd want to know, for the paperwork if nothing else. Isn't there a line on the form that says, like, "Etiology"? Me, I'd want to get all the information I could about a thing like this, to avoid it ever happening to me. Now that it *has* happened to me, I can tell you, it really affects your life. I mean, would *you* want to be on the cross-town bus when the fleet was in town? Wouldn't you want to stay in on prom night?

It just so happens that I know exactly when I acquired oral clairsentience, which is what I call it when I talk to the lady because she doesn't seem like the type who would be very comfortable with "blowjob." She looks like she *needs* a blowjob, to tell you the truth. I have never said this to her, though confidentially, I really feel like a blowjob expert now, like I have a source of knowledge about sucking guys off that is far deeper than almost anyone else's. Hey, and I thought I was a professional *before*! Well, I was, but in a very shallow way. Sometimes I think I should go out again, you know, get out of retirement. I bet I'd be absolutely great now. I'll be honest, mostly I was only so-so before, but like I told you, too many guys don't even *want* blowjobs, really, much less know the difference between a good one and a lousy one. It won't surprise you that most guys have had lousy ones, right? The surprise is that they so often accept them from professionals who, you would think, would have some pride. But I'm digressing again.

OK, I was on E, and this guy was kind of a client, but also kind of a friend. Did you know the working girls thirty years ago used to call all their clients "friends"? Then the '80s hit and it was like every girl on the street got a briefcase. It was weird. Those were friendlier times, and I often think the general caliber of blowjobs might have been a little bit better, though I can never know for sure. I was on E with this guy, a nice guy, and of course on E you think Jack the Ripper is nice—I would never, ever take that stuff with someone I didn't know, don't think I was always indiscriminately doing drugs like some girls—and we were fooling around. Everything felt so wonderful. I'll be the first to admit I'm not always in my body, which is one reason E is a pleasure—well, *was* a pleasure, I don't know whether I'll ever do it again, after what happened. I was sucking my friend's cock, just a nice, average, nothing-special cock, but on E I really liked the feel of it, really wanted to have my mouth around it, feel the cock flesh stroking me back, feel his pleasure coming through my tongue and twining itself around my pleasure. And you know how warm you get, how your skin has new powers of perception that you try to maintain after the high fades, but somehow you never can. I think a cat feels like that all the time, but with us, after the high, our fur turns back into scales.

Nothing weird ever happened when I did E before. And I didn't notice anything special at the time. Maybe the trip lasted longer than usual. Maybe I lost myself to pleasure a little more than I ever had. For sure I liked sucking his cock better than I had ever liked it before. And after it was all over, I had this power. I found it very disconcerting at first, and I had to get off the street right away because I couldn't do it any more—when I tried to give a blowjob it was intolerable, like speaking into a mike with feedback screeching you into deafness. I worried about becoming a human circuit for whatever energy is special to blowjobs. I don't know if we're cut out for that. So I went and saw the lady at SSI.

Well, that's about it. The only other interesting thing I've noticed is when the blowjobs wane. I'm sure it's not that my powers ebb and flow. I have charted this extensively, because, well, it's about all I have to do, and surely this must be important knowledge, or will be someday. I have come to believe that in a better world we would all be appreciated for our special powers. So sometimes I notice that there are few blowjobs going on anywhere in the city. Very late at night they tail off a little; that's when I get most of my sleep. And there's a lull mid-morning, but not as noticeable. But once in a while, inexplicably, there will be an extreme lull, almost nothing happening anywhere.

Then there seems to be an upsurge in traffic accidents and assaults. I know someone out there will consider this important information.

CAROL QUEEN got a Ph.D. in sexology so she could impart more realistic detail to her smut. She's the award-winning author or editor of eleven books, including *Real Live Nude Girl*, *The Leather Daddy and the Femme*, the *Five Minute Erotica* series from Running Press, and *Exhibitionism for the Shy*. She also directs the Center for Sex & Culture in San Francisco.

ANONYMOUS

HERMAPHRODITE

I had sex with a hermaphrodite
A raging raving beauty
Slicked-back black hair
Flaming brown-eyed cutie
Small perfect breasts
Stuffed under her Miracle Bra
Thin black miniskirt
Smelled like the cha cha cha
My name is Ezmerelda
She trilled like a dainty bird
Crawling writhing claws scratching
Slurped and growled and purred
She pulled me behind her
With her skirt still on
So I couldn't see
What was underneath
She bucked pulled pushed
Clenched begged moaned
I bucked pushed pulled
Grabbed grasped and groaned
But I was getting suspicious
What was she hiding under there
I tried to feel tried to touch
I wanted to know I swear
She pulled away sharp
With a loud popping sound
I snapped out of her
Then she pushed me down
Flat on my back on the bed

She was bullriding love baby
Ballerina cowgirl maniac
Don't mean maybe
Wait a minute I said
Hold on a second I said
I want to make you happy poppy
She rumbled from the bed
WAIT A MINUTE
I threw her off me
HOLD ON A SECOND
Condom glistening romantically
I want you to take your clothes off
She looked at me desperate and sad
Got real quiet, shrunk right up
I felt awful I felt bad
There was something under there
She really didn't want me to see
But as bad as I felt
I just had to see had to see
Hey look I don't care I said
You don't have to show me
I think you're great really
I'm just dying with curiosity
She sighed, reached down
Took off her thick black panties
Very slowly pulled them off
A sanitary napkin looking thingy
And then there it was
A penis, smallish and adorable
With wee balls tucked under
Like an adolescent boy
She lay down on the bed
On her belly on a pillow
Adjusted her astonishing package
And gave me a show
There was her vagina
A real proper woman's vagina
She reached back for me
Pulled me right behind her

She squeezed the life right outta me
While grinding into the bed
Until she shook and screamed
And threw back her head
I followed her to ecstasy
A ride on her shooting star
Roller coaster tiltawhirl
Down Hermaphrodite Boulevard
I am from Barcccccccelona
She looked at me and said to me
I came here to be a movie star
My name is Miguel Phillipe Marrimi
My father said I was a curse
He wanted to give me away
Tried to put me in an orphanage
But my mother said no way
She said I was a miracle
A gift from God she said
He would scream and shout
I want it dead I want it dead
He called me a freak
A shame to the family
He blamed my mother
He beat her he beat me
When I got enough money
I left my home and my family
I came to Hollywood to be a star
She smiled sweetly
She slipped back into her mini
What a stunning sight
I kissed her she took her money
And vanished in the Hollywood night
I am filled with a deep sweet
Delicious delirious delight
That I got to make love
To this beauteous hermaphrodite

XAVIERA HOLLANDER

FIVE THINGS I LEARNED BEING A HAPPY HOOKER

1. **Sex sells, but you have to wrap it in the right package.**
   I was a hooker. I was a madam. I sold sex over the phone. But it wasn't until I wrote about it that I became a millionaire. *The Happy Hooker* came out in 1971. For years people came up to me and said, "I read your book, and I loved it." In the late '80s and '90s, people would come up to me with a book to sign and say, "I found this in my parents' bedside table, I stole it off them, I read it, and I love it." Now I have people coming up to me saying, "I found your book in my grandparents' stuff, when we cleaned up the house after they died. I loved it."

2. **Being naked is the great equalizer.**
   If you ever really want the truth from someone, try to get them naked. Civilians, people who aren't in the sex business, don't seem to be able to bullshit when they're naked. I've seen ministers, movie stars, heads of state, and vice presidents when they are naked, and they're like little boys. And a lot of those alpha males, they're the ones who want to be spanked and dominated and told what a miserable piece of shit they are. And they all have money, so they make excellent clients.

3. **The voice is the biggest erogenous zone.**
   People don't realize what a turn-on or turn-off the voice is. If you really listen, you can tell everything about someone by their voice. I used to do phone sex, and I knew immediately what kind of person was on the other end of the line: the soft spoken masochists, who want to be yelled at and humiliated ("Get down on your knees, *now*! And lick my boots!"). And the ones with fragile egos who want to be big, powerful bulls ("Oh, you're so big, honey, you are the greatest!"). People underestimate how hot or cold a voice can make you.

4. **People usually know the answer to their own problems.**

I wrote an advice column for years for *Penthouse*. And of course I've been listening to people talk about their sex problems since I was a happy hooker during the sexual revolution of the swinging '60s. And I've seen over and over again that people answer their own questions, only they don't even know they're answering them. I always thought it was a great pity that people couldn't actually listen to themselves. But then, if they did, I guess advice columnists and sex therapists would be put out of business.

The main sexual problems of people writing to *Penthouse* are:

My cock is too big.
My cock is too small.
I am coming too quickly.
I can't come at all.

5. **It's much harder to be a writer than a hooker.**

I have found over and over again that men are not very picky when it comes to who they fuck. In my experience, they're much more particular about what they read. Men would sooner fuck trash than read it.

XAVIERA HOLLANDER did not invent sex, but she was one of the leading spirits who brought it out of the closet. Her first book, *The Happy Hooker*, sold more than 16 million copies, and she has published seventeen other books, both fiction and non-fiction, which have been translated into fourteen different languages. She is in constant demand as a lecturer (she has spoken at the World Congress of Sexology in Mexico City and Jerusalem) and TV personality, welcomed by such hosts as Larry King, Sally Jesse Raphael, Selina Scott, and Stephen Sackur of the popular BBC show *Hardtalk*. In 2008, she and Katje van Dijk published the first in a series of sex-tip books, titled *The Happy Hooker's Guide to Sex: 69 Orgasmic Ways to Pleasure a Woman*. The book, intended for men, draws upon Xaviera's thirty-two years as a *Penthouse* advisor as well as Robert Sherwood's theory of the triple clit: the brain clit, the heart clit, and the body clit. The book was so well received that they are currently working on the second in the series, titled *Men Have Brain Clits Too*. In June 2008, the documentary about her life, *Xaviera, the Happy Hooker: Portrait of a Sexual Revolutionary*, directed by Robert Dunlap and produced by John Patti, won Best Feature Documentary at the Philadelphia Independent Film Festival.

SEBASTIAN HORSLEY'S GUIDE TO WHORING

What are the benefits of whoring?
The thing about whoring is that you can get the sensation of sex without the boredom of its conveyance. And what I mean by that is that brothels make possible encounters of extreme intimacy without the intervention of personality: You get lust over love, sensation over security, and you fall into a woman's arms without falling into her hands, and this can only be a good thing.

Is it expensive?
The difference between sex for money and sex for free is that sex for money always costs a lot less. So we establish that, because sex that you can get for free always ends in misery, children, divorce, mortgages, and suicide. Whereas fifty pounds for a fuck, well, you're not going to get unhappy about that, are you?

Does price reflect quality?
I have slept with absolutely beautiful, gorgeous girls for twenty-five pounds, thirty pounds, and I've slept with pigs for a thousand pounds. So there's no real correlation at all. You would think that if you go to a high-class brothel or you go to the high-class escort agency in the yellow pages you would get a more attractive girl for your money than you would going to Hull. But it's not true. So the key is to shop around.

Where can I find a prostitute?
Here are your options. You can go onto the Internet and get a prostitute that way. Get the yellow pages; go to E, not for "erection" but for "escort agencies." You can go onto the street and solicit that way. You go to the walk-ups in Soho or Shepherd Market; there are plenty of places like that. Alternatively, you can go to saunas, there are loads of saunas in London,

in fact all over the country. I recommend the *McCoy's Guide to Adult Services No. 1*; it's basically the guide for the professional fornicator.

What is the protocol?
Well the rules of a brothel say that you should always tip the maid. The maid will ask for, and usually expect, a tip of two pounds; that's absolutely fine. Don't go over that. You want to tip the maid, not fuck her, and always be polite, to the girl.

Is it wrong?
Well as far as the morality of the whole thing, a man who moralizes is usually a hypocrite and a woman who moralizes is invariably plain. Morality is about opportunity. It's just as difficult for an attractive person not to have sex as it is for an unattractive person to have sex. In the ugly, temptation sleeps; in the beautiful it's wide awake.

Can I take my girlfriend?
Sometimes I have gone alone, because that's what I want. And other times I have gone with my girl and muse, Rachel. As you can imagine I've met quite a few working girls over a thirty-year period of whoring. You know, every day, that adds up to quite a lot. And Rachel has known girls in the industry, so you build that relationship. Sometimes you go in and you'll get stuck in. Other times you can, you know, watch, you can not get involved. Details are always vulgar.

How should I broach the subject?
If she's your wife, you've got trouble haven't you? People keep asking me if I believe in life after death, and I don't believe in life before death, but one thing I can tell you is that life after death is as improbable as sex after marriage. So if she's your wife, then the first bridge you've got to cross is the fact that you're not doing it anymore, 'cause that's probably what's going on. But the prostitute probably would be a really nice little thing to get you started, wouldn't it? Well just ask her! "Darling, do you want to go to a whorehouse? Yes or no?" It's really quite simple, isn't it?

What if I want a more unusual girl?
There are all kinds of places catering to, really, the most extreme perversions, you know, from S&M to people who are kind of physically deformed,

all different types of things. It's a huge market and it caters to everybody, which is quite nice, really. In that sense it's democracy at work.

In conclusion

Thank you for reading Sebastian Horsley's Guide to Whoring. I hope you learned lots. I hope that you've realized that sex is one of the most beautiful, wholesome, spiritual things that money can buy.

SEBASTIAN HORSLEY traveled to the Philippines to be crucified, as research for art he was making. After he was nailed to a cross (refusing any kind of sedative), he passed out unconscious. The event was recorded on film and in photographs. These, and the paintings he subsequently made of crosses, were exhibited in London. Horsley wrote a column in the *Erotic Review* as well as a sex advice column in *The Observer*. After graphic discussions of oral and anal sex and angry complaints from readers, he was sacked. *Hookers, Dealers, Tailors*, a retrospective by Horsley, was staged at the Spectrum London gallery.

On March 19, 2008, Horsley was refused entry into the U.S. on the grounds of moral turpitude. After eight hours of questioning, he was placed on a plane and sent back to London.

CASTING SHADOWS

Venice, California, 1996

I sit on a concrete block, smoking, ruminating. *How did this happen? How did it all fall apart so quickly? I mean, one minute I'm a hot-shot entrepreneur and the next I'm squatting in a house that's about to be torn—*

The phone number hits my inbox. I hop over the remnants of my tragically ahead-of-its-time e-commerce venture, whip through the trash-bag front door, and cruise down to my new office: a sticky Venice Beach payphone.

Unlike me, Phil is a successful Silicon Valley executive cashing in on stock options. But despite our class disparity, we've got something in common. We're both jocks. Closet cases. Undetectable. His confident surfer drawl washes over me like the crest of a wave. He sounds just like the guys I hang out with at the beach. My anxiety settles to a simmer. I'm not alone.

Phil's about ten years older than me. He's married with four young kids. He says he's never hired a male escort. Sure, he's been looking for a while, but after seeing photos of me and my yard-sale surfboard, he insists that I'm the first real athlete he's seen in the business—the first guy with whom he feels a connection.

Phil has a secret that he claims never to have discussed with anyone until now. Long as he can remember, he's been inexplicably aroused by sports injuries.

Back in front of my computer, I find a couple of websites devoted to worshipping broken limbs on the mend, and there are photos galore. A woman with a mullet crutches through Walmart. A tiny Asian man in an elbow cast orders a Big Mac. No, this kink is hardly the sole property of my new best buddy. I'm sort of intrigued.

For our first meeting, Phil pulls up to the San Diego bus station in a snazzy rental car. *I wonder if I'll be attracted to him.* I get a flash of his pearly whites and big forehead through the passenger seat window.

Still can't tell. I get in the car, shake his hand, and buckle up. My adrenal gland squirts a heavy dose of adrenaline into my bloodstream. The whole thing's a big rush, like sports.

Phil drives to a suburban delicatessen where he parks, leans over the leather armrest, straps a splint onto my leg, hands me two wooden crutches, and suggests that I go order some lunch.

I toddle across the parking lot while concerns with my own pleasure, my own level of physical attraction toward Phil, get kicked around on the asphalt with the pebbles. I push open the door with the crutch's rubber bumper, twist through the glass door, and make my way over to the counter. "Chicken salad sandwich and a cream soda, please."

"That'll be $9.57, honey," says the cashier, a dead ringer for Florence Jean Castleberry.

"Sure, no problem," I lean on my crutch and fumble with my wallet.

"Let me help." Flo zips around and picks up my tray in a motherly fuss. "Where are you sitting, sweetie?"

Phil's brown Cole Haans tap anxiously on the linoleum floor. Flo sets down my food. She raises a suspicious eyebrow.

Eyes darting between us, Phil forces out a preoccupied, "Uh, yeah, hi."

Flo walks away.

"Dude, that was so hot," whispers Phil. "Dontcha think?"

I open wide for the sandwich. *Do I agree? Was it hot? It's not like I got an erection or anything. I don't know, I guess it was hot.* "Totally," I say with loaded chipmunk cheeks.

Phil exhales, leans back in his chair, and crosses his tanned arms behind his head. He seems relaxed for the first time since he picked me up. I must have done something right. I proceed to open up, downloading the important parts of my life, like I always do, to anyone who appears to be listening.

"I'm going to a conference in Manhattan in a couple of months," he interrupts. "How 'bout I fly you out there and put a *real* cast on your leg?"

"Sure" I say, crunching celery bits. "Sounds fun."

I have no idea what to charge for the afternoon's benign charade. In my mind, Phil and I share secrets, which basically makes him my (only) friend. Besides, I'd only entered my name on that escort directory in order to send traffic to the Ten Bucks to See the Naked Surfer site that I'd thrown up for survival. Luckily, Phil slips me five hundred dollars when he drops me off at the Greyhound station.

I white-knuckle the bills from San Diego to L.A. but when I transfer westbound my grip loosens and my jaw relaxes. Then I feel weightless, like I'm lifting right off that bus seat and out that tiny sliver of window. Five hundred is just enough for me to move off the street and into that little studio I've been eyeballing—the one right on the sand with enough room for a futon *and* a computer—the one that is about to become my stage for the next calendar year as I broadcast my life to the entire world.

• • •

OK, I ADMIT it. Even before I plug it in, that smooth little ball-camera made my dick jump. Turns out I'm not only a closet homosexual but a budding exhibitionist to boot. And thirty minutes after rubbing my junk into the little glass eye, my inbox is clogged with credit card receipts and what seems like hundreds of emails from guys around the world telling me that *I am hot*.

I feel like I've punched a hole in the universe. All the attention I ever wanted from my brother, my father, my coaches—served up in a matter of minutes. *Who needs Hollywood? I just hit the center!* I wipe the lube off my hands, pull up my faded blue lightning bolt board shorts, and stumble out the door in a daze. Heart pounding, I rollerblade to the far end of the pier and draw in a huge breath of salty air. There I watch droves of Hispanic families making their weekly mass exodus from the sand. On either side of me, old anglers cast fishing lines. I tower in the middle of them, a big blond alien on wheels.

• • •

CYBER PEEPSHOW TECHNOLOGY is in its infancy, and almost immediately, fellow geeks swarm in to build banners that link me all over the web. I send out a Surf and Sex Report, announcing weekly ocean conditions and show times. Dissected into parts and squeezed through the wires, my club membership numbers soar as the general public begins purchasing home computers and cashing in on free AOL hours.

I am living large, riding high on a steady diet of wheat grass, waves, and '70s porn. When I'm not on camera, I am mixing techno music on my laptop or eating soft tacos at the end of Washington Boulevard. I am always in shorts. I don't ever want this to end.

I email my biological family on the East Coast and announce: "I finally realize what I am. An artist!"

Silence.

But no matter, I am at an all-time creative high. I enhance my shows with cheeky themes and supporting props. In "Campout," I stealthily emerge from my sleeping bag with a flashlight before beating off. In "Working Stiff," I pose as a salesman in my old button-down shirt before beating off. In "Super Heroes," three-inch Aquaman and Superman action figures battle it out on my rod before—well, you get the picture. I hold up perky little signs like, "Hey Walter, thanks for the pie!" and "This one's for you, Tatsuro!" Pretty soon I am selling used underwear and Ziplocked body fluids, translating my website into kanji, and doubling my schedule to accommodate four major time zones. I am sun drenched, sea salted, and *alive* when the phone rings.

"How's that leg feeling?" Phil pants excitedly. "You hurt it pretty badly, huh?"

"Oh man, it hurts real bad, dude. I think it might be broken." My voice cracks. It's the first I've used it in weeks.

"Well, we need to get you into a cast immediately," he says. "I know a great doctor in Manhattan. How's next Tuesday?"

New York City

I am exhausted but ecstatic while being whipped in a taxi around the dark parks and lit-up skyscrapers. Phil, still dressed in a pressed olive suit after his conference, meets me in the lobby. We take the elevator to his suite where I set up my laptop and camera. I give him a Yankees cap, turn his back to the camera, and, as if commissioned by the Manhattan Medical Channel itself, I webcast the casting—live from the Plaza Fucking Hotel in New York City.

I lean back and relax in the shadows while he slathers cold goop over my thick, muscled thigh. In the silence I realize that for the first time in months I am not an object. I am not alone on my little stage, looking the other way as faceless voyeurs privately project their fantasies. I am another artist's canvas, and this works for me today. I am being used for some sort of higher purpose that neither of us knows anything about.

Once the black fiberglass is set and the camera is off, Phil takes me to dinner and a Sandra Bernhard show. Hanging ten paces behind me, Phil watches as notoriously aggressive New Yorkers make way for the injured surfer. Turns out the public attention is the thing that *really* sends Phil into orbit. When we return to the room, he jacks off in a chair while I remind him of the blue-haired lady that held the door open and the handsome young usher that asked, "What happened to your leg?"

That night Phil and I sleep in a king-size bed with a healthy three feet of space between us. My knee itches and I can't turn over on my side. But even so, there is something strangely comforting about being restrained. With my options limited, I am safe somehow. Or maybe it's the thousand-count sheets.

We repeat the evening's performance twice in three days and the whole time, Phil never comes on to me. I've grown accustomed to regularly scheduled masturbation, so by the third night, I'm horny like a sailor. *Why isn't he hitting on me? Why isn't he making me show off for him?* Money from the casting session is rolling in but I miss my voyeurs. I am convinced there's something wrong with me, like I'm dirty or gay or something. I need to get back online.

At three o'clock on the morning before take-off, I wake to a strange sensation. As I lie on my back with my eyes open to the darkness, it dawns on me that Phil is quietly humping my cast. With the hard black barrier eliminating any possible sensation, my mind drifts toward contemplation of the things that keep men apart—wives, religious doctrine, social mores, waitresses named Flo—or could it be something deeper? A state of being that others are all so quick to label *homophobia* or *the closet* when it in fact exists *outside* the realm of liberal politics: the simple desire to *be* a man despite the fact that one *desires* men.

Of course neither of us ever addresses the incident (that would be way too girly!), so other than the drama of lugging huge Hefty bags of cast scraps through the crowded lobby, we part discreetly.

Riding back through the city, this time in a fancy limousine, I can just imagine that Phil is satisfied, eager to return home and love up his wife and little surfer babies. And me? Well I just clutch my bills and gaze out the window thinking of the beach, my webcam, and the little taco stand down the street. Staring at the endless herd of worker bees buzzing about Fifth Avenue in their crisp white shirts and shiny black shoes, I'm Steve McQueen in my blue jeans. I am the international man of mystery. I have a secret, and boy is it a doozy.

JUSTIN JONES is the pen name for a writer who currently splits his time between San Francisco and Big Sur, where he is furiously penning a scandalous book about his semi-scandalous life as an Olympic hopeful turned dot-com drone turned traveling escort.

SELENA ANNE SHEPHARD

PRETTY PERSUASION

beginning

I skate around the mall
with a walkman tuned into
subversive sounds
I am in search of secret passageways
people of unusual genders
spaces of unabashed desire
The teenage girls with
nasty tongues never look at me
yet they tell me stories from afar
strange, exotic tales
they could never have gotten
from television
they dress in layers
in bizarre mosaic patterns indecipherable
I listen for simple truths
yet hear only complex lies
which, of course, are much more trustworthy
I purchase working class lingerie
(I mean, underwear) at Sears
from a salesgirl who KNOWS
but will never tell
I plead with her to scream it out
reveal the source of her despair
but she just laughs heartily and
steals away into the hardware section
I call the security guards
who arrest me for wearing plaid socks
with a leather skirt

I manage to escape between the cracks
and return unscathed to the scene of the crime . . .

middle

I light a cigarette
though I don't know how to smoke
it seems natural at the time,
I cross my legs
right over left,
left over right,
then I refasten my garter,
smooth my skirt,
fluff up my titties

I'm anticipating something
but I'm not quite sure what it is
a recurring moment, perhaps
a (parenthetical thought), maybe
the merger of parallel lines
that's it, the merger of parallel lines

I remember vividly the secret dance
I used to perform
when I was nine and yearning
so awkward
so strange
so utterly incomprehensible
yet it could not be denied
it had a raw beauty to it that exhilarated me

I check between my legs
to see what gender I am today
I find nothing in particular except
an old beat-up baseball mitt
and two dozen rose petals
"I must be a boy," I say to myself,
though I can't be certain,
I never am, but I never give that away
there are much better things to give away
imaginary kisses
telltale signs
sideways glances

I dream of climbing Mt. Everest in my Maidenform bra
I never reach the peak
I wake up in a cold sweat . . .

end

We make love in a vacant lot
as it was meant to be
cold asphalt below
full moon above
crickets chirping madly in the background
He is my dada Daddy
I am his exotic drag princess in heat
when we kiss, our fantasies collide
explode
immersing us in minute particles
of lust and longing
He touches me as if I wasn't there
when I cry out for more
he gives me less
the pleasure is all too much
so I revel in the pain
He draws his sword
and I my water pistol
we duel for hours into days
he backs me into a corner
I dive between his legs
and make a run for the abandoned space
between provocation and allure
between outrage and surrender
between perception and scandal
He calls for me
he pleads for me
he paints his face by numbers
and recites nursery rhymes for me
remembering my name for the first time in weeks
I reach out and pull him deep within
and hope he hasn't forgotten how to swim . . .

SELENA ANNE SHEPHARD figures that, at this point in time, she is exploring erotic, psychological, emotional, and maybe even spiritual spaces betwixt and between transvestite and transexual, making her living as a cocky gal (dressing up en femme every day, creating sexy videos, or doing fun sessions with admirers or other T-girls), but still appearing as a male a fair amount of the time (wearing blue jeans and sweatshirt and such). She has been dressing up since she was a kid and is continually learning new ways to do the Transgend-Dance . . . Oh, even now, it can be confusing, anxiety inducing, and hard to fathom, but playing "Girl" can have a power and a thrill that being a guy has hardly ever given her.

THE BEAT: ON THE PAIN OF LUST

AT THE CHARMINGLY average small-town fag bar, Cyd is on the dance floor for about half a second before he dramatically collapses to his knees in front of Warren, legs disappearing under him like a folding chair snapping shut. A sly pleading look in his eyes completes the performance of affected little boy innocence. A small but unmistakable spark of lust ignites. I look away.

We're knee-deep in queers and whores celebrating the end of a national forum for sex worker organizations in Australia, dancing to Beyoncé remixes and being choked by The Beat's fake smoke machine. I half hope he'll give me that pleading look, half hope he won't. I know my weakness for kneeling boys, especially a smart, cute, trannie-boy bottom like Cyd who subs for a living. I know the way that lust feels like a demand, a craving, a tyranny. Most of the time, I'm happier without it.

But the next time he drops, Warren takes Cyd's hair and yanks his head back and forth, faking a rough face-fucking. Cyd yields completely, surrendering his body to Warren's fist. Their faces widen into bright mischievous smiles.

Fuck.

A storm of want explodes from my cunt and pulses up to my heart and there it is again, my need. I gasp and back into the wall behind me, groaning, "Holy fuck, that's so hot!" under the music. *Fuckfuckfuckfuckfuck*. I've stopped dancing, I look like a maniac standing there with my hand over my mouth gasping and moaning. I'm overwhelmed with the need to crush something. Immediately.

I both love and dread this explosive storm of sexual energy. Five minutes ago I was bright and composed. Now I have hundred-mile-an-hour winds to harness and direct.

I want to slam into him. I want to use my full force to dominate him—safely and consensually. But Cyd hasn't offered his body to me, so I quickly begin implementing Plan B: I restrain myself. I bite down on my finger. I take deep breaths. I try to get calm while I scan the room looking for any soft surface to hit: a couch, a padded bench, a willing human, anything. Anything that will let me unleash the storm.

I avoid looking at him but he appears in front of me, fixing his best puppy-dog eyes on me and dropping to his knees, giving me that helpless look that has worked a million times before on a million other dance floors.

Lightning has to strike somewhere. I don't even know it's happened until I look down at my own hand, as though it is someone else's, gripping his hair tightly and shoving his face down. Thunder in my heart, my hands grab, pull, push, and stroke. My mind moves in quickly to calm: *Woah, ease up. Is OK? Is anyone going to be hurt or upset by this? Are we all sober? Be careful, go slow, check in.*

I let go and take a step back.

He gets up close and invites me to hit him. Or maybe he doesn't. Maybe he just gives me a defiant look, points to his chest and gets in close enough so that I can strike him. So I do, the back of my hand flying out against his chest. I grab his chest binder, shove him against the wall and do it again. I watch his face to make sure he can take it and that I'm not scaring him. Again, I stop. I lean my back against the wall and lightly press my fingertips into it. I want to keep track of those hands. *I want this. I don't want this. I want this. I don't want this.*

I quickly rifle through my ethics checklist: *Will we be offending, insulting, or hurting anyone*? Don't think so. *Could this fuck up any of our mutual friendships?* I'm not positive but again, don't think so.

"I'm trying to resist," I say. Well that's fucking catnip to a pro like him. A moment later he's in a nearby corner of the dance floor, shaking his ass in my direction. I look at Warren, panic-stricken. "*Now what?*" I implore. Warren points toward Cyd and nudges me in his direction: *Just go for it.*

It's the permission I need. In that second, the room closes in, the music disappears, and all that remains is this body in front of me. This ass that's in the air and what I want to do to it. I want to see him wince. I want his eyes to soften and glaze. I want to push, crush, and break.

In a single movement, I lunge toward Cyd and order him to face the wall, which he does with a knowing smirk. I tug his mobile phone out of his rear pocket (but leave the coins) and tuck it into the top of my red halter dress. In a trance of pleasure, I beat his ass as it's presented to me, his arms over his head. Every few minutes I notice others watching but for the most part there is nothing but us and I disappear into the full force of my body. I let myself become the pure rhythm of aggression. My blood floods with calm. Enraptured, I hit him over and over, alternating the force of the blows and rubbing softly now and again to give him a break and let him know I am there with him. He entices me to go harder.

I feel like I could rip flesh from bone until I collapse in a heap, content and satiated, his blood drying in the corners of my mouth, but for now I am satisfied to hit until the little plastic ring on my right hand breaks in two, I've expended all my fury, and he still hasn't even flinched. He turns around smiling and when I go to hug him, I'm surprised to note that my eyes are heavy and slightly unfixed. It only takes me a minute to come out of my semi-stupor but I'm done for the night. My limbs are light, my heart is steady, my head is clear, my cunt is satiated.

What was *that?*

Physiologically speaking, his ass was my Valium. When I was a teenage girl, speaking to my crush could induce such a fierce rush of excitement that I hyperventilated and got a pounding headache. Composure was impossible. My body went on high alert, sirens would scream, lights flash, heart race, fight or flight.

In our bodies arousal is identical to excitement, which is identical to stress. Physically, it's all the exact same thing, although we interpret some excitement as "positive" and some as "negative." Because I'm extra sensitive, when I'm turned on, I'm over-stimulated and uncomfortable. When I'm really turned on, I might as well be in a state of emergency. My fight or flight response is triggered. In the past, fucking resolved the emergency so I tried to do it as soon as possible. When I got less interested in fucking, "fighting" (in a controlled way) stepped right in. In this view, desire is just a physiological (over)reaction to a stimulus, a disturbance of our physical homeostasis, and affectionate brutality is my natural calmer.

But I've always loved the more subtle sexual exchanges like making out or teasing someone. Because I'm a hooker, a professional domme, and a slut, people have a hard time believing how thrilled I am by little things like standing near the object of my desire and noticing the way they blush, how the red creeps up their cheeks, the way they avert their gaze. For me those can be the cause of stomach-churning excitement. Of course, I never feel anything quite this exciting with clients—because, while I often have fun, there ain't no raging desire most of the time and even if there was, the guys are kind of a sure thing.

So why all the drama? Beyond just the biomechanics, what *is* desire and why does it cause so much trouble? My favorite understanding of lust comes from Buddhist philosophy. Lust is understood as just one form of wanting, which is seen as the principal cause of suffering. If we can avoid wanting, we avoid all manner of pain. It's strange for a queer slutty sex worker to think that desire is a cause of unhappiness, but I think I came to this because of my deep involvement with desire.

Desire places a demand on me that can be exhausting and has gotten me into endless scrapes. When I was younger I lost friends and lovers because I couldn't resist giving in to the demands of my desire, and I've stayed in at least one (OK, maybe three) bad relationships because the sex was stupidly hot. You know exactly what I'm talking about. Sexual desire is fun—but it's motherfucking trouble, too.

This year, thanks to an extended trip abroad (and unanticipated celibacy), my sex drive became much quieter and life did indeed get more peaceful and less complicated. There is more space in my relationships with people. I feel less dragged around by my cunt. I have felt so much freer that I continually mulled over celibacy, wondering if it might free me even more from the yoke of lust. But I had this nagging doubt that for me, celibacy wouldn't reduce my want, it would just suppress and deny it. In addition, I just couldn't do it. I was sure that my cunt wasn't gonna allow that shit for long. I'd end up cheating on her and I have too much respect for her to do that. I have precious little desire now—but when she emerges, she's still fucking fierce.

So is desire undesirable? Rather than deny or eliminate desire, I, along with many Buddhists, distinguish between "skillful" and "unskillful" desire. Skillful desire is that which helps calm the mind and focus it on the present moment. It is a kind of desire without attachment and possessiveness (awesome; Buddha was down with non-monogamy!). It is not fearing or denying desire (which *might* mean no celibacy). The challenge isn't to eliminate it but to manage it, lightly and ethically.

So my intention is to become more still, more content without constant sexual excitement. I don't chase every hot little thing that crosses my path. I avoid complicating things and act with honesty and integrity.

When I finished with Cyd, I had the kind of deep calm I sometimes feel at the end of a meditation. In fact, I'd just done a "spanking meditation." Mindfulness meditation is simply the focusing and calming of the mind in order to allow clarity, and it can be done while doing anything: walking, preparing food, talking, parenting. So why not a dance floor spanking? Done safely and ethically, sexual domination requires complete attention to the present, focus, and alertness (good aim helps too). And it renders me deeply calm. *Voila!* A skillful expression of desire and a meditation all wrapped up in a dirty little queer package. My dharma teacher is gonna love this one.

Maybe I go to too great of lengths to justify the satisfaction of my desire. But Buddhist philosophy is explicit about respecting difference and not clinging dogmatically to a narrow interpretation of the canon. In both beating someone's ass and sex work, I'm using Buddhism to help guide me in making ethical choices about something rarely addressed in most sex-phobic religious traditions: having a full-blooded, complicated, perverted, professional, and deeply non-normative sex life.

JULIET NOVEMBER is a white radical queer femme writer. She (usually) lives in Toronto and writes about sexual politics.

5

THE SAGE STORIES

INTRODUCTION

David Henry Sterry

This book really started when I sold my memoir *Chicken*. I was so grateful, I made an agreement with the universe: I vowed that I would do something to help people in the sex business. And people who were raped and victimized, like I was. Those two groups, contrary to popular opinion, are not the same, although naturally there is some overlap. I wasn't sure exactly how that desire to be of service would manifest itself, but I knew how great and amazing it made me feel to finally tell my story, to write down the worst, and best, things that ever happened to me. What a blessing and relief it was. How it helped me untangle the knots in my soul. How it helped me become someone who isn't actively trying to destroy himself. Who can feel happiness and joy on a daily basis.

I kept searching for a way to help. Living in San Francisco, I did outreach on the streets handing out socks and condoms. After a while, I came to the realization that socks and condoms were all well and good, but I really wasn't helping that much. Then one day I contacted Norma Hotaling, who runs SAGE. I asked if maybe I could start a writing program in the basement. She agreed.

Every Tuesday afternoon in the basement of SAGE on Mission Street in San Francisco, right across the street from a porn emporium, my ex-literary agent/now wife (she fired me as soon as we got married) and I ran a writers' workshop. Old, middle-aged, and young; black, white, brown, red, and yellow; urban and rural; men and women; gay, straight, and transgendered; college educated and high school dropouts; upper class, middle class, and from dire poverty, the writers had one thing in common: They'd all sold sex for money.

Every week we'd pick a subject and read a piece of writing about it, from *The Catcher in the Rye* to *The Adventures of Tom Sawyer* to *Permanent Midnight*. Then we would write. Then we would read our writing for each other.

My wife, who had absolutely never sold sex for money, was shocked to discover that the level of writing talent and storytelling skill was often

higher in that basement than it was among the published authors who sent her manuscripts in her capacity as a literary agent.

We began doing this as giveback work, to be of service to people who needed our help. To our great surprise, we discovered that our time in the basement ended up giving to us, being great fun and making us better humans. So many times we came in grumpy and cranky, with nasty crab cakes in our pants. After our hour in the basement we always, *always* felt happy to be alive. And we noticed the same thing in everyone else who spent that hour with us in that basement.

Bear in mind that all of the stories written at SAGE are first drafts, written in forty minutes. Which, to my mind, makes them even more remarkable. And because many of these people don't have email addresses or reliable telephone numbers, there was no way even to do second drafts or edits on the pieces they wrote. I look at these stories kind of like the recordings of anonymous but brilliant musicians that folklorist Alan Lomax made for the Library of Congress. I believe that, raw as they are, they're a true piece of Americana.

Scientists did a study in which they had people write down the worst things that had ever happened to them. They found that immune systems were boosted. No vitamin C or chicken soup. Just writing. Well, after two years in the basement, my immune system was like the locks on Fort Knox.

CARLA CRANDALL

I first met Carla in the basement of SAGE. With those fine-boned features and the peachy, creamy aristocratic complexion, she looked like Meryl Streep's younger cousin. From the very beginning, she was one of the shining lights in that basement on Mission Street, and she was there every single Tuesday, come rain or come shine. The first time we met Carla she was the picture of health, wrapped in cardigan and corduroy. She smiled so sweet and easy that it was impossible not to like her. Slowly, over the months, she revealed her crazy addiction and fall from *Long Day's Journey into Night* suburban lunacy down the rabbit hole into the madness of mainlining heroin and selling sex for money. She was deep in a rehab.

When I'd say, "It's time to start writing . . . *now,*" some people would gnaw on the ends of their pencils. Not Carla. Carla would be off to the races, pen scribbling feverishly, and she wouldn't quit even after I said, "OK, time to stop." And her writing was always so to-the-bone. There was an elegance and a poetry even when she was writing about the darkest shit there is to write about.

I became friends with Carla. I tried to help her write her memoir. She would call me at least once a week. Sometimes she was sweet, engaged, the Carla I met in that basement. Sometimes hysterical, out of money, out of an apartment, out of luck, out of her mind. Sometimes incoherent, medicated to the point of stupor. Carla relapsed. She was on so many different meds that it was dizzying just to listen to her list them. She was getting disability from the government, but being in the system is a nightmare in the best of circumstances, never mind when you have a giant monkey on your back and up your ass.

She grew emaciated, as if she had created her own little Auschwitz for herself. At times like this, she could barely write a whole sentence from beginning to end, and I swear to God it broke my heart into a billion pieces. One of the last times I saw Carla, she had just been evicted from a truly disgusting dive in the cankerous groin of the Tenderloin where used syringes and condoms play together in the street. I got a frantic call. It was Carla. Could I please hold onto some of her stuff while she was transitioning? So I met her in the city and she gave me a bunch of purses. Some old, some new. Some gold, some blue. Some leather, some pleather. I tried calling Carla back a couple of days later, but her cheap shitty disposable cell phone had been disconnected.

A year later, as I was preparing this anthology for publication, miraculously I got a call out of the blue from Carla. I was so happy she wasn't dead. I invited her to come and read at the Sex Worker Literati event I had put together. She's clean again. Sober. She looked her old self again, and it made my heart so happy. Carla had never read her work in public. I explained this to the audience, asked them to be gentle with her, as it was her first time. They were extremely sweet, and Carla totally rose to the occasion.

And I gave her back her purses.

ONE DAY SOBER

A LETTER FROM one of San Jose's men's facilities that I received years ago still has me reeling. At the time I had no idea what it was to be incarcerated. "I've got a plan, Baby, and it includes you." Before he got to that point, the letter had opened with a huge, "Whew, was I ever glad to hear from you! Came just in time, because next week I'm being sent to the gas chamber." Typical Dennis humor. Out of eight years that we were together off and on there was one sober day. On that day, I said to him, "I used to think you'd never quit." For a split second—half a split second—I saw something before me that was a once-in-a-lifetime thing. For a man who joked his way through life and made a career of getting a rise out of people, I saw a moment of vulnerability. His face fell. We were always quick to shut that off around each other. That night, at that stupid coffeehouse in my corporate work outfit, when we made contact, and when I said that and it was apparent that I had struck a nerve, Dennis showed quiet pain—the worst kind. Not the kind of pain that screams, "I'm the pain, I'm the pain!" but the kind that lurks there constantly, eating away at the soul.

Like when the party's over, it's over. It was over three years later when he got out of Soledad and was told he would have to serve another term at an Arizona facility. He said, "That's it." The day he left the country to go to the U.K., never to be seen again, I was too absorbed in painting my toenails to notice when he went out the door.

A BLESSED DAY

A BLESSED DAY. Sobbing attack due to the movie *What's Love Got to Do with It* (seeing Ike beat Tina Turner to a pulp notwithstanding). Looks like housing is covered for the next couple of weeks. I spent my first night at the Ambika Hotel and it was great. Anthony was at GA at 1 P.M. as planned. He complimented me on my shoes. His eyes said the rest . . . but not enough somehow. He held me *really* close. It *would* take the financial crunch off if we shared a place (split the rent)—everything's a mess as far as GA goes. When SSI is going to kick in and save the boat from sinking altogether I have no idea. I'm wondering if what I want, what I *deserve* in a man is simply too much to ask. He's so depressed I hate to see him that way. I called his hotel from my dad's cell and no answer—he's asleep, or out, or in the shower. He said he was depressed because he wanted to kick it—and me—and it wouldn't happen because he had no choice. So I hadda take the train down to Sunnyvale where Dad is. An hour and a fucking half ride and no trains this time of night. I didn't get in until 10:42! Then I had to take a subway to Market Street then a fucking cab; couldn't wait on that goddamn 19 bus. Won't walk this hour anywhere. I was supposed to go straight to Anthony's hotel but he didn't answer when I got off at SF State so I just went home.

I told him today was my domestic violence class at SAGE. I'm too tired to get into it. Basically he . . . fuck. I had to pass through San Mateo, the county that fucked me in the ass with sand and no lube . . . seven months in jail behind stupid dope paraphernalia—one day in solitary confinement (maximum security, i.e., Jeffrey Dahmer cell—the guy who was killing his dates and eating them for dinner). David used to joke about that to no end. That and the poor five- or six-year-old girl (what was her name?) who was found brutally murdered. She was a child model . . . actually put makeup on her, put her on display—Ramsey was her last name. "I killed her," he said one night when he was drunk. "I fucked her in the ass and boy! Was she tight!"

GOD, WE LIVED AS LARGE AS WE COULD

WE WERE WASTED in Erick's studio—on the floor in hysterics. David was hilarious! I laughed to tears.

Back to the current man in my life. God, it's hard to stay awake. Anthony.

Anthony won't answer his phone. It's driving me fucking crazy. I saw Mom for a minute. I told her I thought Anthony wasn't "emotionally available" at times. She said, "Well, keep in mind he's got his mental health problems too—you have to be there for each other." Makes sense. More about her but now I'm about to conk out.

I feel so alone. That's when you're supposed to pray and remember we are never alone. There's God, I thought quickly as I walked down Polk Street, wearing my big, bulky, hooded sweatshirt—from the payphone—last attempts at reaching Anthony and Carolyn. Neither answered. Then from Subway—where they accept food stamps. Ten dollars is now my fucking balance. I'm having a hell of a time coming up with $$ to feed myself and support my cigarette habit. Dad's helping. Carolyn, bless her heart, gave me seventy dollars. I'm really penny counting, coupon clipping. (I used to laugh at people who collect coupons and take forever at the register, holding up the whole line. Now I am one of them.) If Baker House continues to totally screw me over and not give me my goddamn money . . . don't want to go there. I had a grievance form sitting next to me on my great bed. I had a lot of shit next to me. Reminded me of the living the high life with Kent. We went through seven thousand dollars in six weeks. First stop was the Hyatt Rickey's in Palo Alto. God, we lived as large as we could.

Anthony still won't answer his phone.

WART

I WAS IN Dermatology at SF General trying to do something to my wart; my oh-so-bothersome clump of skin on the left foot . . . from the homeless days. I got the wart in December, the month I was on crutches for two weeks—bad strep throat and hence couldn't talk at all for at least a week—strung out as a dog, my ninety-day detox (methadone detox attempt #502) wasn't working—couldn't come up with twelve dollars a day some days . . . but I really can't be without it; I have to be good to my liver. No money for that or dope. I'd have been dope sick and suicidal for days on end. The worst month of my life. If not the worst, a close runner-up.

Mary at rehab is a miracle. A thousand gifts from God have been coming on a daily basis! With each passing day the crying bouts lessen and lessen. I don't have to keep my occasional weed-smoking from Marcia. We smoked one *together* last night! The Hindu guy who is the manager was shit-faced drunk last night.

My foot hurts whenever I let myself sit still for a few seconds.

So much to say and so little time. God do I have a bone to pick with so many people. I'm grateful to God for bestowing all these gifts on us; don't get me wrong . . . but damn, other people get under my skin. Sometimes I don't know if it's my paranoia acting up again or if it's real—this negative energy I'm getting—and I'm so sensitive to other people's energy.

I feel like a lot of people think of me as a "drama queen" or at the very least, overly dramatic, or that I say "crazy" stuff just for the shock value, and I swear to God that's not who I am! In fact, the less attention I get from people the better—especially when I'm going through my emotional episodes.

Baker House *finally* processed my motherfucking rebate check—the assholes. Tomorrow will be laundry day and grievance-against-Baker-House-writing day!

I had come from Palo Alto. I knew I hadn't dealt with that ticket, the five hundred dollars due last year—one I have a warrant for—I didn't even look out the window. Too painful. It was where Kent and I would wait for Jose to sell me dope. Kent is now in place with the rest of my dead people, but it's a pleasant thought . . . I hope you're resting in peace. I still need to visit your mother . . . the only one left in the whole family. A very, very wealthy but profoundly lonely woman in her nineties.

Seroquel's making me see double, I took seven 'cuz I was depressed . . . forgot to finish my thought. I am not alone. God and my imagination; just like when I was a little girl . . . so many dreams swinging out of the mood.

I left SF General before they called my name and now my fucking wart is killing me. Remember baby, not writing is not an option. You must. It's your way back. But my baby is my obstacle. Now it seems to have contracted the flu—probably from the Hindu guy (manager) at the Ambika. A terrible loneliness attack happened Saturday.

Yesterday was heaven. April and I made love-magic peace. I couldn't take it anymore. I had to taste her literally and figuratively. Today I'm sick. I need to be in my room recuperating.

What I really want to say is dangerously close to what I come up with when I've been nodding my ass off on heroin.

I'm scared to death that she'll somehow drift out of my life, and I cannot tolerate even the thought of that. She has changed my life regardless of anything. I don't care what anyone says—my mother, Michael D at Baker—they are just jealous that she showed up in my life, not theirs!

I'm forcing discipline on myself. These days if I don't write it's never due to lack of something to say—my God it comes pouring out of me—the well is never dry. Having her around, waking up with her in bed next to me is a Godsend. I'm still out of ginkgo biloba, which I'm convinced was responsible for my marked improvement in the memory department.

I was telling her about Anthony checking himself into the Psychiatric Emergency Services (PES) at SF General, where I've been a dozen times—this is only his second time—when she demanded, "Did you tell him yet you've been taken?" I said—more like mumbled under my breath—"not yet" because I was really—I mean my head was spinning in confusion—lots of layers of thought. Thoughts bombarding into each other like meteors into planets at this point . . . it was well into the afternoon. She saw me when I first came over in a little black dress; it was so cute. She quickly threw on a VL sexy black velvet dress, put on dramatic bright cosmetics to her already pretty face. She looked great by the time she was done. We walked around the park that's smack dab in the middle of the SF Public Library, City Hall across the way, Bill Graham Presents theater, the Asian Art Museum and the new heart sculptures, and we fed the pigeons.

Anthony indicated in that brief (always brief with him) telephone conversation that he regards me being with a woman while we are committed to each other as "cheating." It was just one of the million things I tried to talk to him about. He always abruptly cuts me off with, "Not now." Then, when? I finally had the nerve one day to ask him. I spared him "healthy communication" because it was apparent he was already depressed as hell. Especially the April bone, which would upset him even more. He checked himself into PES, at least he said he would. He's resorting to his old, known (hence safe) ways of coping, e.g., smoking crack (he said it was a one-time thing), going to the psych ward for a place to sleep, eat, and have shelter. He will not admit it, of course, but hospitalization, even (God forbid) another drug rehab program would probably do him some good. Like everything else I've advised him about in the past few months it was like talking to a wall. Maybe he's one of those men who have pride about asking for help, listening to or taking advice from a woman.

Hey! Didn't I say I wasn't going to write about Anthony? I guess I needed to go there still. It all pertains to April. She's just like me in so many ways. Very intense, all or nothing with a black view of the Universe. She said, "I want all of you or nothing."

The other day we walked to Tom Waddell's Health Clinic (my appointment with my shrink), and an actual doctor, M.D. or Ph.D., has to fill out the paperwork to verify the fact that I'm nuts, i.e., depressed, suffering from anxiety etc., and hence unable to work. No SSI award letter or anything on that front came. God, am I pissed off.

But, at least yesterday was heaven.

My April! What am I going to do? I have to tell her to slow down—way down—this AIDS thing cannot go un-talked about any longer.

The girl is moaning about her body piercing belly-button infection in the puncture room. She is now my "girl friend," "wife" sometimes she calls me—I haven't had the talk I always have with my female lovers which is basically: I am not gay—can't be—tried to be, but I can't help myself, no matter how many problems are associated with men I'm still attracted to them. I can see myself marrying one some day. But (and there's a big "but"—no silly pun intended) I am attracted to women—some women—just like with men—there are only some men I'm attracted to. I am always honest with women from the gate about all this. If a man comes along who I think may be the *one* I have to be true to myself and pursue him (if it's reciprocal) but I don't want what I have with women—the emotional, spiritual bond that manifests itself physically—to stop. I want my cake and want to eat it too. Trouble is, not all men or women share this philosophy. I really do have a potentially life-threatening disease (Hep C) and very likely HIV:

1. My behavior when I was H-addicted was deplorable—can't get more high-risk than what I did with those needles.
2. I had totally great but totally unprotected sex with April last weekend. April is dying, so she says, and it really appears that's the case based on how sick she always is—very sick, throwing-up sick and everything—maybe not everything—I don't know everything. We need to talk. What goes with full-blown AIDS.

I already decided that if it turns out I face a long, drawn out, slow, agonizing death from *anything* I'll off myself either with a few shots of 100 percent pure china white 1+ or bark up the Hemlock Society tree that Tom at Baker was talking about. I'm pretty convinced I have HIV. I've been saving the test for when I reach the point when I am OK with either outcome and I think for the most part I am. I loved what Jim, the guy from Wisconsin who leads the Life Ring Group, said last time about how he had to embark on his crack-smoking addiction to come to recovery and learn the tools he needed to cope with life. It confirmed what I thought about myself years ago—about me and my affair with H. I needed to experience addiction so I'd end up at Mariposa in San Jose, to be blessed by the presence of my Health Redemptive teachers. For sure I'd have killed myself long ago with depression if not for them.

THE LAST CRACK HOUSE HOTEL

My hat's off to anyone who can live in small quarters with someone like me. Other people are just too much for me to deal with. I've long since realized that I have so much chatter with myself, that I don't need chatter with another human being. If I'm going to harm myself I'd like to have the privacy and integrity to do it by myself and not have anyone who might walk in on this ghastly phenomenon.

That's why it is hard to look at these bright and sunshiny ads on craigslist to no end. They show a beautiful kitchen and then promptly inform that there is no smoking, drugs, pets, or some shit like that. They always announce things like, "Come hang out with us. Enjoy our barbeques and views of the ocean," and you can tell these are functioning people with jobs and lives and I just want to puke because I want the right to exist how I want to exist or not exist, the right to complete hermitage.

But this is San Francisco, the land of twenty-eight-day throw-outs and shady managers with varying levels of drunkenness and inhospitality. Lately, in my current place, I'm met with a strong stench of alcohol and pee all over my toilet. Any way you look at it, someone is either drunk or missing or deliberately saying "Fuck you" to the manager, or entire floor, like the blood smeared all over the bedroom wall following an all-night screaming match.

At the last crack house hotel I lived at, I guess a woman next door had a guy over who didn't pass the drunken manager's criteria, as he was screaming at her in a shrill Hindi accent, "Get that fucking asshole out of here, now!" She screamed, "NO!" and from my room it sounded like the "fucking asshole" was toppling down the stairs.

That was the Ambika Hotel at Larkin and O'Farrell.

THE MAGICAL YEAR

It was a hot day in summertime 2002. I was with my career-criminal boyfriend. The only reason we were there was the free coffee the bookstore offered upstairs. We needed coffee desperately to make the methadone kick in. I saw a book I wanted. It was a toss-up between buying the book and getting some dope. I bought the book. Over the years, like virtually all of my personal belongings, the book was lost—a casualty of being thrown out of a recovery home. But here I go, like my mind always does, veering off course. It's always a challenge for me to jerk myself out of the gloomy storm clouds and root myself in the here and now.

A safe place for me was the two-bedroom apartment that I shared with my girlfriend Nancy in the summer, fall, and winter of 2000. That was the magical year. It was also the year that I fell apart, when my friend killed himself in December, and I plunged myself all the way into my addiction.

JUSTIN

Justin is tall with large spectacular hands and a sweet soft Southern drawl. He always had a big grin for us, greeted us with the warmest of hellos, made a point of asking us how we were doing, what we were up to. I could never quite reconcile the gentleness of his voice, his manner, and his words with the stories he would tell about being a crazed methamphetamine addict staying up for weeks on end, wandering the mean streets busting heads, taking no prisoners. But that's Justin.

TINY

TINY, A GOOD mother . . . that she was . . . she had a litter of five. All of them looked like every mutt in the neighborhood. Tiny was very small—part Chihuahua, I believe. Her puppies were so beautiful. We kept them by a wood-burning stove in our three-room shack.

Eight o'clock in the morning: time for me to go to school. Cold winter days I would hate. Kids would always tease me for smelling like a smokehouse. On occasion, Tiny would walk with me to school.

But not this morning. She wasn't about to leave without her babies. She was a devoted mother. She would challenge a bear behind those puppies. I wanted to ask my grandmother, the only mother I ever knew, if my mother, my real mother, loved me the way Tiny loved her babies. But as a kid I dared not ask that question. It was a sin to ask adults questions. As my grandmother would say, "I'll beat your ass for asking grown folks questions."

Over time, Tiny's puppies all died. They died one by one, and I felt sad. Tiny never stopped being my best friend. She answered the question for me. My mother wasn't able to be by my side. I often heard Granny say, "I hope I don't have to turn my baby over to the care of God."

It wasn't until I was a middle-aged adult that I heard a pastor explain the meaning of those words. As a colored kid back then I didn't know my mother had problems. I guess my grandmother loved her daughter so much that she asked God to take her. I heard a preacher say the very same thing over 3,000 miles from where I first heard Granny say it. It meant that my grandmother hurt so much from my mother's problem to where she didn't know what to do anymore. The day my mother was killed I saw hurt but could not feel any pain. I felt more for my grandmother than the death of my mother. However I didn't understand why and everything went numb. I didn't know how I felt, but I knew it wasn't good.

SOFT PORN IN THE LIVING ROOM

As I recall Full Figure is what caught the lustful eye of the slim, dark, and handsome guy.

"Pee Wee could you come here a sec?"

"Here Boy, fasten my bra."

Only the small hands of a boy would have slipped and let go of the bra.

"I'm sorry."

Wow, oh my God, look at the size of those things. My, Grandma, where did you get those things? God forbid she could hear my thoughts. This was my grandmother, and I knew right then and there what I wanted when I grew up. I really loved those days when Aunt Sissy came to visit. Not a mouse or a stir or a sound . . . soft porn in the living room.

I watched through the skeleton keyhole.

Days, months, and years took their course. Thumbing through the JC Penney catalog reminds me of those moments.

Can't wait 'til I grow up.

COLORED

AS A COLORED kid growing up in a small town, population eight thousand, "Afro-American" was a few decades down the road. "Colored" was what ABC, NBC, and CBS called us, and those were the only channels that we got on the black and white TV that my mother got me. I was proud of that television. That was one way my mother showed love; she couldn't say it. I never really heard the words "nigger" or "junglebunny" much. I thought that was odd—most of the northern states have blacks against whites. Cuero, Texas was the name of my hometown . . . I did know about poverty and segregation, though I didn't know what the *words* meant yet.

Despite the problems in the world, most folks in Cuero knew everyone else. The railroad tracks seemed to separate blacks and whites. My grandmother worked for the McClunges; they owned a grocery store. They didn't seem to mind my grandmother's lifestyle at all. I was always embarrassed about the way we lived. I didn't realize that it was a lifestyle that hundreds would pay thousands for today, and a lifestyle that I truly miss. As independent as my grandmother was, she could not get by without the help of our neighbors. Because they would just do things for us without asking. From fixing things at our three-room shack to leaving food by the door.

That's what it was like being a poor, colored boy growing up in Cuero, Texas.

BOYS SHOULDN'T KISS THEIR FATHERS ON THE LIPS

I'M ON A crowded bus in the wintertime in Detroit, Michigan. It's about a week after the first snowstorm of the season. What was once a blanket of white lying like silk on the ground has turned into mush. Black, muddy mush filled with the grit and trash of the urban streets. It makes me feel kind of sad and lonely. It makes me wonder how something that was once so lovely could so quickly turn into something so ugly, sad, and depressing.

I'm a kid seven years old and thinking about love and not sure what to make of it. This is a different kind of love unlike any I've ever felt! Definitely not like the kind I'm used to. I am used to the hugs and kisses of loving parents. Hugs in the morning and kisses at night. However I can only give Dad a kiss on the cheek at night because boys shouldn't kiss their fathers on the lips—not at this age anyway. Besides, even if I was allowed to kiss him on the lips I'm not even sure that I'd want to because he's well . . . older. He's older than the dads of the kids my age. In fact, he could be my mother's father. I always wondered why she calls him "Daddy" just like my brother and I do.

"Is he your father too?" I asked my mom when I was about four or five.

"Of course not, quit being silly . . ." was the only reply.

Anyway the love I'm feeling today is once again quite different. It's physical; it's making my body change. Why is this happening as I look at the black man on the Detroit public bus with the pretty green eyes?

The bus was always full of black men and women when I returned home from where I attended a school full of white kids. Kids as white as the freshly fallen snow which had blanketed the streets a week ago. The snow that was once so beautiful . . .

If the black man with the pretty green eyes was my father (after all, he appears to be the age that a kid like me's father should be), I'd kiss him goodnight on the lips every night.

TIME IS RUNNING OUT

OH, I HAVE a secret. In fact my heart is pounding and my stomach moves around as I get ready to write about it. It is the biggest secret of my life. My father, who are you? Faceless man I've held a hundred conversations with. What happened to you? Are you good? Are you as bad as they all say you are? How many stories are fiction, how many truth? I've never even seen a picture of you. Do I really "look just like your damn father?" There is a famous story where you cut a screen and kidnapped me from my bassinet, and it took a week to find me. Why did you do that? I search for clues. Was it because you were angry at my mom and her relatives? Because you wanted to protect me? Because you were high?

So many stories, so many questions—do I dare try to find out for myself? I don't think I'm that brave. I'm caught in my own web of indecision.

But mostly, I want to know: Do you think of me on my birthday? Do you love me? Are you still alive?

I wonder if it is meant for our paths to cross—but time is running out, Father. I've been waiting for forty-five years; I guess I can wait a little longer.

THE MAN OF MY DREAMS

HERE I AM. Alone. Broke. Standing on Santa Monica Boulevard looking for Mr. Right. Who will I see today? Will it be a banker, a musician, an accountant, or maybe even a movie star? I get cruised by the gas queens. We call them that because they never stop—just slow down and speed away. Wow! Who's this guy? He pulls by looking at me, hard. I wait for him to pull over but he doesn't. Maybe he'll pull around again. Sure enough, he comes by again. Nice car. It looks like he's pulling over. I slowly walk to the car, noticing its nice, new look. It's a two-seater, a Mercedes, and the guy behind the wheel is cute. Nice muscle definition, short haircut, military style—I'm attracted to him.

I lean into the car and say, "Hi! Can I hop in?"

He leans over and pushes the door open and in a husky voice says, "Sure!"

I slide into the car noticing the smell of new leather and admiring the way his jeans cling to his well-muscled thighs. He tells me his name is Dan and that he is just about to go overseas to Desert Storm and wants male companionship one last time. My defenses go down. I don't say anything. I can't believe my luck. I've just been picked up by the man of my dreams. He tells me he's staying at the Holiday Inn on Hollywood Boulevard, and would I like to come over? I can't say "Yes" fast enough.

He says, "I know you're probably working so I'll give you one hundred dollars to stay the whole night. Is that OK?"

Still no warning signs pop up. I say, "Sure, I could use the money."

Nineteen years old, and here I am selling myself to survive. We drive towards Sunset and he has to stop the car at Fountain Street, what's this?

Four Lincoln Town Cars come out of nowhere, each with three or four people in them. They jump out and approach the car.

"Take it easy," my dream man tells me.

I see something hanging on chains around people's necks. Badges. Oh shit! I am dumb, dumb, dumb. I look at the man next to me and think, "Boy you are *good*. I can't believe it, you completely slipped through my defenses."

CO-CO COUNTY BOY

I'm on the yard. Today's my first day here. Am I safe? I did the crime, but can I really do the time? I look around me in the yard and there they are. The yard is filled with criminals just like me. Or are they really like me? Can they see what I am inside? I hope not. What will happen if they find out I'm different? After all, I like men . . . will my thoughts betray me? I better not smile. Guy comes up to me and says,

"What's up Wood? Where you from?"

"Contra Costa County," I tell him.

So he says, "Another Co-Co County boy, huh?" Then he tells me where my homeboys kick it in the yard and I walk over. Am I walking with a swish? Am I mincing?

I try to walk like the men around me.

FIRST LOVE

MY FIRST BOYFRIEND was Mike Aliré. He was the class clown. Big troublemaker. I'm not sure why I liked him, but figuring it out would probably explain a lot. He constantly picked his nose. He wasn't a dirtball, he was actually really cute. He would fish out these long, gooey boogers and smear them down the pale green wood paneling of the school. He also had a habit of making sex noises when he was walking around: Oh! *Oh*! Oh! Oh, oh, *oooh*! he would call out, and the teachers would never say anything about it. I bought him a ring once. I got it for a quarter out of a candy machine, but never gave it to him because I was embarrassed. I'm not sure when we broke up, but I think it was sometime after he and Cesar Robles took me on the quad and took turns humping me, while the other one held me down.

Eventually, Mrs. Taylor, the principal, discovered them and pulled them off of me. But I don't remember either of them getting in trouble for it.

MAKEUP

I FIRST MET makeup as a little girl. I'd watch Mom painting meticulous, black perfect arches—great strokes of eyeliner, just like Cher, and perfect lips in siren red. Makeup first kissed my cheek when I was about eleven. We had to meet in secret; otherwise there would have been trouble because we weren't supposed to be seeing each other. It was fun—I fell in love with my Maybelline sky-blue—couldn't get enough. Makeup was good to me—helped me feel better when I wasn't feeling so hot. It helped me to face a not-friendly world at times by letting me hide behind it for a while.

Makeup and I are old friends now. Sometimes we don't see each other for weeks at a time, and as time goes by I've replaced makeup with new loves. But I can always rely on makeup. No matter what, makeup will always be there for me.

FOOD

I FUCKING WANT to stuff my face with a dozen donuts and then a whole chocolate cake, mmmmmh. I haven't had cheesecake in forever. Light, crispy tortilla chips and fresh salsa, hell, even cheap taco picanté sauce. I don't really care. I just know I love food. I also hate food. I hate the fact that since I was four I've used food to get attention, to escape, and to numb out. I've used food to suppress my pain.

There is, or can be, a beautiful ritual around food—especially around the holidays. Spending time with family and friends, preparing the meat and the desserts, enjoying lavish food using the china, drinking out of the crystal, sitting in a formal dining room, dining at the best restaurant in town. Getting all dressed up to go.

My rituals with food are not always so beautiful. I'm sad. I'm craving sugar.

SARAH TESCH

Sarah is another fantastic enigma wrapped in a riddle. If you rounded up a hundred random Americans and put them in a lineup, you would never in a million years pick her out as a hooker. Which, I guess, is part of the point of this book. She comes across as thoughtful, introverted—someone who might play bass in an alternative rock band. It's only after you get to know her a little bit, and take in the sly, sardonic corner-of-the-mouth barbs that flow from her steadily, that you realize she has been to hell and back many times.

A BIG OL' SECRET

I OFTEN THINK that I'm just a big ol' fake. Draped in a facade of desperation. Sometimes I think I'm always acting and I hate myself for it. Whatever person lives within my costumed existence must be a weak and shriveled fetus of sorts. I'm frequently rolling in introspective revulsion. I watch Her/Me. Sometimes She is Miss Shy and Bashful. There She is: Miss Brazen and Fearless. Here She is: Miss Sweet and Seductive. There, She's Miss Dependable—I'm never sure if She's Me.

Me is a big fat secret. A secret even to my own curious thoughts. A secret buried so deep that I can only imagine that it must be the ugliest, most fetid and wretched thing.

I pluck about my day, vacillating between personalities, before I eventually initiate the relentless pouring of whiskey down my gaping gullet. Then the secret reveals itself to me, to my blacked-out person. I never remember, but I leave clues for my conscious person. Scars and blood. Red eyes and cheeks. Just a big ol' secret.

A VERY BAD PERSON

I DON'T HATE cops. And I'm not anti-authority. I have a number of friends who are all, "Fuck the Pigs." Their harrowing encounters justifying this stance range from too many parking tickets to a cop pushing them at a protest or something. Myself, I've been fucked with and helped by cops.

Cops are people, and just like everybody else, a good many of them are assholes. The difference with cops is that they have more power than any given pedestrian. Anyway, I felt compelled to preface this story with that.

Four o'clock in the morning. I'm in a hotel. High and wasted. I decide I should go home before I put myself in some stupid situation again. Call cab. Cab comes. I pass out in back. Oh fucking well, poor cabbie . . . Such is the hazard of driving graveyard shift. Get me to my destination, wake me up, and make me pay.

Cabbie has a different idea. He pulls over, somewhere in my slumber. I wake to him crawling on me in the back, grabbing at my thighs.

I punch him in the face. He punches me in the nose, I proceed to bleed furiously and black out.

Next thing I know, the cops are there. Handcuffs. Good ol' cabbie called the cops on me, saying I assaulted him. He was probably worried about what to do with me if I remembered about my smashed nose and bruised thighs, so he took action first. I'm wobbling and incoherent. Cabbie is explaining to the police that I brutally attacked him and he had to defend himself.

Memory exits then enters again. I'm in this bed and a woman who looks like that lady who was in *Poltergeist*—the one with the weird voice—is holding a piece of toast inches from my face and shaking me. I don't want the toast and am wondering why I'm bloody and dressed in hospital scrubs. She says that if I don't eat the toast I will never get out of here. I don't know where I am, but I know I want to get out. I eat toast. Lights back out. Lady leaves. Couple of hours later, lady comes back in and tells me that I'm in some isolation room at detox.

Another couple of hours and she judges me fit to join the others in the group area, where there are TVs and magazines. It seems like paradise for a while.

Then she shows me my room. It's small and there's a bed and a shelf. It's greenish blue. She shuts the door behind her and delivers her soliloquy.

"You are a very bad person. You attacked that man. You've done a lot of bad things and you will continue to do bad things. You have a very big problem. You have to stop being this way. You're going to either die or kill someone if you keep going this way. You are sick. You are very, very, very sick!"

The cabbie didn't press charges. No shit. I got out of there thirty-six hours later. On the computer I looked up the cabbie's court record. You can do that in Wisconsin, I don't know about here.

He had been convicted of sexual assault on a child. Good thing they have the cops out there to keep people like me off the street.

ANONYMOUS WRITERS

The woman who wrote this piece didn't say anything to me for a long time. No "Hi." No "Hello." Nothing. She has a big face and big hair. She takes up a lot of space physically, although she isn't fat. Her features all gravitate toward the middle of her face, and her default mode seems to be a glowering scowl. Being who I am, I thought she completely and absolutely hated me. But as the months went on, she softened toward me. When she saw me she would barely move her head and cock one eyebrow—the smallest hello I've ever gotten. But somehow it meant so much more to get a hello from her than from people who give them away cheaply.

BITCHES

BITCH. IF I had a magic camera, right now, I would use it to "appear" all the bitches in my life, starting with my mom. All the bitches that have stolen from me. Why do women do that to each other? Why are we *so* scared that we feel we will *never* have enough unless we steal from the other women in our lives? Why have we learned to take instead of give? Why do we always have to live in fear? Who the fuck originated the idea anyway? "Hey, I'm feeling disenfranchised, I think I'll try to take from someone else—something they really need for themselves, then I'll feel better. Or maybe not, but even if I don't they'll be just as miserable as I am!" Right on!

Now comes Chapter Two. You know, Chapter One: "Piss and Moan." Second Chapter: "Oh No! I'm a Bitch Too!" I didn't look hard enough at the magic camera's photograph. There I am. Yeah. There in the back row. The second one from the left. Ah, hell . . . I hate like fuck to be included in that photo. I just want to sit on my pretty white pony and know that I'm better than all y'all. But, you know, my mama didn't raise no fools did she? She could take better than the rest—why, she was so good she could charm the honey out of the hive and *convince* those bees that it was in their best interest to give it up! Man, she was slick. Do you think she was going to leave this earth without training her firstborn girl to follow in those footsteps? Not on your life! I hate to admit it, but now that she's gone where does that leave me? The queen is dead; long live the queen!

So, here's the dilemma: I want to stay mad—*pissed*—at all the other bitches out there. After all, their primary purpose has been to make my life fucking miserable.

So, Chapter Three: "Where the Fuck Do I Go from Here?" Cough—Tenth Step—cough. No, no, I *want* to stay mad! It feels good to be mad, powerful to be mad, I don't want to take a look at me. Cough—Tenth Step—Tenth Step, cough, cough.

See? That's the problem. I want to stay mad.

But then the little voice comes in: "Would you rather be mad, or would you rather be dead?"

DEAD MAN WALKING

I'M IN A borrowed car. The person who lent it to me did so with extreme reluctance. "Uh . . . yeah . . . I suppose you can borrow the car, but don't . . . you know . . ." He doesn't finish the sentence but I can feel the unspoken words. "Don't fuck up again. Don't do something stupid again. Don't fuck my car up."

So, here it is, a couple of hours later, and I'm high like a kite with a tail, full of mind-bending chemicals. I'm driving the borrowed car. Without really thinking consciously about it, suddenly I'm in skanky Crackville, on the wrong side of the tracks, where track marks fester on funky arms, streetlights are shot out, abandoned buildings sigh like old men with cancer and broken limbs and organs that are all shutting down. And, *voila*, there she is—tall and tan and young and lovely, the girl from Nasty Ho-town goes walking, and when she walks each one she passes goes, "Yo bitch, how much?"

I stop the borrowed car. As soon as she gets in I know I've made a huge mistake. I should not be doing this shit. And yet, I am powerless to stop myself.

"Got a place?" I ask.

"Yeah," she purrs in a register lower than it has any right to be. Then I look through the haze of my high and my desire. Adam's apple. Wrists. Dude looks like a lady. Or rather lady is a dude and I don't care. I really don't. I try making some small talk, but he/she will have no part of it. Name is Angel. That's about it. So Angel directs me to a block where darkness squats over everything like a giant dark octopus—you can sense the menacing tentacles but you can't see them. Angel tells me to stop. I stop. Fast as a snake capturing a hypnotized mouse Angel grabs my keys. Then punches me in the nose. Those male hands come in handy, busting my schnozz pretty good. Angel wants my fanny pack. I know there's a couple hundred dollars and an ounce of some killer bud in the bag. I jump out of the borrowed car. Suddenly the whole neighborhood is swarming with people nightcrawling toward me like zombies hungry for my flesh. I have never felt so white. Angel screams at me to give up my bag as the gang circles me, tightening the human noose. I try to negotiate.

"I'll give ya twenty dollars if ya give me back my keys." Warm blood oozes down my face and I can taste the red metal of my bleeding. From nowhere, a large man raises a lead pipe. I can see it in motion but I can't get out of the way. BLAM! The heavy lead slams into my skull like a head-on collision. I don't even feel it. I come from a long line of thick-headed idiots, so my coconut splits a little without really cracking. Blood soaks my shirt. But the mood changes. No one can believe I'm still standing. I give them my fanny pack in exchange for my keys. Someone throws a rock at the car. Someone else bashes in the parking light and steals the side mirror. The borrowed car is a mess. Luckily, I looked like a dead man walking, and my friend was polite enough not to say, "I told you so," in the face of my ravaged, savaged face.

BRITTANY CAUFMAN

Brittany is a wee slip of a waif. Sometimes she looks twelve years old, sometimes fifty. She is a sweet little girl and a foulmouthed urchin. She is someone you want to take in your arms and hug. Brittany has an ethereal quality, like she's from another planet. She floats through rooms with big glazed dazed eyes that focus in from time to time, and then drift away again. At the time she wrote this piece, she was seventeen years old. And pregnant.

RAPED NINETY-SEVEN TIMES

Brittany Caufman was born on St. Patrick's Day, 1986, to Cindy and Jimmy Sterlock as Kasey C. Sterlock. When born, she had a twin sister named Brianna. At age two years, she was adopted and at that point, renamed. By this time she had already had both hands broken. By the age of ten years, she had been kicked out of her adoptive parents' home. She started on drugs and became a prostitute. She was raped ninety-seven times by age sixteen, shot four times, and stabbed numerous others. She has now been engaged for four years and is trying to get her life straight. She plans to start a business soon and now has three daughters aged seven, four, and two years old.

ANONYMOUS WRITERS

The woman who wrote this story penetrated deep into my heart. She is a classic big-boned beauty, large and in charge. Loud, brash, spewing profanity, overflowing with life. She's someone who will slap you on the back and ask with a cockeyed grin, "How's tricks?" Which, in the basement of SAGE, takes on many levels of meaning. And definitely someone you'd want on your side in a dark alley. So it was quite totally shocking when this tough tough nut allowed herself to crack open, and after she was done reading, there were many tears shed around the table.

THANKS A LOT

I SAW MY mother in Reno last weekend and she looked a little better than last time. This isn't saying much, because the last time I saw her she was on her deathbed from an abscess that spread into her heart and also weakened her pelvis bone so badly it broke. The only thing that saved her life is that she went to jail. It's so hard to see her in such bad condition.

She knows that I'm clean and getting ready to have a baby but that doesn't stop her from doing a shot of heroin right in front of me.

I can't believe she said, "Too bad you can't try any 'cuz you're pregnant."

Thanks a lot.

Surprisingly, watching her do a shot repulsed, rather than triggered me. Seeing all the open sores all over her body, legs so swollen that when she took her socks off you could see indents from them. She stabbed herself with that needle for over an hour while blood ran all over her body. It was like looking at a mirror of me in my addiction. She finally gave up. Well, actually the rig clogged so badly that adding water wouldn't help anymore. So, of course she had to fix up another one and decided to muscle it.

RABID DOG MARINES

I SET THE camera about four feet from me, just enough room to focus and just far enough for the shutter cable to barely reach. I called him, it was 7 A.M., he's still at work.

"Hey it's me, come over when you get off, I need your help with a photo project. Bring your glock and pick up some scalpels if you can."

I wanted to show some abandon, hollowing myself out to be a vessel for something else, postmodern romanticism, so when I arrived I had to carve the letters M I N E into my chest. As the blood tricked out and dried in garnet beads on my tits I made him sit behind me with a gun to my throat. I clicked thirty-six frames, I was done. This was hollow.

The denial of the self, becoming a vessel for anything other than your own will, this happens in the Marines too. Unfortunately I didn't have my camera with me when they circled me on the deserted beach like rabid dogs. Pacing back and forth, letting me know that they always get what they want, so I should give up now. I should have known better than to go swimming at three in the morning. I tried to get away. When one of the seven disagreed about their conquest, he stood in front of me, and I don't even remember his name.

"Just leave her alone," he yelled.

"Ohhhhh, you like her, you want us to leave her alone," the ringleader spat back.

And with that they attacked, their anger distracted, forgetting about me, dissent within their ranks much more interesting than the half-naked girl swimming alone at 3 A.M. And so, they turned on their own. Daring to disagree with the act of frat boy rape. Pummeling him and knocking him to the ground, he begged for them to stop. And I ran.

HIS BUDDHA PENDANT

I SMIRKED as soon as I heard the subject. I didn't need to search any files or compare hatreds; I knew immediately who I should write about.

But I started to search the files anyway, I'd rather not write about him. Him. Alex. His real name is Alan Man, but he never told me that, his license plate did: 9HRZ500.

I didn't know much but I knew that he was a jeweler and made a lot of money, yet five years later he still refused to tell me what store he owned.

Maybe cuz he knew I hated him, maybe he knew I wanted to kill him, or show up at his house with a DNA sample and give it to his wife. But then again that wouldn't work either. He hated her, that was obvious, but I didn't, I felt sorry for her, just like I felt sorry for myself.

Besides, she probably accepts it. It's common sociological knowledge that in Hong Kong it's perfectly normal to have a satellite family. You have your main family, the wife, house, kids, dogs in Danville. The satellite in the city; the lush apartment, young naïve girl, money.

I've always wanted to kill him, but as cliché as it may sound, he knew Kung Fu. I knew if it came to hand-to-hand combat he would kick my ass. I don't want to touch him anyway. I could shoot him, but that's too loud. Cyanide in an oyster, I can get that from the darkroom.

He moves his Buddha pendant on his necklace to the back when he fucks me; it's been in his family for decades. He says he doesn't want me to fuck anyone else. But why not, I'd never done it for money until I met him. I crossed that line; why not exploit it? So he turned me out but that doesn't mean he owns me.

THE KAY BUFFINGTON PHOENIX MURDERS

I GOT UP this morning and my arm and hand hurt like hell—so painful it took several hours to get the pain worked out. But I didn't care because I woke up happy—what a concept. Who ever thought that could be me . . . that I could wake up without that dragon of impending doom slopping his head around toward my face and breathing his fire down my throat and turning my insides into ice? I actually felt happy—not the manic euphoria that I was wont to feel off and on sometimes for no reason at all but usually because I was getting my way and finally the world would be all right. No not that. Just your regular run-of-the-mill smile-in-the-mirror kind of happiness.

I've been staying with a friend for the past week. She left her husband two years ago; the divorce—long, drawn out, and nasty—was final about two months ago. She had been with him for fifteen years! The last time he hit her she had him arrested and he spent a few months in jail . . . not long. He called her shortly after the divorce was final saying, "I just wanted you to know I don't have any hard feelings. How are you anyway? I just wanted to check on you to see if you needed anything." Several phone calls later—"Oh you're short this month; let me help you. I'll get a few groceries and drop them by."

A week or two ago she and I are hanging out, "Jeanne, you know I slept with Andre the other night. I didn't want to feel like I was lying to you or keeping something from you."

This morning after an hour or two fluttering around—you know, just being happy, she gets up and clearly something is bothering her. Finally, out it comes, "Andre and I are supposed to go to look at an apartment today. I don't know what to do, you know. He's still drinking but he promises me, and now I'm not drinking so I won't be doing bad things all the time."

I don't say anything, just finish making the pancakes. When I finish I go boot up Google. I type in Kay Buffington. Nothing. I try Kay Buffington, Phoenix, murder. Nothing. I try *Arizona Republic* newspaper archives then type it all again. There it is: twenty-three grisly pictures that should never be seen but must be seen. A Phoenix woman is brutally murdered by her boyfriend. After systematically breaking every bone in her body he loads her body into the trunk of his car and drives to his friend's house. The twenty-three pictures shown here were confiscated as evidence by Phoenix police. Story after story.

I tell my friend to come here, I want you to see them. She sees/reads a few and gets up.

I ask her, "Do you know that the leading cause of death for women our age is murder by their partners?"

GETAWAY MONEY

FOR ABOUT SIX months when I was with my ex, Jason, I put money away. I think deep down that it was actually "getaway money," you know, to escape from him. But I pulled it out one night after we had smoked all the drugs and been to the casino. It was about one thousand dollars. He wanted to be pissed at me for having this secret stash—but how could he be? I handed him the cash; just gave it to him. We bought something to eat and then more drugs.

THE SLANTED CHURCH

I once had a camera, Canon I think it was. I was experimenting with black and white film. As I was walking past Safeway I decided to take a photo of a church located on Church Street. As I took the photo, I didn't think much of it, but I did make sure to keep the photo free of any advertisements. When I had the film developed at Walgreens, I shuffled through the pictures, choosing my favorites through visual criticism. As I came upon the one of the church, I discovered an artful flaw. The picture was slightly out of focus, as if the camera had been slightly moved to the right, giving it a haunted gothic look. Also, an overhead light from the Safeway parking lot brought another strange element in. It was as if I had taken this photo nearly a century ago with a camera from the future. I asked myself if, upon request, "Could I achieve this effect when taking another photo?" Something told me no. After several photo sessions with that same camera, I achieved other strange effects by accident. Later that year I pawned that camera for drugs.

DAVID HENRY STERRY

JUST TRYING TO KEEP IT REAL

DATELINE: NEW YORK—Yankee Stadium erupted last night when forty-seven-year-old rookie David Henry Sterry won the World Series almost single handedly. Not only did he pitch a no-hitter, he hit five home runs, made an unassisted triple play, and saved an orphan who was choking to death on a hot dog. Sterry, the oldest rookie in baseball history, was named MVP of the series and was carried around on the shoulders of Yankee veterans Derek Jeter, Bernie Williams, and Alex Rodriguez. Owner George Steinbrenner handed Sterry a $10 million cash bonus and offered him a lifetime contract worth $100 million and keys to the stadium so he can play there anytime he wants. Afterward in the locker room, amidst champagne flying, the Coors twins took Sterry into a room where they had a private celebration, from which Sterry emerged with a large smile. His wife reported that she was no longer concerned that Sterry has sex with movie starlets and other assorted hotties: "I know he loves me deeply, I'm secure in our love and only want whatever makes him happy." Then she gave him a huge smooch and they hugged, soaked in Dom Pérignon. Afterward, Sterry was asked about his earth-shattering greatness. "This is not about me," said Sterry with his trademark humility. "I dedicate this to all the boys and girls who have no love—who have no home. I urge Congress to cut the military budget in half to provide care and housing for the homeless and pay teachers what they deserve, and to get rid of all the pimps, pedophiles, and predators. I urge the Arabs and Jews to live in peace. I urge the U.S. to legalize drugs and put the money freed from this insane war on drugs into setting up rehab centers for addicts and education programs that accurately depict the good and bad elements of drug use. The IRS should be abolished, replaced by a 20 percent flat tax. I urge President Bush and Dick Cheney and Donald Rumsfeld to resign, and for Morgan Freeman, Noam Chomsky, and Warren Buffet to take their place."

Amazingly, Bush, Rumsfeld, and Cheney immediately resigned, while Israel and Palestine agreed it was time to make peace. Congress sprang into action and in an emergency session, cut the military budget and decreed that all the money would be spent on housing the homeless and attacking those who prey on the young and defenseless. Drugs were legalized later that night, with all "drug war" funds now being earmarked for education, training, and rehab. And in a surprise move, the IRS decided to disband itself and issued a formal apology to Sterry's wife for their harassment of her and agreed to pay back all the money they had sucked out of her, and to further compensate her for the time she spent submitting to their petty tyrannies. Sterry was awarded the Nobel Peace Prize. "I am so grateful," Sterry said. "And I'm just gonna try to keep it real."

FLIP THE SCRIPT

THE SCIENTISTS AT UC Berkeley took one hundred homeless people and one hundred rich people who can't understand why the bums just can't find a job and decided to "flip the script." The wealthy were asked to voluntarily give up their lavish homes for twenty-four hours, grab a shopping cart, some Goodwill clothes, a couple of banners, and a cardboard sign and get a taste of what it's like to struggle. On the other hand, the homeless were cleaned and bathed, groomed, dressed in the finest fashions, and were told they could live it up for a day in the homes of the more fortunate. These volunteers were monitored to see how they could adapt to their new environments. The poor seemed to have no problem adjusting. There was a lot of eating, drinking, and goings-on but no complaints. They appeared to be very content. The rich, on the other hand, had a little trouble adjusting. Most refused to go to the bathroom in public places—certainly not on the street, but when nature called they found it difficult to relieve themselves because not even the Chevron would unlock the door for them. A lot were shocked to be treated like they were a waste of space. Seventy percent wanted to quit after the first twenty minutes, and 52 percent just stood up all night long in protest of sleeping on the ground. Most had nothing to eat because they were simply too proud to beg. At the culmination of the experiment, 100 percent of the poor enjoyed the experiment and 100 percent of the rich did not. As a result of this effort, nothing has changed in the world, but the scientists were entertained.

6

National Summit Of Commercially Sexually Exploited Youth

SUMMIT INTRODUCTION

David Henry Sterry

As a result of my work with SAGE, I was, as I mentioned earlier, brought to Washington to teach a creative writing workshop at the first-in-the-history-of-America National Summit of Commercially Sexually Exploited Youth, sponsored by the Justice Department. However, the young women I worked with all week ended up teaching me a lot more than I taught them. They were between the ages of seventeen and twenty-two, they were from all over the country, and they were all survivors of shocking abuse.

The first day of the writing workshop, they took one look at me and saw a Stupid White Man. One of their tricks. What the fuck did I know about them? Why the fuck should they write a bunch of shit down? I told them my story and showed them my book. Their eyes went wide. Then it was like we were girlfriends. And the stories poured out.

I read great stuff from great books to them. Then I asked them to write about their favorite music, things that pissed them off, things that make them happy, people who hurt them, people who helped them, and, of course, how they got into the Life. As these street-hardened, nail-tough girl-women read their stories, they broke down weeping and wailing, collapsing in the arms of their friends, new and old. As we spilled our guts on the floor, they collected in a giant toxic pool and flowed out, and we became a part of each other, connected by rivers of exploitation, abuse, and horror.

On the last night of the summit, there was a public performance. It was one of the greatest moments of my life when I watched these young women, my new crew, who had so quickly become such a deep part of my life, stand behind the podium and read their work. They were funny, they were fierce, they were soft, and they were hard. They opened themselves up and let people look inside. Many times as I looked out at the crowd, I saw dozens and dozens of hands simultaneously reaching to wipe away tears.

To watch these young women evolve from shy, uncertain, reserved, defensive, guarded, and nervous to that moment when they stood up reading their intensely intimate pieces was breathtaking. I could actually see them gaining confidence right before my very eyes, as they basked in the wild applause of the audience. Suddenly they were worth more than just some ho to have sex with. There were getting love for their words, their stories, themselves.

Afterward we walked to DuPont Circle for a candlelight ceremony to honor those not able to be there, those without a voice, and those who are no longer with us. Walking down the street, I noticed a new head-held-high pride in their stride as we bopped and goofed and laughed through our nation's capital.

With the circle of candles throwing soft droplets of light, we sang an old spiritual about overcoming trials and tribulations with faith and love. As voices sang and rang, booming through DuPont Circle, the electricity swept around our circle and went shooting across the universe.

I was inspired every day by these girl-women: by their honesty, their humor, their courage in overcoming years of horror at the hands of adults, many of whom were responsible for loving and taking care of them. They broke my heart, made me sob uncontrollably, laugh hysterically, and understand the world in a profound new way.

I am honored and privileged that these young women let me into their lives. I give much love to all of them.

JESSICA BERTUCCI

I made an immediate connection with Jessica, and I've now worked with her for the last couple of years developing her story. Jessica definitely checks "other" in the race box. In her eyes resides the blood diamond hard look of a cobra, and she could absolutely kick your ass. She talks with a staccato urban inflection that's like a semi-automatic weapon. But what I loved first about Jessica was that beneath that titanium shell was a warm, soft, sweet, tender center.

I worked hard with Jessica on her story. She is a hard worker. And on the final night of the conference, when tough-talking, wisecracking, hard-boned Jessica read her story about her dad, you could hear the proverbial pin drop before she brought them to their knees in her jaw-dropping finale. As soon as she finished she broke down and ran off, followed by three of her new best friends who caught her in the hall and formed a tight hug circle around her, embracing her in their comfort as she shook and shook with convulsive sobs, downloading more and more of her misery.

When she looked at me, there was a smile on Jessica's face I had never seen before.

HELPING DADDY PAY THE RENT

IT WAS TIME for another weekend visit with my dad. I was just a little kid. He lived in a filthy, run-down, two-bedroom apartment with his main bitch and her five kids. I begged my mom not to take me but she did anyways.

Oh, by the way, my dad raped me when I was two years old.

So we arrived, parked the car, and I am still begging, "Please, I don't want to go."

My step-mom said, "Stop whining."

So we were greeted by my step-bitch, Ramona, at the front door.

"Come in and sit down," she said. "Your dad will be right back."

Well, my step-mom did not like my dad so she took the opportunity to leave without hearing his filthy mouth. So the night went on, and on, and on, and I proceeded to crash on the couch and not long after I heard my dad and his friend in the living room with me, while I pretended to be asleep. They were smoking crack, drinking, and having a good ol' time. Suddenly I was blindfolded, confused, and scared.

Next thing I knew, my dad was sitting next to me, whispering in my ear, "Don't be scared, you're helping Daddy pay the rent."

Oh, by the way, I was nine years old.

Then I was a ward of the state.

The second year there I started doing prostitution. I was twelve years old. I was always big for my age.

I had my first miscarriage when I was thirteen. It was my pimp's baby. I had four pimps between the ages of thirteen and fourteen. I was with Pimp Jody for three days before he found out I was fourteen. He was gonna ship me off. But it was too dangerous because I was so young. Finally, I ended up with Scorpio. One day I was seen talking with another pimp, and he put me in the middle of a circle, all the girls around me. I got beat for ten hours straight, no lie. They took turns beating me. They beat me to a bloody pulp. You see, I stepped on toes. I learned then it's better not to step on any toes. When I worked for Scorpio, he took all my money. I had time to hide it, smell it, and give it up.

He had the girls do my hair, he picked out my clothes, and then he put me on the street. I was so young, it was easy to get dates. I used to think of leaving all the time, but they scared the shit out of me. A lot of girls got shipped off. They wired back their money. There was someone watching them all the time.

It's weird, even now, that I got saved by getting sent to jail.

People need to experience ho-in' for themselves. No, actually I wouldn't want anyone to go through that. It's just denying reality. That's like saying the government is not corrupt. Everyone knows it is. But opinions are like assholes, everyone has one.

TOPAZ

Topaz is like an overgrown puppy, hands and feet still a little too big for her long lean lanky body. She has a way of slitting her eyes when she is evaluating a situation that makes her inscrutable. She's someone who can shrink and expand seemingly at will. I've seen her scrunch into herself in a chair, disappear so it's like there's no one there. I've seen her take over a whole room full of oversized characters quick as an eye blink. Topaz sneaks up on you. She can be silent for a very long time, so you think she's zoned out into Topaz Land, and then all of a sudden she'll say something so perfect and funny that after you laugh, you shake your head, like, Do not judge this book by its cover.

WHEN A MAN PUTS HIS HANDS ON A FEMALE IN ANGER

WHAT REALLY MAKES me very upset is when a man puts his hands on a female in anger. I guess I feel this way because as a young child my father beat me with a belt, shoe, iron, extension cord, broomstick, or metal fold-up chair. Back then I used to just sit there and take whatever beating I got, I didn't really start fighting back until about a year ago. No, my father is a big man, but the way I was feeling, I really didn't give a damn about what size he is. After a while I just got tired of getting blamed and beaten for every little thing. My mother would try to intervene but she was so little, she really didn't make much of a difference. I was so fed up living in that house. I started not going to school, staying out late, smoking weed and drinking, running away. After I got arrested I decided that I will not destroy my future over some bullshit. My lawyer had warned my father that if he ever put his hands on me he would be going to jail. That was one of the main reasons why I dislike seeing men abuse women. Ever since those experiences with my dad I never tolerated any boyfriend of mine abusing me in any way. Any cursing or disrespectful tone will get you out of the picture. I don't and won't accept any forms of abuse. No one deserves it and there is not and will never be an excuse for a man abusing a woman.

THIS ONE'S FOR YOU, BITCH

Do you like the word BITCH? Huh, bitch? No. Oh really? You loved to call me one even though I kept telling you that wasn't my name.

Why did you trick me into selling my ass for you when you knew what I was getting into? Do you think using and abusing females, particularly underage ones, makes you a bigger man? WELL IT DOESN'T! It just makes YOU the bitch.

Do you love your mother? Obviously you don't because if you did then you would have never put so many young women's lives at risk because you were too DUMB to get a real job.

Who in the hell gave you the authority to use physical force to discipline me? Who told you that you have the power to execute judgment? Are you God? HELL NO! So stop acting like it.

Are you slow or just plain stupid? Did you really think you could get away with sexually exploiting females? WHAT GOES AROUND COMES AROUND! BITCH.

Can you tell that I have no love or respect for you and that I never did? Ha! If you can't then you're really as dumb as I know you are. I can't say I hate you because the Lord says to love thy neighbor. I can say that I hate everything you have done to me and put me through. You took away my fuckin' childhood and made me see and do things I had no business partaking in. I hate the fact that I had to go out every night and put my life on the line for YOU while all you did was sit comfortably at "home" and wait for me to bring you "your money" you fucking bastard. Not once was you there to protect me like you said you was when I met you, you fucking liar. WHY DID YOU DO THIS TO ME? I have a lot of anger in my heart that only Lord knows I wish I could take out on your bum ass but that's God's job. Lucky you.

Hope the rest of your life is as miserable as you have made mine but one thousand times worse. Have fun in hell you ignorant, child-abusing rapist. Life's a bitch. Ain't it BITCH?

THE STRUGGLE

IT REALLY HURTS when you try so hard to impress everyone by doing your best and all you hear is "you're so stupid," "you dumb little girl," "you fuckin' ho," and other discouraging words from the people who are supposed to be supporting you and be by your side through anything. How is a child expected to be successful and happy in life when love is not shown in the way it's supposed to be shown? If you don't receive love and support from your family, who would you turn to?

I got into the Life at the age of fifteen. I thought that I was receiving love from a dude who really didn't give a shit about me. I was held hostage and forced to sell my body to benefit my pimp in return for a place to stay, food, and clothes. I never really saw any of the money I made. All of it was given to my pimp each night. I was beaten for stupid reasons all because I still had a square mentality and wasn't hip to the rules of the game. I was very "uncooperative" my first few weeks in the Life. That's mainly the reasons why I got most of my beatings. I was physically abused at home, so I wasn't tolerating a dude, who wasn't any parent to me, beating on me. I would fight back and get beat worse. I used to get dragged up and down the stairs. I got punched in the face and all over my body. I was beaten with a leather belt with metal rings on it after I got out of the shower. I was almost drowned to death. I was cut with a switchblade on my thighs, and basically just slapped and kicked around like a misbehaving dog. I was raped about four times and my pimp set up two of them. The life I was expecting to live wasn't what I thought it was going to be. I felt better off on my own. I was stuck between a rock and a hard place. When I got arrested for prostitution for the second time, I made the decision to exit this lifestyle once and for all. It wasn't as easy as I thought. Although I am living with my family again and things have gotten better, I am still dealing with issues and aftereffects of the Life. Currently I am being harassed by people who are acquainted with my pimp all because I am no longer with him and he's locked up because of promoting prostitution, raping underage girls, and endangering the welfare of a minor. I get threatening phone calls and there are people watching me everywhere I go. Is a teenager supposed to go through a struggle such as the one I have experienced? Does the family life play an important role in a girl's entrance into prostitution? Statistics show that 80 to 90 percent of females in the Life have been physically or sexually abused as children. Would it be wrong to say, "Hey, thanks a lot dad!" In my opinion I don't think so, but in reality I can't put all the blame on him. But I can say that I wish that parents would be cautious of the things they do or say to their children. It could put their child in so much danger that they never could imagine. I'm just thankful that I can now share my experience with others so they won't have to go through the struggle as I did.

BRENDA

IF I COULD I WOULD BUT I CAN'T SO I WON'T

It was September 17, 2002, the day I met my first and only pimp and my life changed forever. After meeting my pimp, I was never the same. I had to sleep with a lot of different tricks to earn his money. I always had to worry about my pimp and make sure he always had his money. I had to worry about tricks who wanted to hurt me and the cops who did whatever they wanted. I did not realize the danger that I was putting myself in. There was even a time when a cop came up to me and arrested me. He took me to the police station to ask me about one of the girls out on the track. She was killed by a trick inside a hotel. He choked her to death and laid her body under the bed. The only thing I could say to him was that I saw her before. She never talked much.

I have been arrested eight times for prostitution. It messed up my life. I was blinded by my love for my pimp. I didn't want to prostitute but I did. He was nice to me.

Once I started it was like I couldn't stop. It was like I was addicted. I saw the money and it sucked me in. I didn't really think about where the money was going to, all of my money went to my pimp. I guess I still felt special because I knew him before he became a pimp.

My pimp was my first real love and it felt like I couldn't leave him. I believed that I needed him just as much as he needed me. When my pimp got in a really bad car accident I stayed by his side when no one else was there. I stayed with my pimp for a year and I have gone through so much with him. It was not an easy year. I was by his side all the way good and bad, rich and poor. When he was in the hospital in a coma I was right there with him. I was the one holding his hand, praying that he would wake up. I stayed with him the whole time when everyone else bounced knowing that he might not be the same again. I was the most loyal person he could ever find, and I did all this out of my heart, even though he would still beat me and I was still unhappy. It seems like I could never be good enough for him to appreciate me and that's when I decided to step out and be away from him.

I still feel like I miss him and love him. It seems like I can't change how I feel on the inside, but I am going to start from the outside and work my way in. I decided to change my actions first. I know that everything takes time. It just won't happen overnight. It will take me a while especially when my feelings are involved, and I still feel close to him. It is really hard for me to deal with this even as I write this story. It is not a nice feeling. I miss him so much.

Whatever relationship we had, good or bad, it was all I had. It was my first relationship. I find myself thinking about him over and over.

When I try to do things just to take my mind off him, sometimes it doesn't work. If I could change anything in my life I would never ever want to fall in love with another person again because it is too much pain. I am scared of getting hurt and abused again. Right now I feel nothing lasts forever, no matter how much love you have for that person. That is just how I feel. The bad thing about it is that I am in love with the wrong person.

If I could change him I would.

If I could I would but I can't so I won't.

I'LL SELL WATER TO A WHALE AND I'LL SELL YOU A DREAM TOO BOO!

THEY WERE SO cute and young. I could have sold them anything: dreams, wishes, hopes, or my mother's panties, and they would have bought it. To me selling dreams was easy. Shit I could've sold dreams to Freddy Krueger and he would've bought them, buy one get one free. But once I figured out I had game, the money started rolling in like I had a nine-to-five. Every week I had another dream and another reason to take their money. This went on for about two years, along with selling weed, crack, and ecstasy pills. At this point I was very arrogant and closed-minded. Then I was hit with a hard reality check. I realized that I was using and abusing my sisters and my peers. So I went to the park where my girls were working and told them it was over. I told them there was nothing to look forward to, at least not from me. I felt really fucked up looking in their eyes and seeing hopelessness, and I knew it was my fault. They took it pretty well but my partners in crime on the other hand . . . well . . . All I'm going to say is all it took to change my life was a black eye, busted lip, bruised ribs, and a broken middle finger. After they jumped me I felt better though 'cause I knew that it was a start to my new life. I mean to be honest I was kinda mad and sad because I lost my street credibility, but I knew in my heart I can earn more street respect doing positive things with my life.

CHANTE

THIS STORY IS about a girl named Chante, she was a very bright, intelligent, smart girl who just got caught up with the wrong type of people. She lost her mother at a very young age and she felt abandoned and all alone, 'cause her family went their separate ways leaving her to fend for herself. She was only sixteen at the time. She dropped out of school and turned to the streets for the love and guidance she was looking for. She started smoking weed and cigarettes and drinking.

One day while she was outside, this guy started talking nice to her. She thought he was cute, so she listened to what he had to say. He asked her how old she was, and of course she lied 'cause she wanted to kick it to him. Little did she know, she was in for a hell of a surprise that would change her life forever.

He was twenty-five and he would get his girls by acting like he wanted to be their man. They was seeing each other for a couple of days until one day he asked her, how does she make money, how do she take care of herself. So she told him by doing odd jobs here and there like babysitting. They both knew it wasn't much so he told her he knew a way that she could make fast cash without having to do little to no work. Of course she wanted to know how, so he showed her.

And that's when the saga begins. He took her to his house one day, where she saw a lot of girls. It was then he told her who he really was, which was a P-I-M-P, and that the girls, as he would say, was his BITCHES, and they went out every night to a track where guys would pay for play.

At first she wasn't really sure if this was what she wanted to do, but after she saw all the money the other girls was bringing him she jumped on the bandwagon. Soon she was bringing in a lot, like the other girls, if not more. She was very happy 'cause he was taking good care of her, buying her clothes, taking her out, doing all the things a pimp was supposed to do, but she didn't know that—all she knew was that her daddy loved her, but that was only because of the money she was bringing him.

Until one day she got arrested for talking to an undercover and went to jail for that night. That was the first time she ever got arrested. Of course her daddy was waiting for her when the judge let her go, only to have her right back out there, after three years of the fighting, arguing, and other bullshit.

She said enough was enough. She had a plan to go to work one night, make some money, and bounce, but it didn't go according to plan, 'cause she got arrested again, and that was it for her. This time the judge sentenced her to go to a program where they helped her out a lot, and she still goes to the program this very day, where she is striving for a better future and life. So far so good, 'cause she hasn't been on the streets since, which is a good thing 'cause all the stories she heard about girls being raped, beaten real bad, or even killed—she did not want that to be her. And as far as her family goes, she's closer to them now more than she ever was.

BEING IN THE LIFE

When I was a little girl I was always outside. When my mother passed away, that's why I started working on the streets of New York City. But when I was fifteen years old, that's how I got with my first pimp. He was the type of person that will let you do anything you want. He let you go to work when you wanted, but when times were hard, you *will* get hit! He would make you go to work even if you were messed up, bruised up, or sick.

Being in the life wasn't easy at all. I had another person that I had gone to because my first pimp was really pounding me all over my body. With this new pimp it was easier because he was like a father to me. Because I had known him for so long, it wasn't hard to work for him, but when I would come home it just wasn't feeling like home to me. I was leaving him to go back to the first person but I really did not want to go back to him because I knew what he was going to do to me: beat on me.

To me, the game wasn't easy because I wasn't making it easy. I wasn't listening and I wasn't going to take NO PIMP HITTING ON ME. Everyone was telling me that I should stay with him because he was the best pimp for me. I still left him because I did not really want to be there; I did not want to be in the Life.

If you are thinking about going into the Life you don't want to!!!!!! It's not something for anybody to be a part of. Because when you want to get somewhere positive in life, you are not going to be able to. You are so much bigger and better than you think you are. Don't do something that you are going to regret in the future; because you will regret it.

UNTIL I REALIZED

Making me feel so good,
It's all that I understood. It's all that I understand.
I never took into my being, that you would ever hurt my feelings.
I was blind by you because you were just a little cutie.
But really also my daddy.
That's why I couldn't see your true identity.
A person who only wanted me
For pleasure, company, money
and not for better.
I finally saw it, when I thought about it,
I never knew love could make me so blind,
I never knew your love was so fake and unkind
until I realized . . .

LOST IN DARK DEPRESSION

Lost in dark depression not knowing where to turn
I opened the windows to my soul to see what I could Learn.
I swept up depression, scrubbed the sadness and the hurt
I put it all in trash bags and set them by the curb,
I found stashed in a corner tucked high upon a shelf
A treasure chest of knowledge that I could love myself
And wherever my future takes me I know that I will win
Because I opened the windows to my soul, and let the light shine in.

JANICE

Janice is an imp with a twinkle who lights up a room when she enters, and she has a motor that just won't quit. I just could not for the life of me see her on the streets. Getting the holy hell knocked out of her. She seemed like someone who should just be getting ready for the junior prom. Which just makes your jaw drop faster when she reads you her story.

TIMES SQUARE

This man found me in Times Square after I ran away from the group home where I got beat and abused and misused sexually. I was twelve and I had to get out of there. I had no choice. So this super nice guy came up to me and asked me did I need a place to stay, was I hungry. I tried to pretend I was waiting for somebody, of course I wasn't. But he wouldn't go away. And he was soooooo nice. He took me back to his place and fed me and bought me clothes, and told me he loved me. I thought I was his girlfriend. One night while I was asleep, a man came into my room and started beating me. I ran in and told my "boyfriend," knowing he would defend me. Sure enough, he came back into the room and told the man, "You paid to fuck the bitch, not beat her, I'm the only one gets to beat her." Which he then did. Split my lip wide open and knocked out my two front teeth. I screamed and cried. I didn't want to have sex with the man my "boyfriend" had rented me to. I had no choice.

Then my pimp found out one of his women was stashing part of the money she earned. So he called a "family meeting." He had all his women sit in a circle. In the middle of the circle, he tied the woman who'd been stashing money to a chair. He covered her in alcohol and set her on fire. "This is a lesson for all y'all," he said. "This is what happens when one of my bitches holds out on me." We had to watch while she burned to death. I was fifteen.

Now I don't take any mistreatment from any man. I don't think all men are bad. Just some people are bad and they want to do bad things to you. I have my eye on the prize and I will not compromise until I realize my dream.

ACKNOWLEDGMENTS

First and foremost, we would like to thank all the writers who contributed to this book. For many it was an extremely courageous act. We are also thankful to Richard Eoin Nash for welcoming us into the Soft Skull fold and to Editor Anne Horowitz for her extraordinary grace, generosity and intelligence in shaping this book. Elise Canon of Publishers Group West, that great friend of writers, cannot be thanked enough for her guidance. We owe a huge debt of gratitude to the SAGE Project and SAGE's late executive director Norma Hotaling. Hawk Kincaid made a great contribution, both with his words and his excellent cover art. Thanks to Leslie Levitas for serving as muse and for a great author photograph. Finally, we would like to thank Arielle Eckstut, the Snow Leopard, for bigness of her brain and heart, for traipsing down into that basement on Mission Street every Tuesday afternoon for two years to work with the writers who congregated there, purely out of the goodness of her heart.